Florida Birds

A Birdwatcher Discovers the Sunshine State

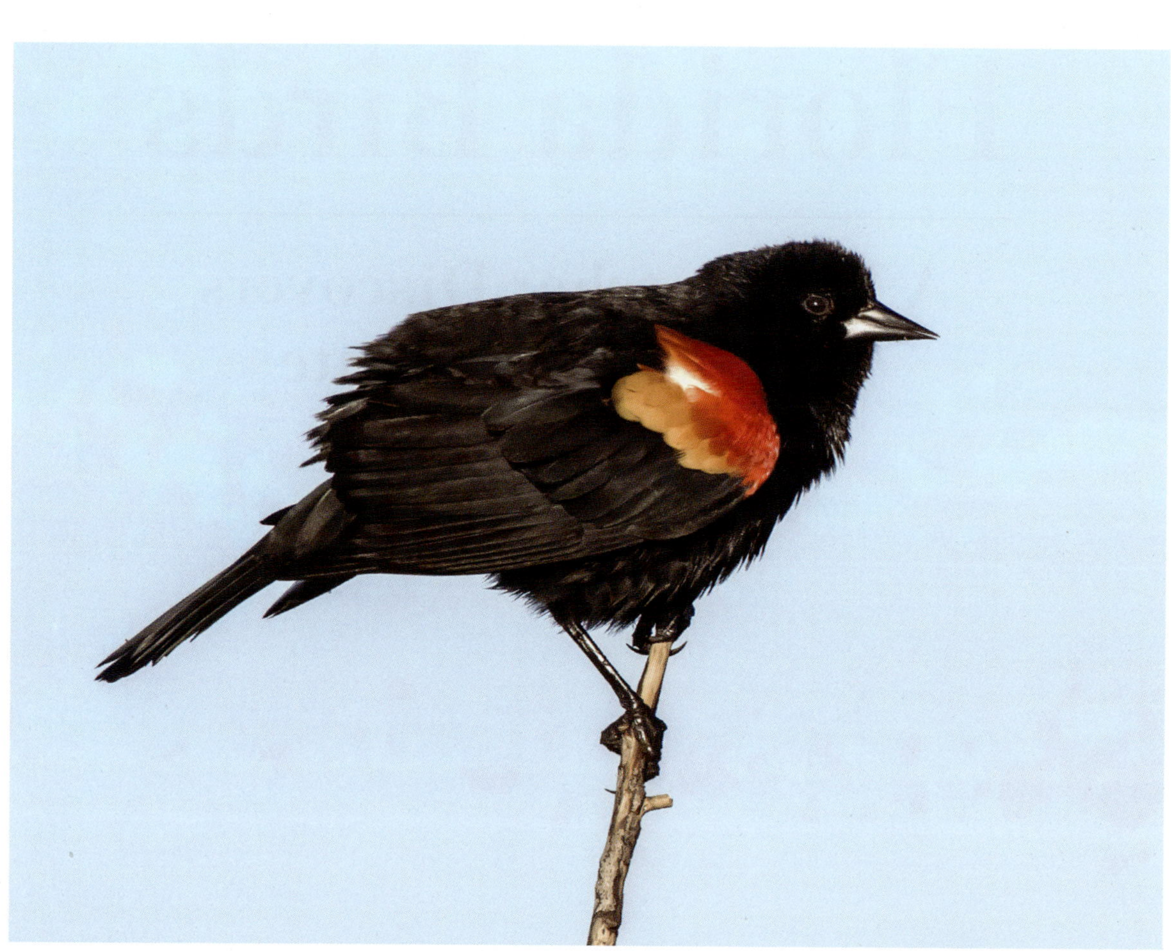

Florida Birds

A Birdwatcher Discovers the Sunshine State

Photography and Notes by Ken Janes

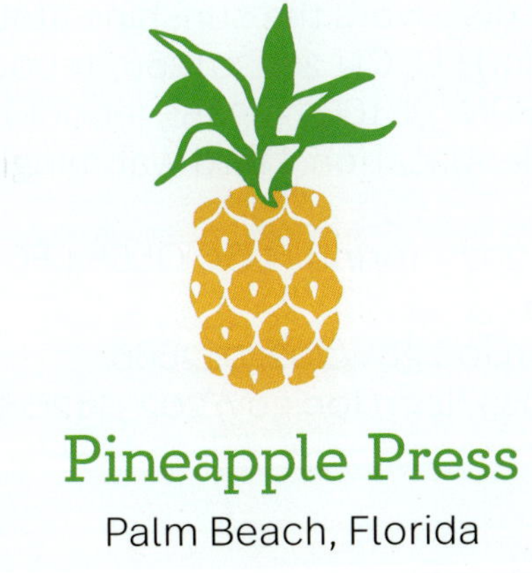

Pineapple Press
Palm Beach, Florida

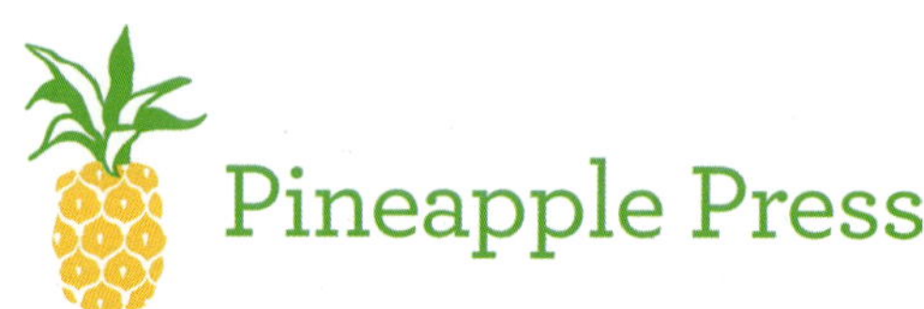

An imprint of The Globe Pequot Publishing Group, Inc.
64 South Main Street
Essex, CT 06426
www.globepequot.com

Distributed by NATIONAL BOOK NETWORK

British Library Cataloguing in Publication Information available

Library of Congress Cataloging-in-Publication Data

Names: Janes, Ken, 1942- author.
Title: Florida birds: a birdwatcher discovers the sunshine state / Ken Janes.
Identifiers: LCCN 2023012666 (print) | LCCN 2023012667 (ebook) | ISBN 9781683343448 (paperback) | ISBN 9781683343455 (ebook)
Subjects: LCSH: Birds–Florida–Identification. | Bird watchinging–Florida–Identification.
Classification: LCC QL684.F6 J36 2023 (print) | LCC QL684.F6 (ebook) | DDC 598.09759–dc23/eng/20230421
LC record available at https://lccn.loc.gov/2023012666
LC ebook record available at https://lccn.loc.gov/2023012667

Printed in India

Contents

Acknowledgments

I must begin by thanking my friend Hugh Beath for his enthusiasm and encouragement in getting this book together. After he looked at my first book, ***Life List: Field Notes of a Maine Birdwatcher***, Hugh became a serious observer of birds in his Florida neighborhood and urged me to create this collection of Florida birds. My birding buddies, Harold and Mona Brewer, have added their support and advice. They are ardent conservationists, and we have spent countless hours in the field, both in Maine and in Florida.

Special thanks go to Val and Bob Marier for their editing skills that make the text much more readable. Val is a talented writer and has meticulously gone through every page looking for the last misplaced comma. Thanks are due my son Matt for his artistic ability in designing and formatting the book. And finally, I would have never finished this project without the patience and continuing support of my wife, Sandra.

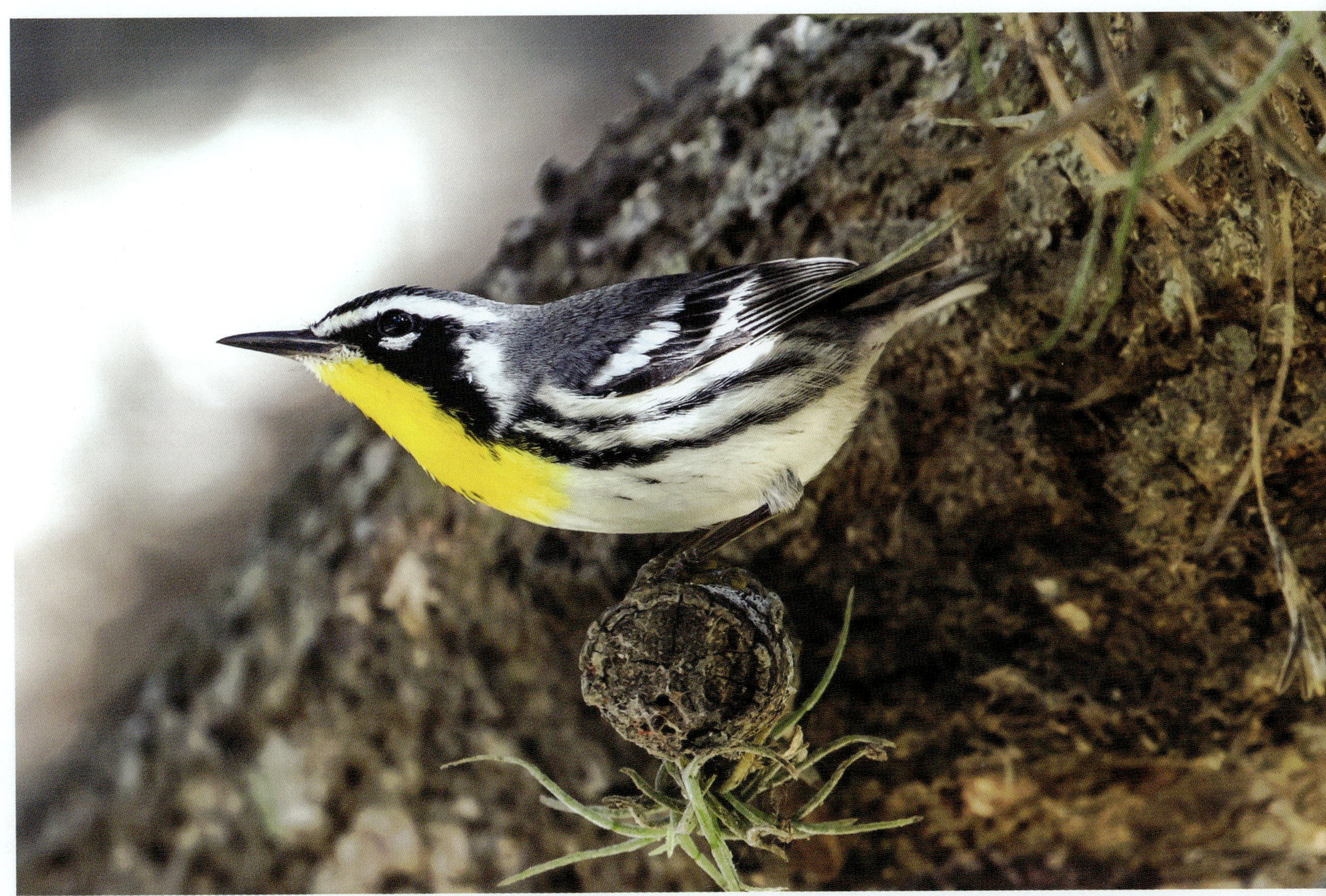

As a birder, the best part of spending time in a different place is finding new birds to identify and study, like this Yellow-throated Warbler. Although warblers are common in Maine, this southern beauty is rarely seen that far north. There is a resident population in northern Florida, but the South Florida birds migrate to breeding grounds in the swampy forests of the Southeast, infrequently venturing as far north as New England.

It took several seasons, but I was finally able to capture a beautiful male in the open, in good light, and in sharp focus. I was thrilled to add it to my life list in 2019.

Introduction

No matter the season, birds are always with us. In my first book, ***Life List: Field Notes of a Maine Birdwatcher***, I put together a collection of my bird photos taken in our southern Maine neighborhood of Kennebunk Beach. Many of the early pictures were terrible and went in the trash, but the final result was a collection of the best photos from six years of daily walks along the beach and down to the Mousam River and its estuary. I called the book ***Life List*** after learning that birdwatchers keep extensive lists of new bird sightings in county and state lists, as well as the all-important life list.

The positive response to the book astounded me. Friends, neighbors, and complete strangers began to notice the birds in our area and would stop me on the street to talk about the egrets that had just arrived in the marsh or the eagle that was soaring over the river. As time passed, I gave a few presentations and did some book signings, attempting to introduce more people to the idea that birds and wildlife were all around us, and that all we had to do was take notice.

Now that we are migrating south from Maine and spending the winters in Florida, my life list has grown markedly. I have added many local Florida birds and also the migrating birds that pass through on their way to the Caribbean Islands and South America. Our winter location in Vero Beach and Indian River County has many diverse places to find photogenic Florida birds. I have spent hours walking, watching, and taking pictures and have imported thousands of new photos into my Adobe Lightroom Library. ***Florida Birds: A Birdwatcher Discovers the Sunshine State*** does not include every bird in Florida, but I wanted to highlight those that are unique and most impressive to a visiting birdwatcher getting to know Florida birds for the first time, and, of course, working on a life list.

Ken Janes
Vero Beach, Florida
Kennebunk Beach, Maine

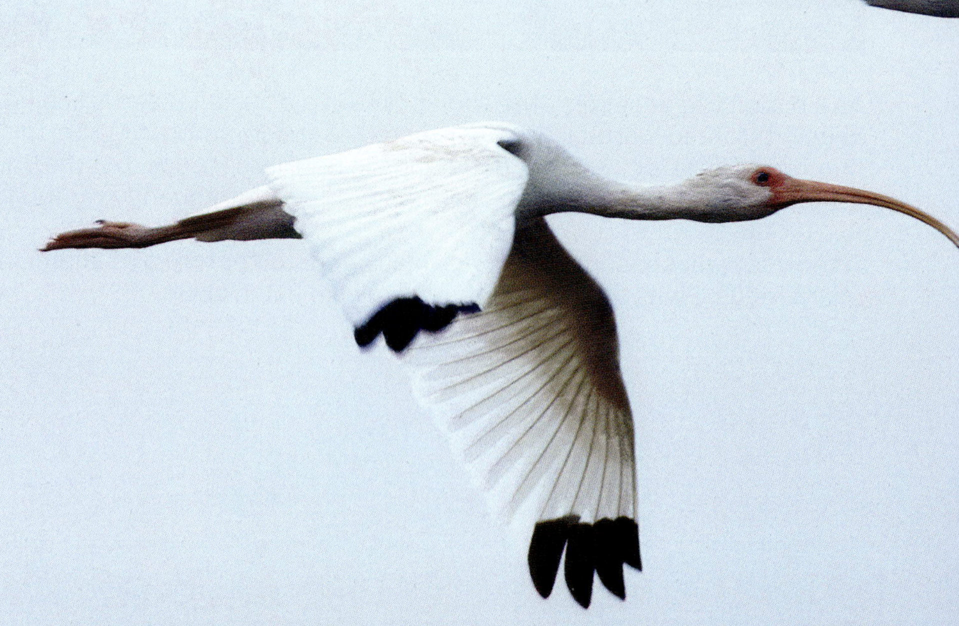

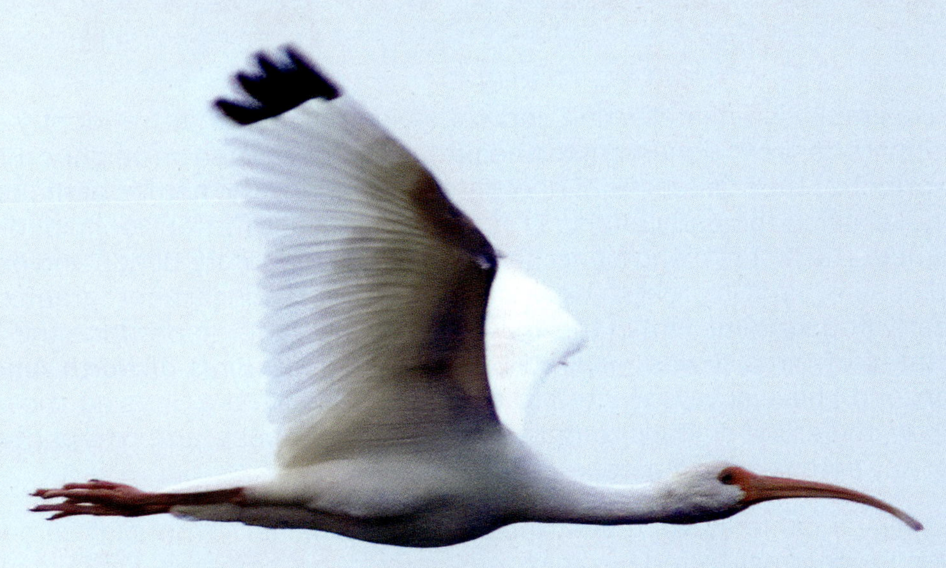

In all things of Nature there is something of the marvelous.

—Aristotle

Bird Photography

Bird photography is an interesting and satisfying pastime that frequently develops from a birdwatcher's desire to document the beautiful creatures seen on neighborhood walks. Some people prioritize the challenges of photography, learning the names of the bird species later. In any case, since the early efforts of pioneers like Eliot Porter, techniques have improved significantly. The first film photographers had to use elaborate blinds and flash photography and find nesting birds in order to have any chance of creating a photograph of a bird in focus. Using early Kodachrome film in the 1940s, Porter was able to produce the first satisfactory color plates of birds. I was inspired by his 1972 book ***Birds of North America: A Personal Selection***, and I have always wanted to make pictures like the ones he showed in that book. Since then, the era of digital photography has come to pass, and bird photography is within reach of any enthusiastic amateur.

The first digital cameras were adaptations of the original 35mm film camera designs from the 1970s. In contrast to today's mirrorless electronic cameras, which can shoot at a rate of twenty frames per second and have amazing autofocus capabilities, the early digital cameras were slower and heavier. Ten years ago, a tripod was necessary to ensure any possibility of sharp focus when using a telephoto lens greater than 400mm. Due to the built-in image stabilization in modern cameras, it's possible to hand-hold a camera with a telephoto lens and still take high-quality pictures. Now, instead of waiting a week to see if the slides were properly exposed, we can analyze an image in the field, make exposure and focus modifications instantly, and take as many shots as we like.

Regardless of the camera used, many of the fundamentals of bird photography remain the same. Even with the best telephoto lens, getting close is mandatory. No picture will work from 500 yards away. You will not get many decent bird photos without patience and persistence. "Stand still and be quiet" was my advice to a friend asking how to get good bird photos.

There are many styles of bird photography depending on the tastes of the photographer. Some people like to create very artistic, dramatic images of birds in beautiful settings. The best way to do this is with a blind and feeding stations. Decorative perches, good lighting, and getting close can produce absolutely gorgeous photos. Hummingbird photography, for example, is nearly impossible without using such tactics.

Other photographers enjoy photographing birds in their natural habitat. Even though it is challenging, taking this type of photograph can be gratifying. Like any other wild animal, birds will not let you approach them, especially if they are nesting or protecting their young. Learning the behavior of a target species and getting in position with good lighting is often the best approach. I'll take note of the location and the time of day when a specific bird feeds, and then plan to be there when the sun is at the proper angle. Waiting quietly and letting the bird work its way into the optimum spot works well. Nothing is more satisfying than having a bird, or any other animal, accept you as part of the landscape and go about its daily activity, oblivious to your presence. One of my biggest thrills was having a Florida bobcat walk out of the bushes twenty feet in front of me, while I was trying to get close to some Glossy Ibis. The bobcat never noticed me, and I had to call out "Hey, bobcat!" before it realized I was there. I got the eye contact I wanted and the best photo I could have hoped for.

There are a few technical considerations in making a good bird photograph. Light is key, and getting the sun behind you is critical. "Let your shadow point at the bird," I was told by an experienced photographer, and that is always on my mind when setting up a shot. In Florida, photographing birds during the middle of the day can be challenging due to the sun's intense shadow-creating effects and overexposure of white birds. The best light is in the early morning and late afternoon, which has the benefit of being when birds are most active. A cloudy, overcast, or even stormy day can result in excellent photographs.

I would encourage every birdwatcher to try photography. There are excellent cameras available for any budget, and the results can be very satisfying. Just ask anyone with a camera, and I'm sure they will be happy to get you started.

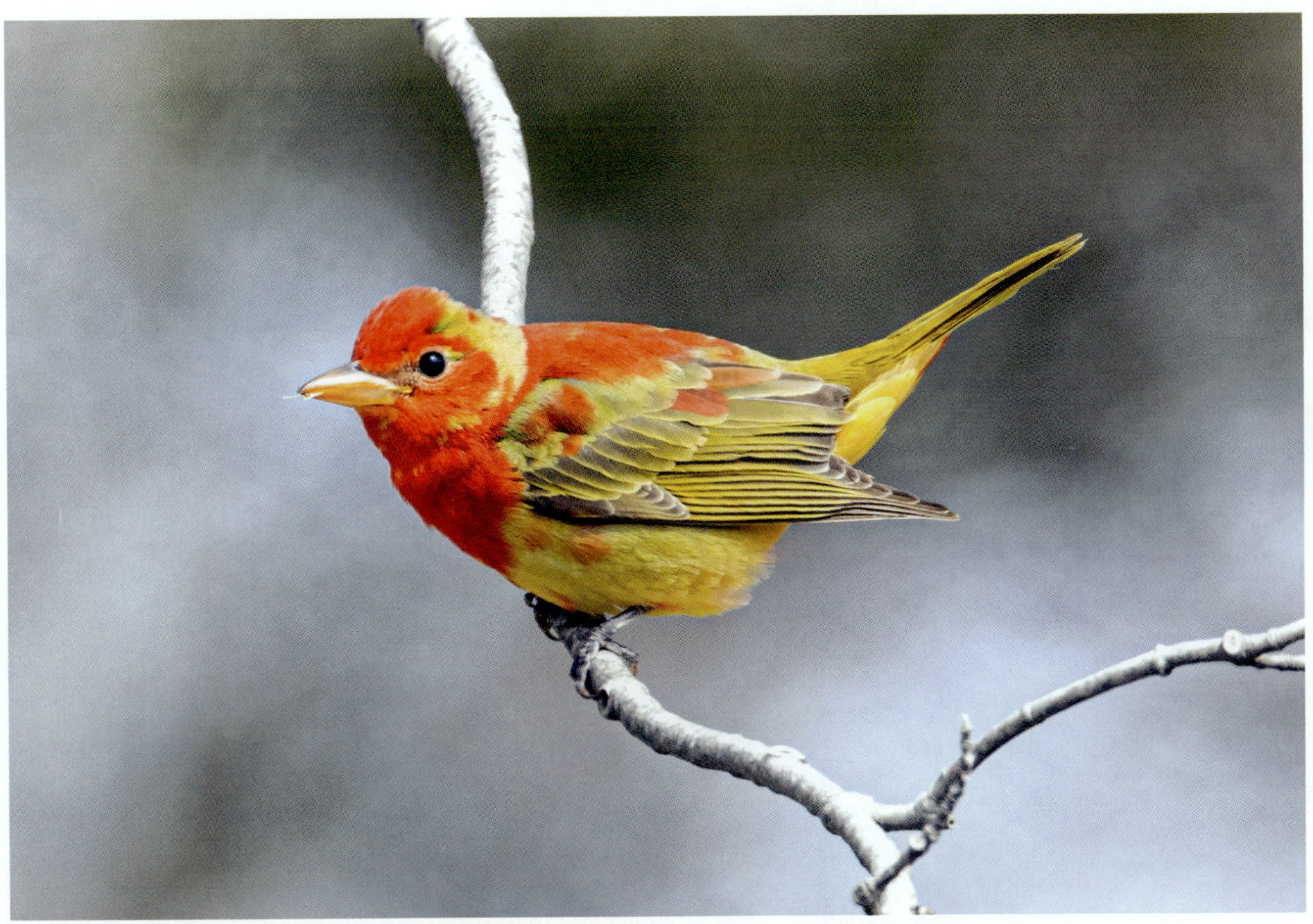

This photo of a molting juvenile Summer Tanager demonstrates why good light is critical to proper exposure. It took some time before the bird finally came out in the open where it was possible to expose for the bright yellow highlights and also get detail in the darker shades of orange. Any other light situation such as shade or backlighting would never had worked as well. All it takes is patience, and the camera will do the rest.

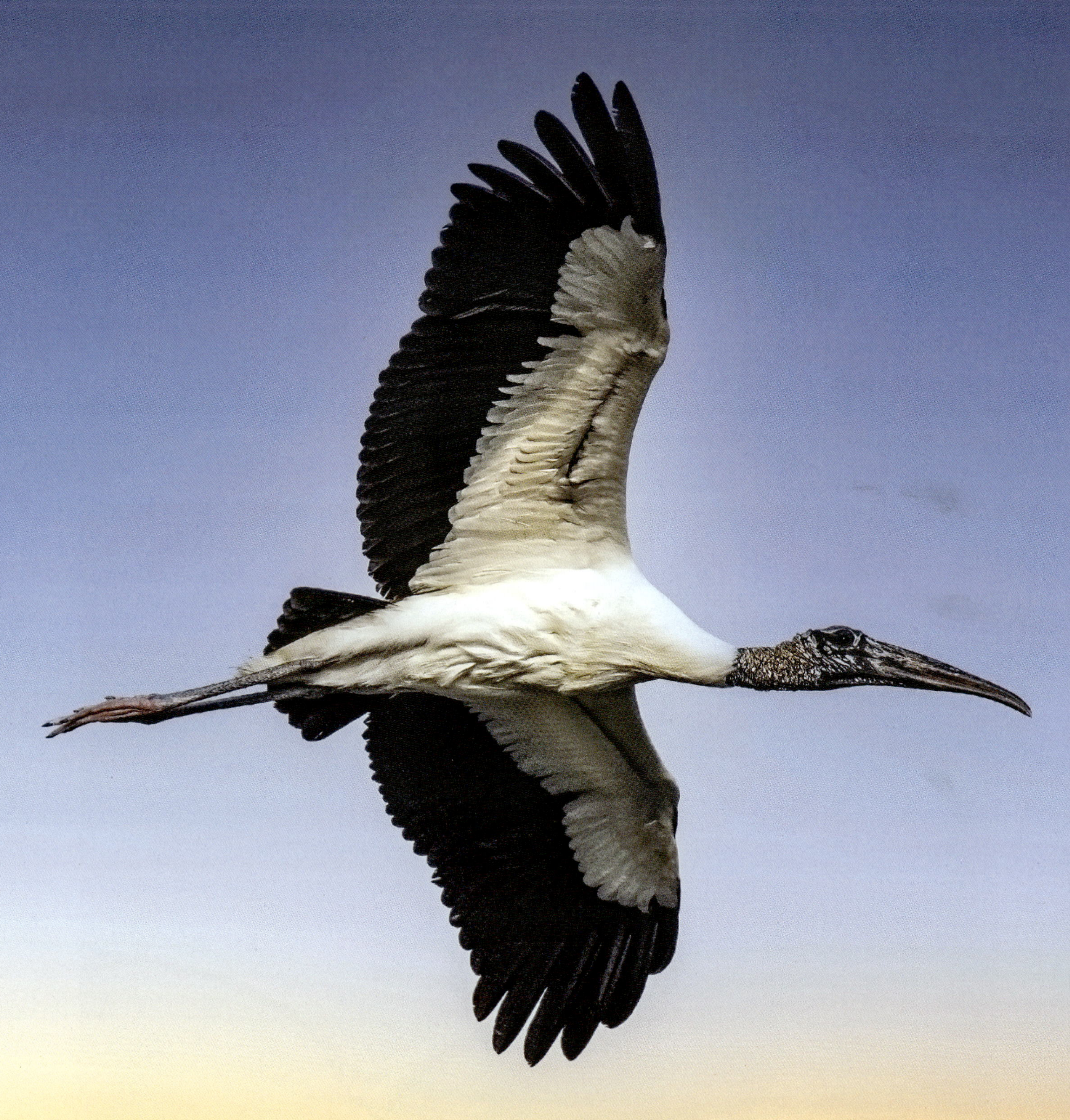

Wading Birds

To birdwatchers, the term "wading birds" means those tall, long-necked birds that are widespread throughout Florida. They are typically the first birds that a novice learns to recognize, and they are fascinating to study in depth. These birds spend the majority of the day hunting, and each has a distinct hunting technique.

Herons and egrets slowly patrol the edges of ponds and canals, occasionally remaining motionless for several minutes before striking prey with their daggerlike bills. Egrets are actually a subgroup of the heron family, and they have similar hunting styles. The egret term refers to all-white birds that develop long plumes called "aigrettes" during mating season.

Spoonbills sift through the water and soil in quest of tiny invertebrates. In Florida, there is only one spoonbill species: the dramatic Roseate Spoonbill. Ibises are smaller birds that use their curved bills to probe mud and shallow water. White Ibis are frequently seen in small flocks foraging across parks and golf courses.

Wood Storks are tropical birds that are uncommon breeders in Florida, Georgia, and the Carolinas. They use their hefty bill to search the water for small fish and crustaceans.

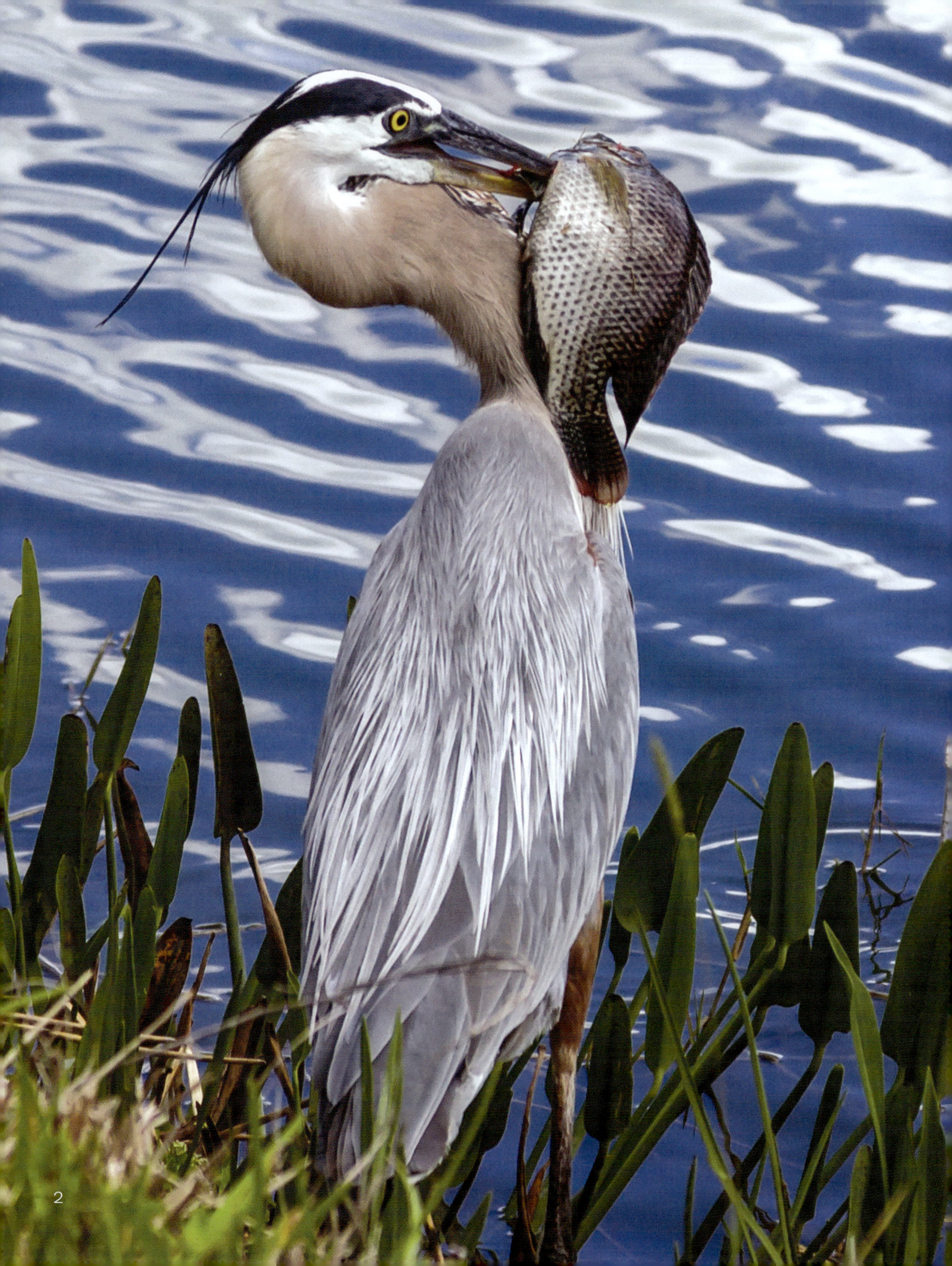

Great Blue Heron

The Great Blue Heron is the largest wading bird. It stands five feet tall and has a six- foot wingspan. Look for their huge size and slow wingbeats, their head pulled back and legs trailing behind, as they fly overhead. They are gray-blue in color with long black plumes on their heads and dark blue shoulder patches. A subspecies that is all white and slightly larger, known as the Great White Heron, exists in the Florida Keys.

These birds are unmistakable as they stand still or slowly move along the edge of a pond or canal in search of food. When a fish comes near, the spear-like bill lashes out and stabs its prey. The heron then flips the prize into the air and catches it headfirst. Using this method, they can catch and eat fish that are surprisingly large. While fish are their favorite food, they are very adaptable and will eat just about anything; snakes, frogs, even small birds or mammals.

Great Blues choose a new mate each year and go through a complicated process of dancing and showing off until they are ready to build a nest. The male chooses the site, often twenty to sixty feet off the ground, then brings material for the female to use in building the nest. This pair built their nest out of sticks in the shared rookery at the West Regional Wetlands on 8th Street in Vero Beach. The female was very picky and threw away many of the sticks brought by the male.

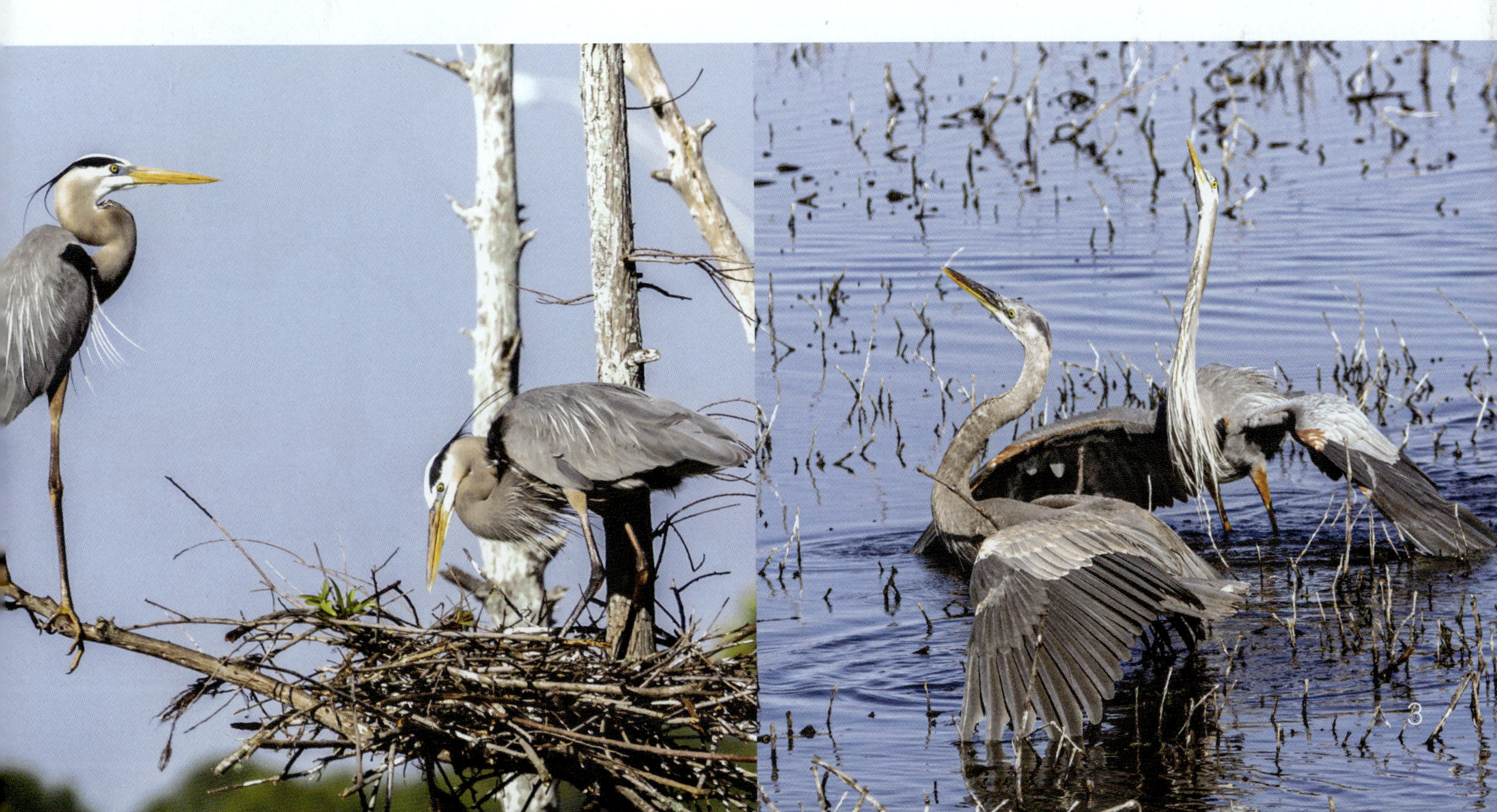

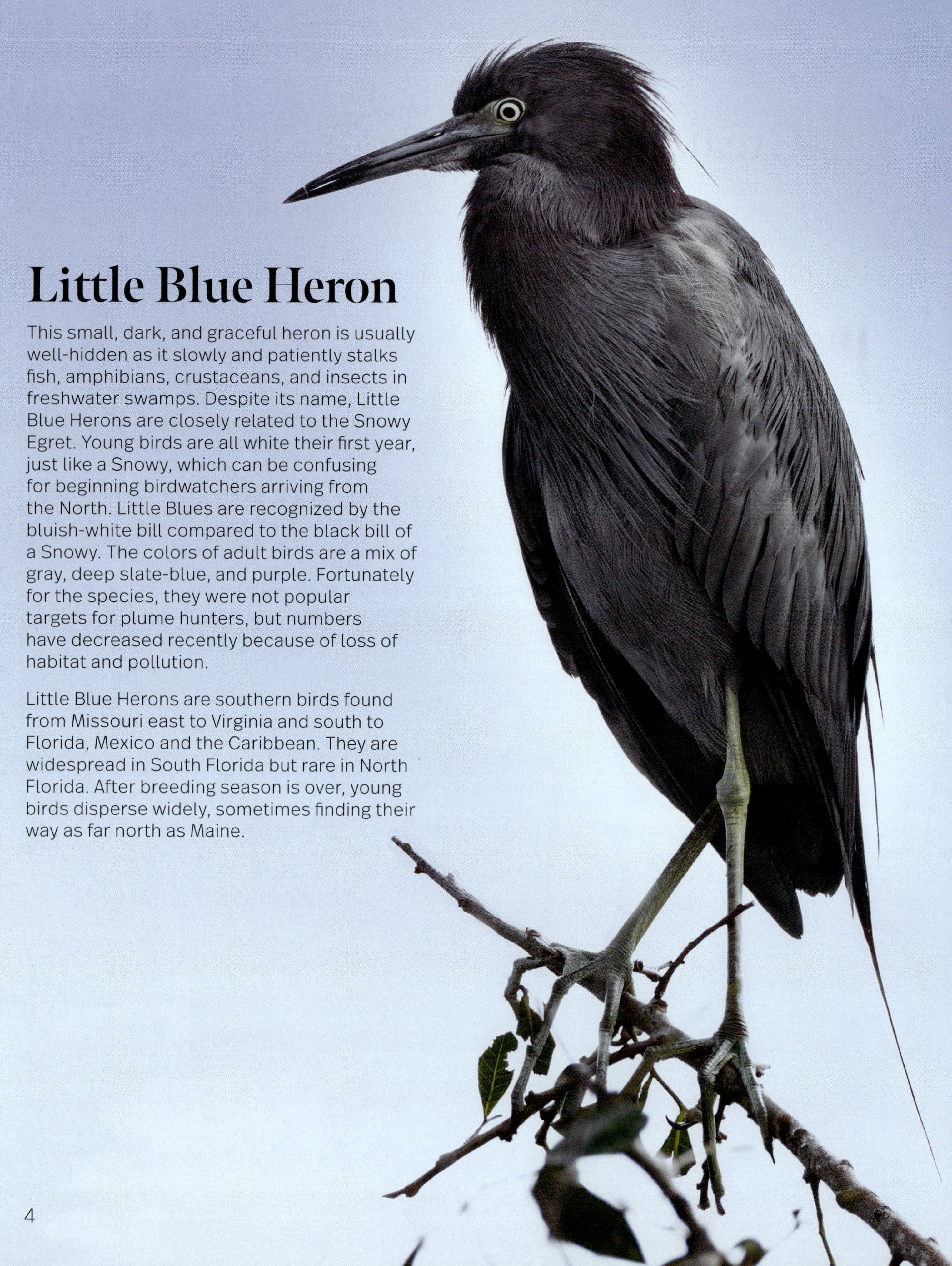

Little Blue Heron

This small, dark, and graceful heron is usually well-hidden as it slowly and patiently stalks fish, amphibians, crustaceans, and insects in freshwater swamps. Despite its name, Little Blue Herons are closely related to the Snowy Egret. Young birds are all white their first year, just like a Snowy, which can be confusing for beginning birdwatchers arriving from the North. Little Blues are recognized by the bluish-white bill compared to the black bill of a Snowy. The colors of adult birds are a mix of gray, deep slate-blue, and purple. Fortunately for the species, they were not popular targets for plume hunters, but numbers have decreased recently because of loss of habitat and pollution.

Little Blue Herons are southern birds found from Missouri east to Virginia and south to Florida, Mexico and the Caribbean. They are widespread in South Florida but rare in North Florida. After breeding season is over, young birds disperse widely, sometimes finding their way as far north as Maine.

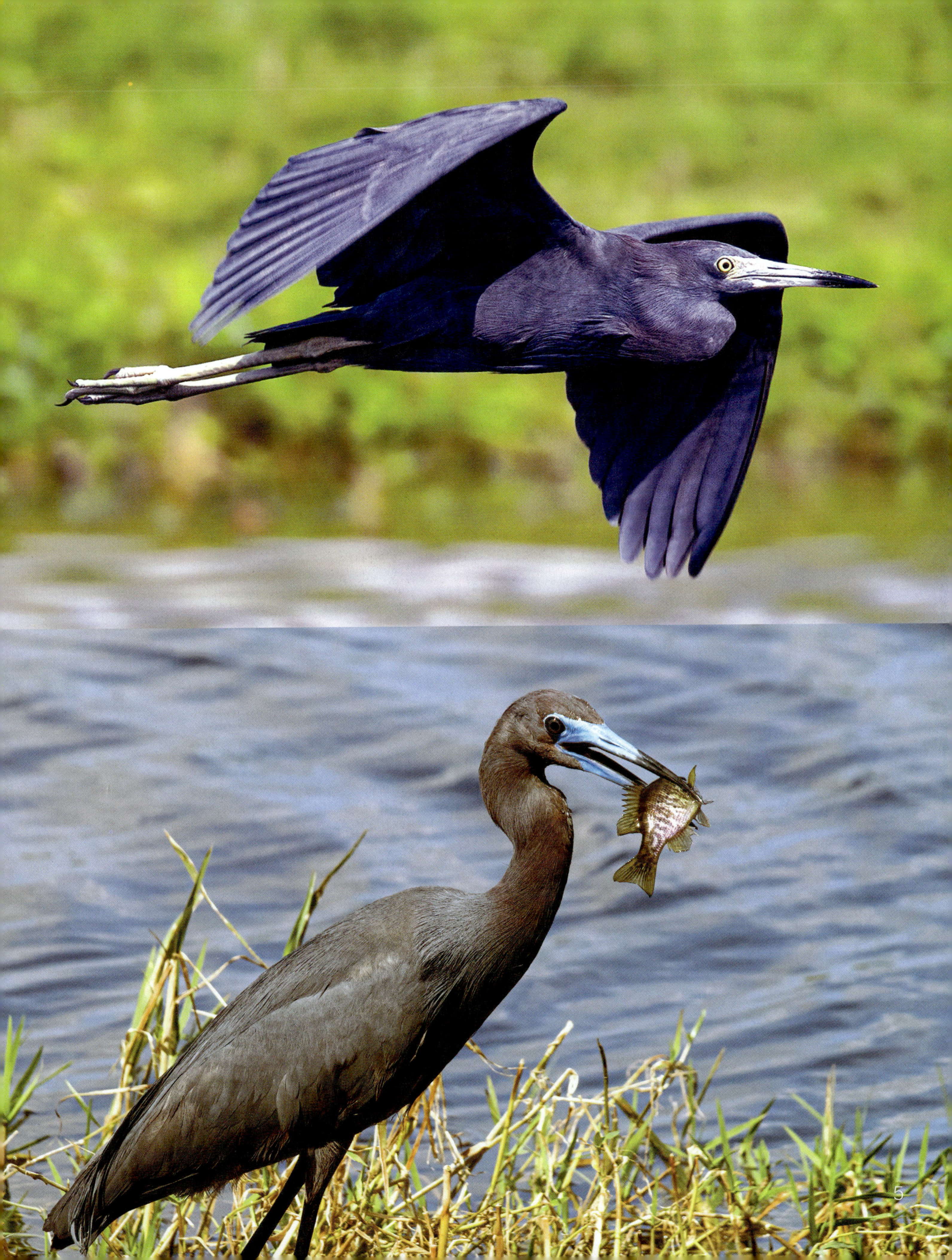

Tricolored Heron

This small, thin bird was previously known as the Louisiana Heron, but the name was changed to Tricolored Heron in 1957. This is a medium-sized, slender heron that is a dusky blue-gray on top and white on the bottom, with a reddish-purple neck area, giving us their modern, red-white-and-blue name. In February and March, when they start to breed, their usually yellow bills turn a deep blue, and they develop a white head plume. These are year-round residents of coastal Central and South Florida, where they are joined by migrating birds in the winter.

Tricoloreds stalk their prey slowly and gracefully through the reeds along the water's edge. They can strike quickly and prefer to eat fish, but they also catch a wide range of amphibians, reptiles, and insects.

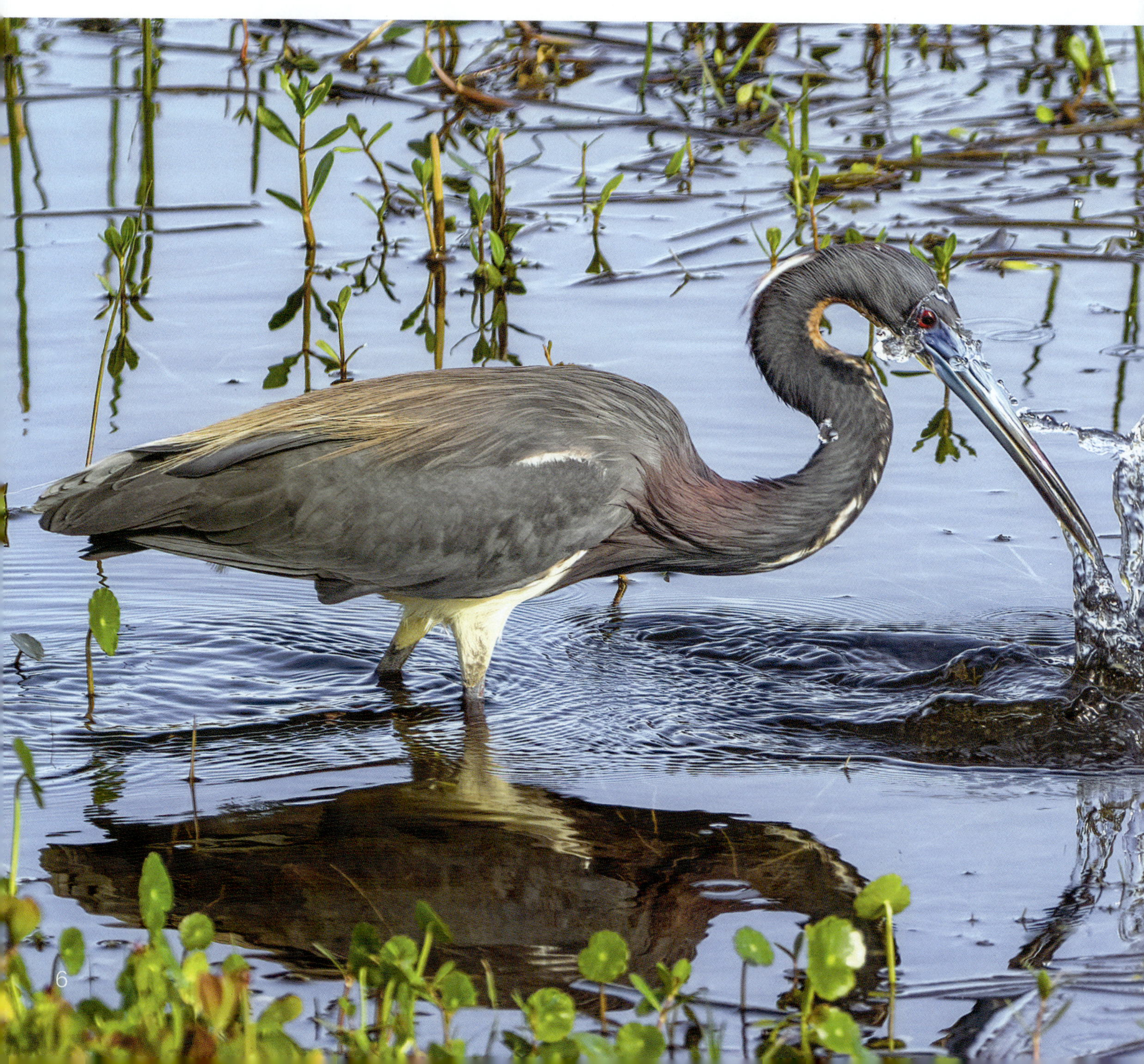

Tricoloreds tend to eat fish they find in shallow water, so they are susceptible to pesticide and mercury exposure, loss of habitat to pollution, and loss of breeding grounds converted to recreational use.

Audubon called this beautiful bird “Lady of the Waters” because he thought it was so delicate and graceful.

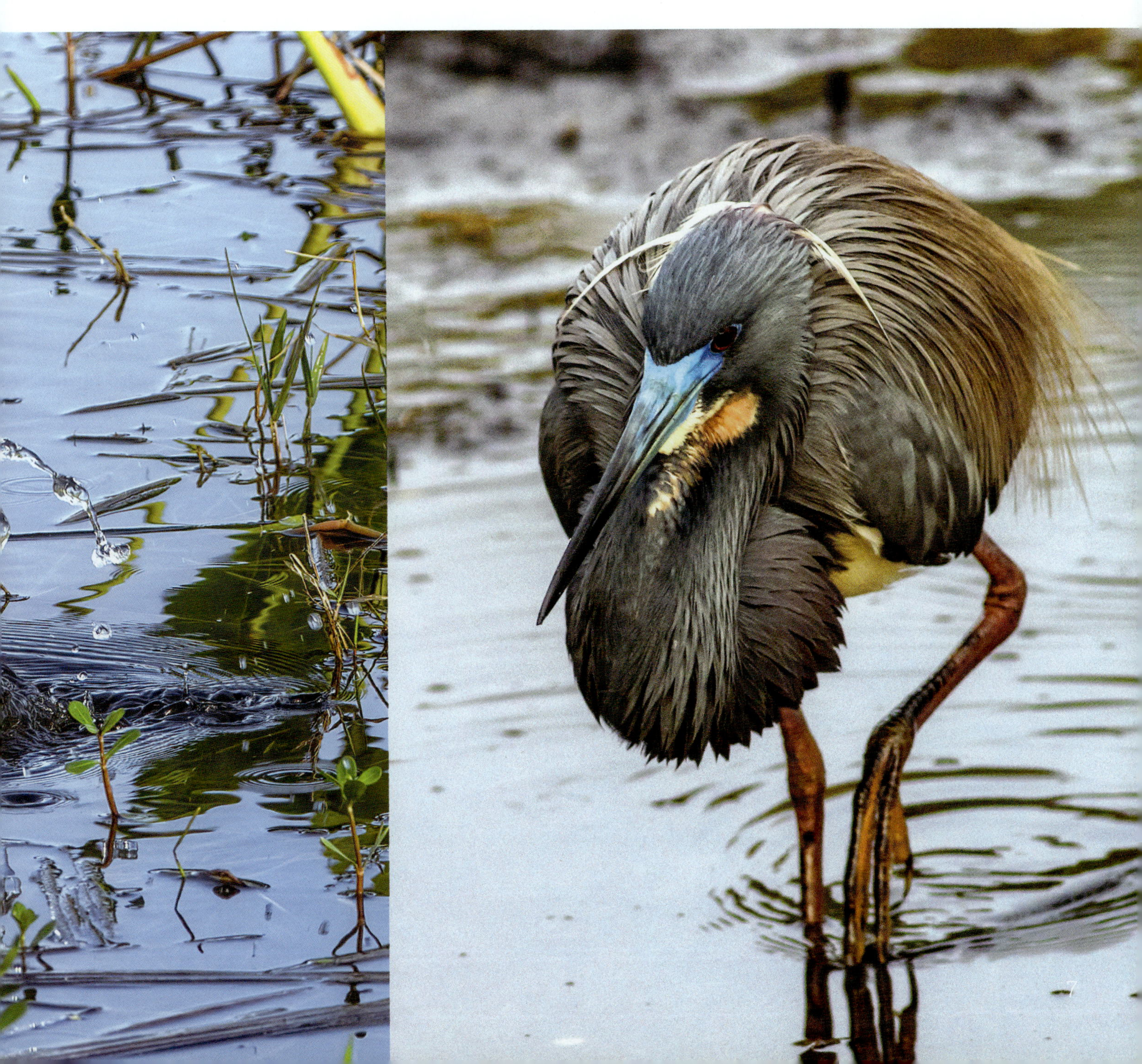

Green Heron

Green Herons are small, shy birds that live near freshwater ponds and plant-filled marshes. They often go unnoticed because they sit motionless for fifteen minutes or longer, waiting for a fish to come within striking distance. They are clever hunters and sometimes "bait" the fish by dropping a leaf, twig, or live worms onto the water.

Their green feathers are actually a bluish-black color with iridescent green highlights. When it's time to breed, their eyes turn a deep orange color. Green Herons live year-round in Florida, but many of the birds we see in the winter are migrating from the northern states to Central America.

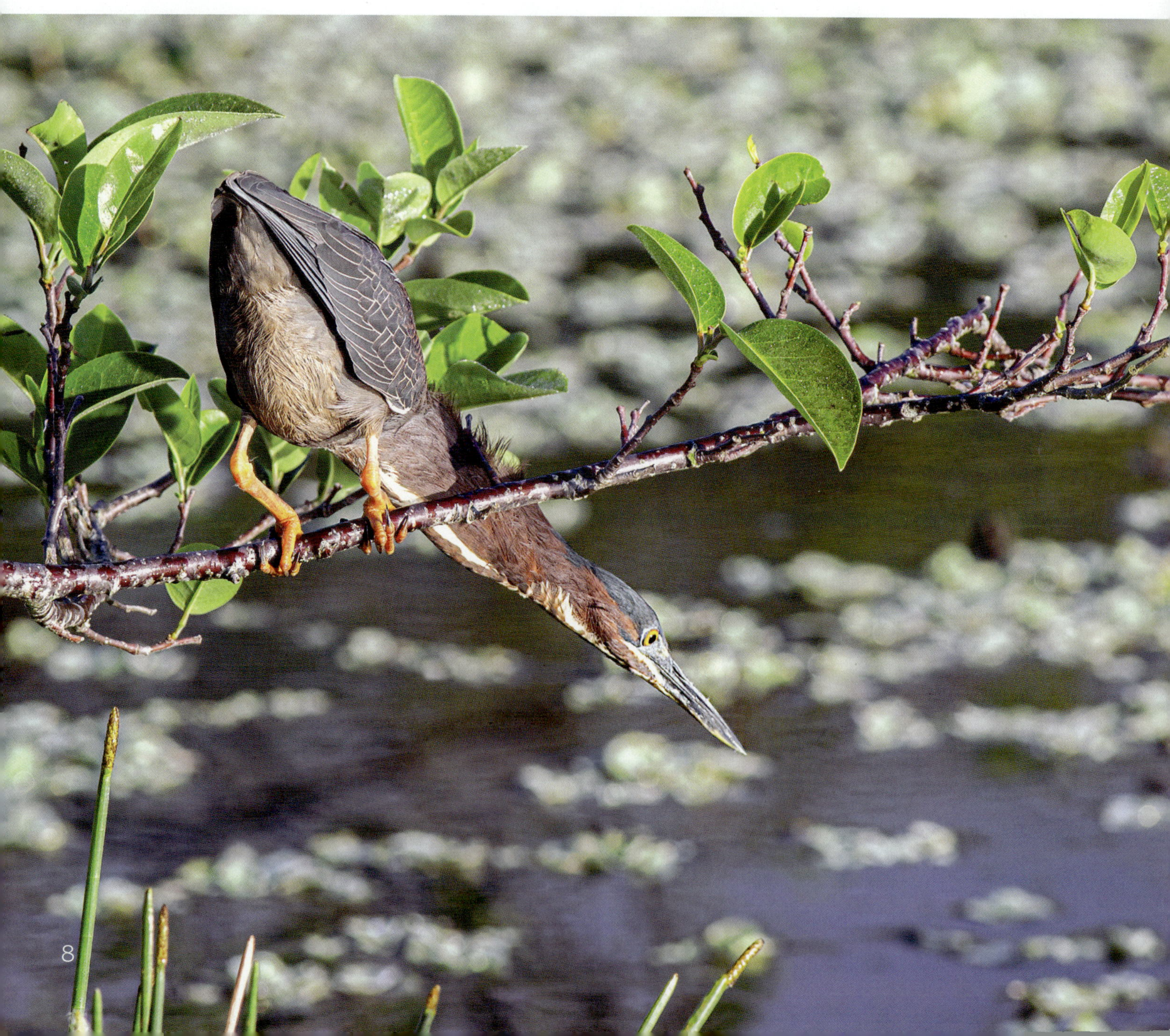

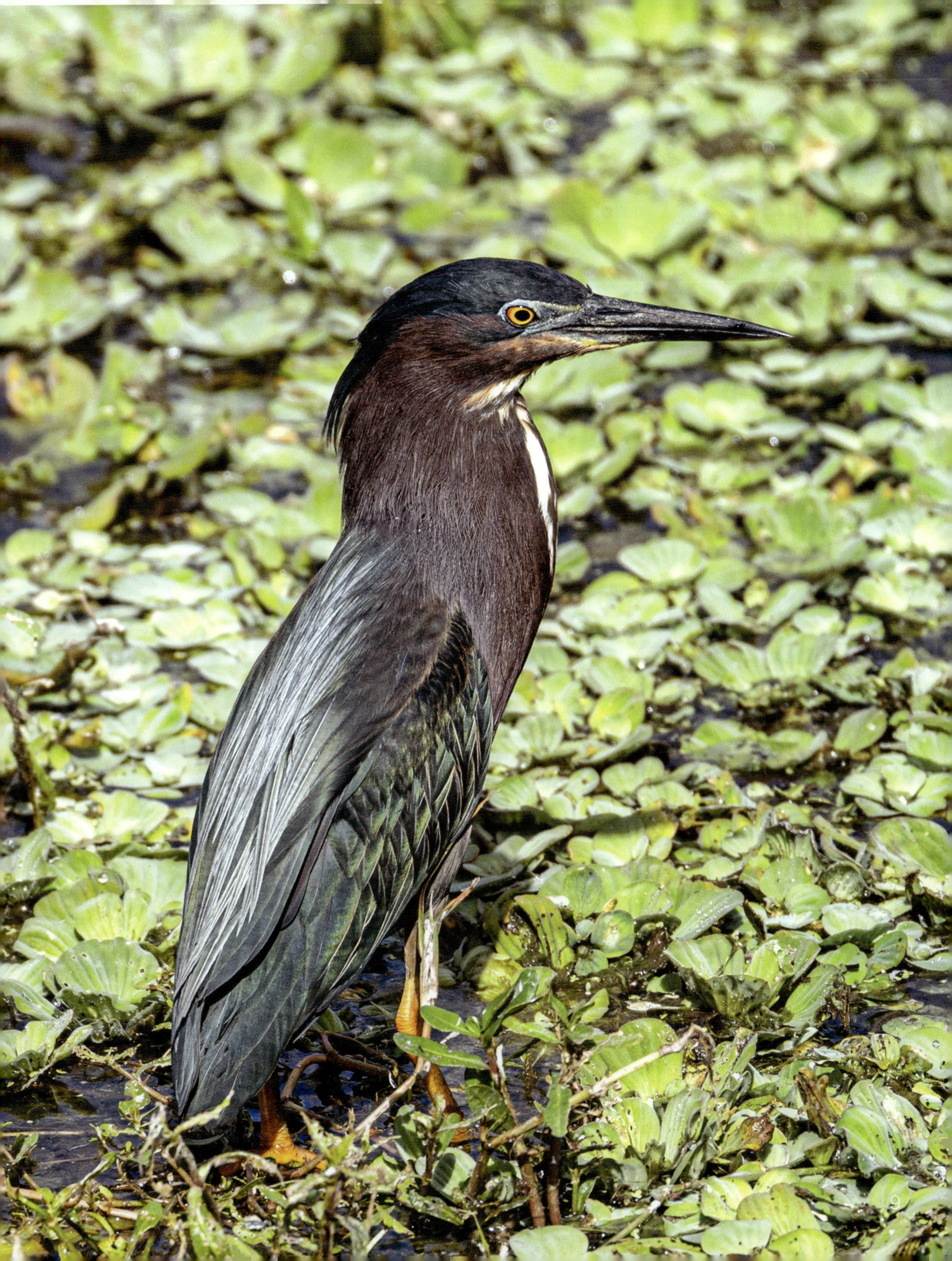

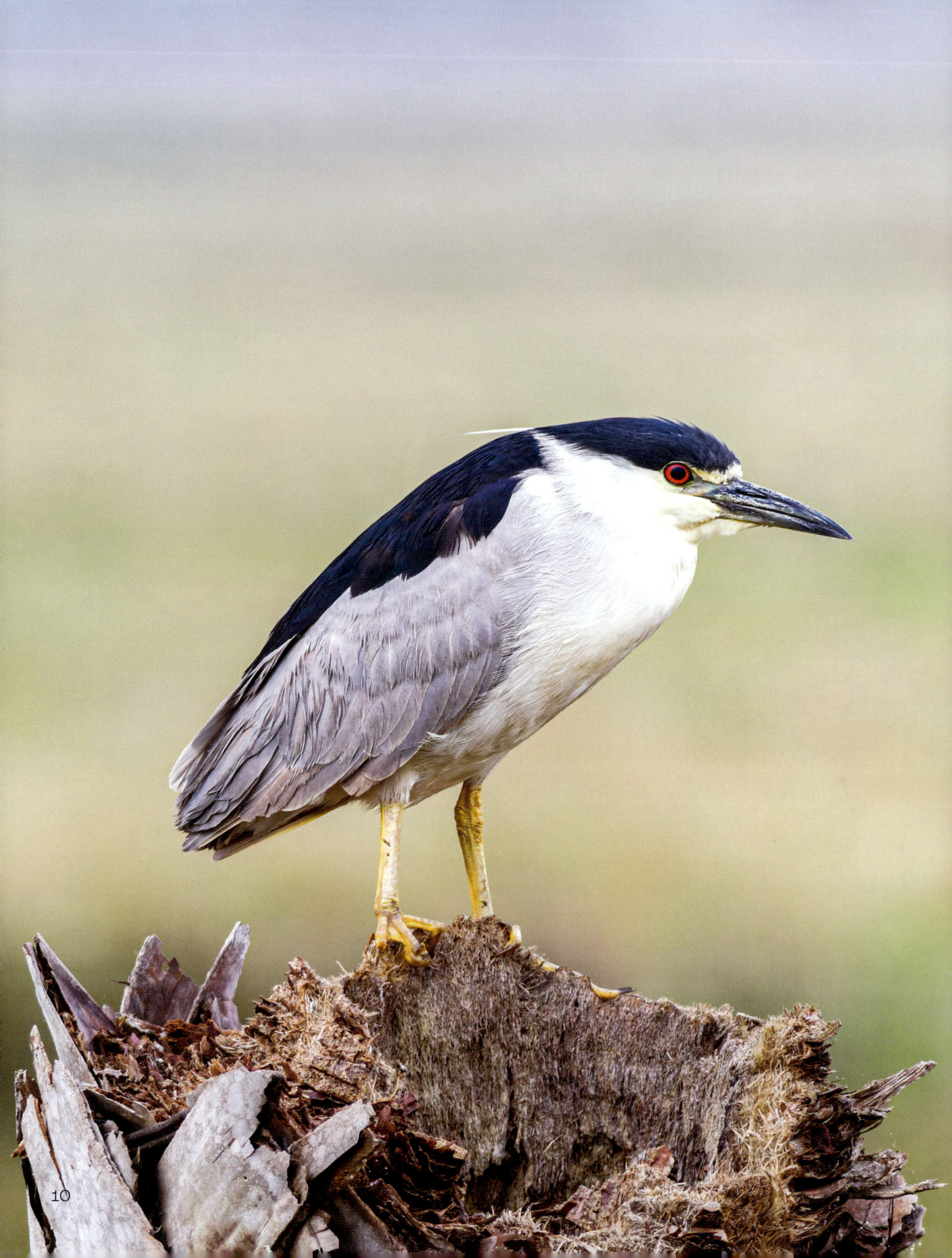

Black-crowned Night-Heron

Both the Black-crowned Night-Heron and the Yellow-crowned Night-Heron live in Florida. Even though they are fairly common, Black-crowned Night-Herons are hard to find because they feed at night. During the day, a lucky birdwatcher might see one resting on a pier or in the mangroves. At dusk, as they fly to their favorite feeding grounds, they make a loud, squawking "wonk" sound. Look for their hunched backs and menacing red eyes. Young birds have the same profile as adults, but their feathers are a mix of brown and white.

Night-herons consume fish, crabs, and other sea creatures, but when they eat eggs, they can cause havoc in tern nesting colonies. Like all wading birds, they are at risk when wetland habitats are changed or destroyed.

It takes young night-herons three years to develop their adult plumage, and birders have a hard time telling the two species apart until they learn that Black-crowned Night-Herons have bigger white spots on the edges of their wings.

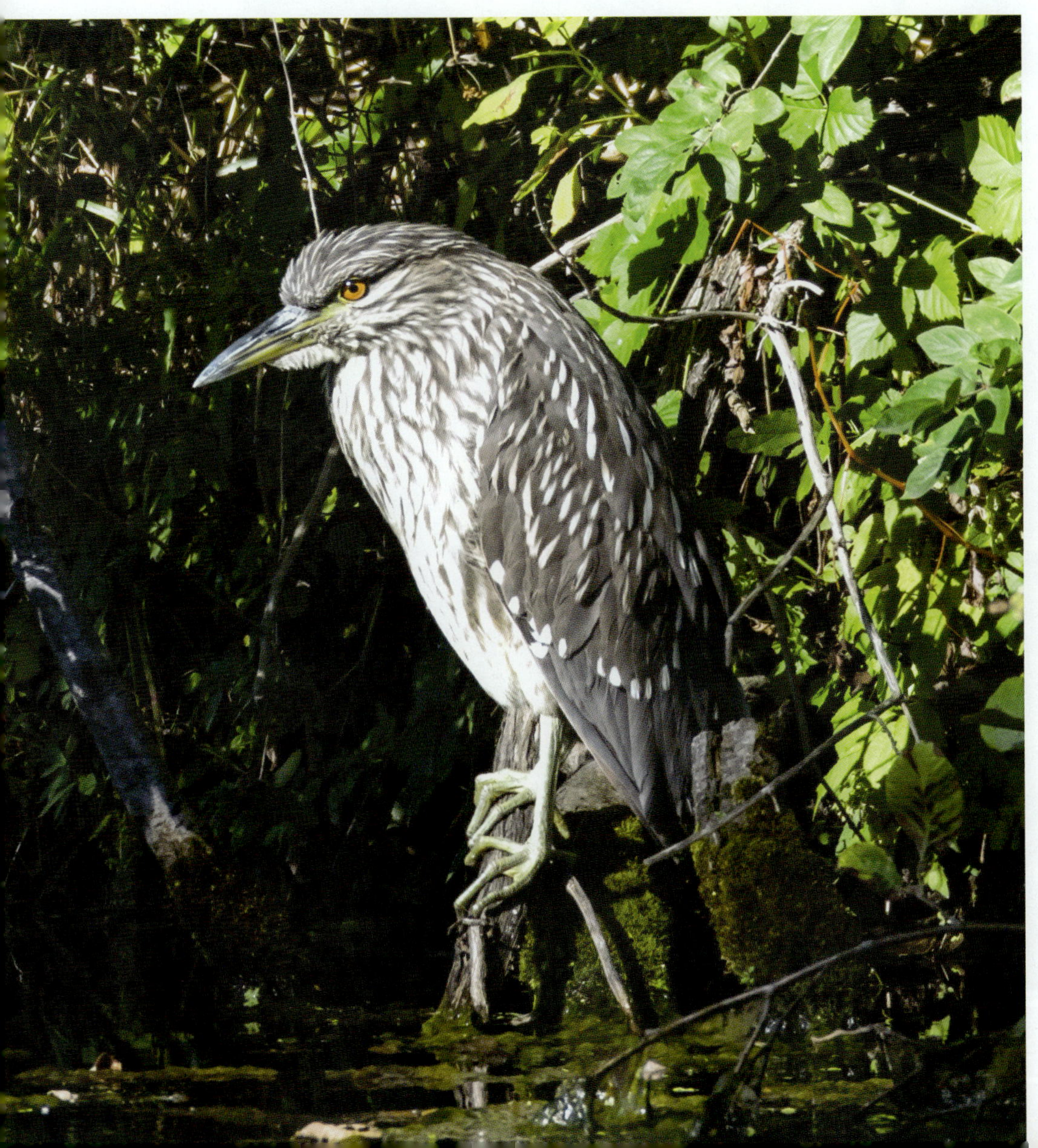

Yellow-crowned Night-Heron

Yellow-crowned Night-Herons can be found almost anywhere, but because land crabs are their favorite food, they are more common near the coast where there is brackish water. They were successfully introduced to Bermuda to replace an extinct night-heron species and help reduce a land crab infestation.

Like their Black-crowned cousins, they are hard to find. During the day, they roost in the mangroves, and they typically eat at night. A high tide that brings crabs out of their burrows will bring them out during the day. This adult bird was catching land crabs on the Joe's Overlook trail at Pelican Island National Wildlife Refuge early in the morning.

Adult birds have a black-and-white pattern on their faces and a striking yellow forehead. The white spots on the wing feathers of a young Yellow-crowned are much smaller than those on a young Black-crowned.

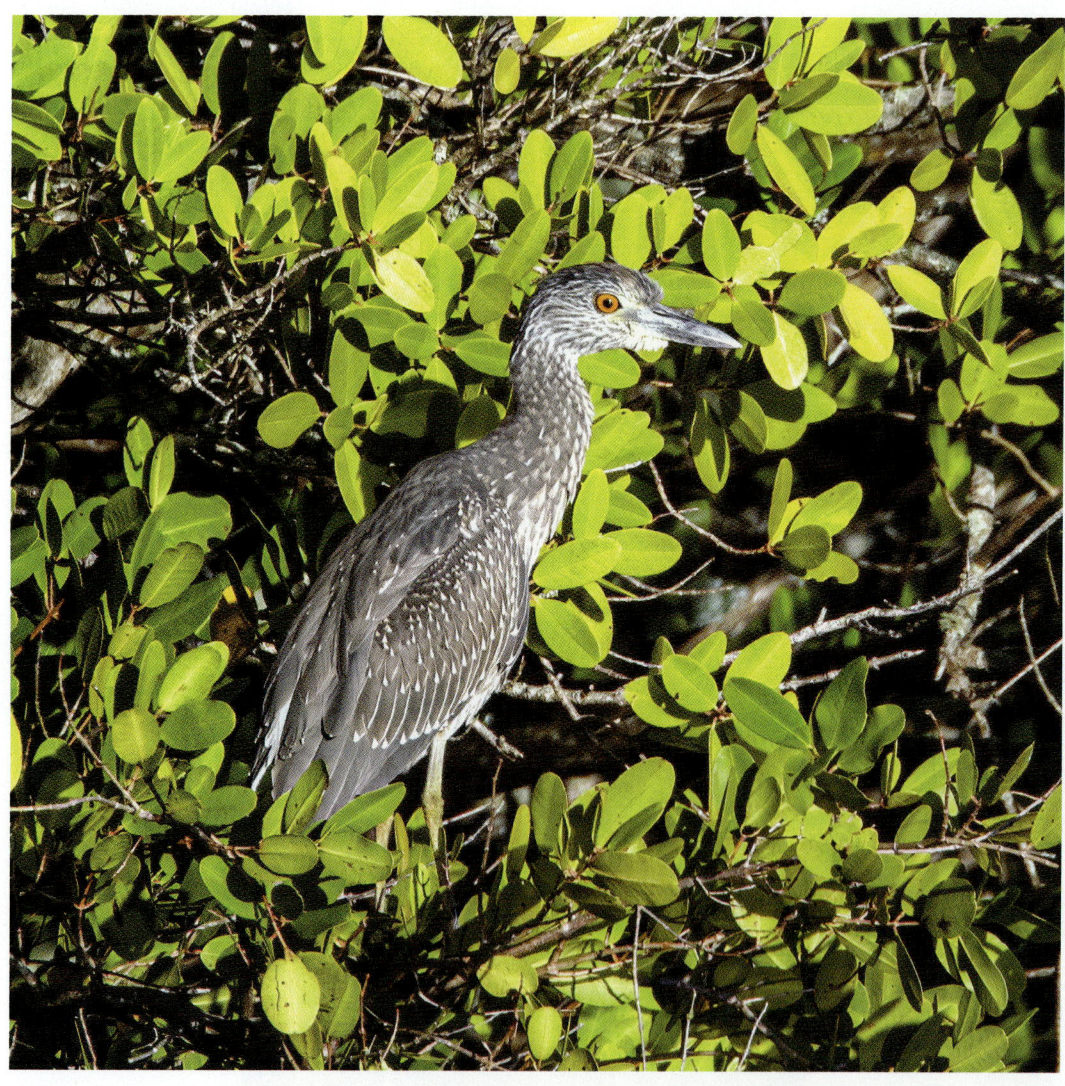

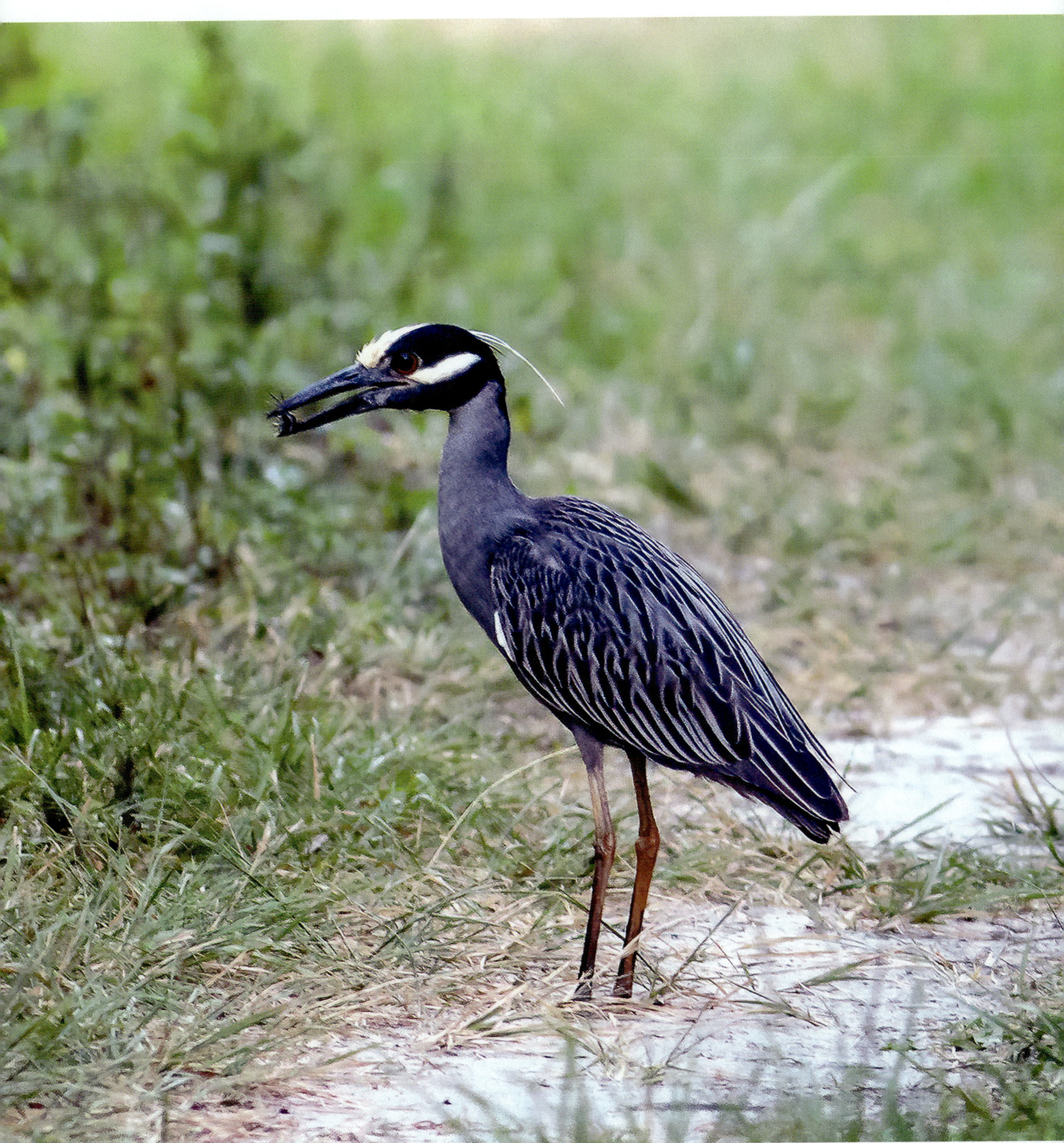

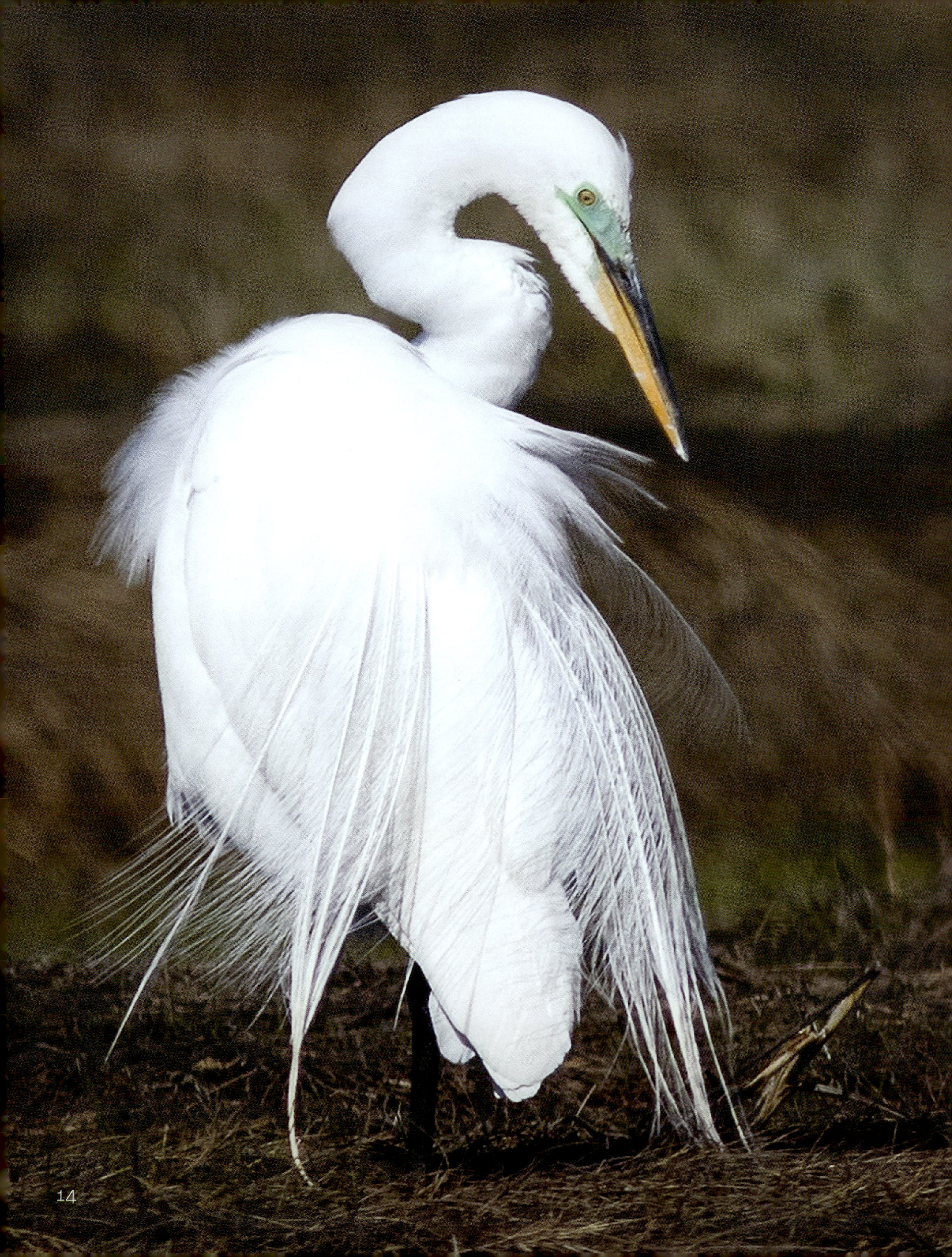

Great Egret

This striking three-foot-tall bird lives all over the world. In the winter, birdwatchers get to see plenty of them in Florida. They can be seen stalking through almost every canal, wetland, and golf course pond until late March, when they begin the breeding season. Some birds stay in Florida for the summer, but many migrate north. They live in large groups called rookeries alongside birds such as Snowy Egrets and Roseate Spoonbills. The famous rookery in Venice, Florida, is the best place to see Great Egrets in breeding plumage. The bird on the left has bright green skin on its face and long plumes indicating it is ready to breed.

Great Egrets usually hunt in shallow water, where they can use their sharp bills to spear their prey. They devour any fish, small reptile, or amphibian that comes within range. I have also seen them looking through shrubs and ornamental plants, hunting anoles, the small lizards that are so abundant in suburban South Florida.

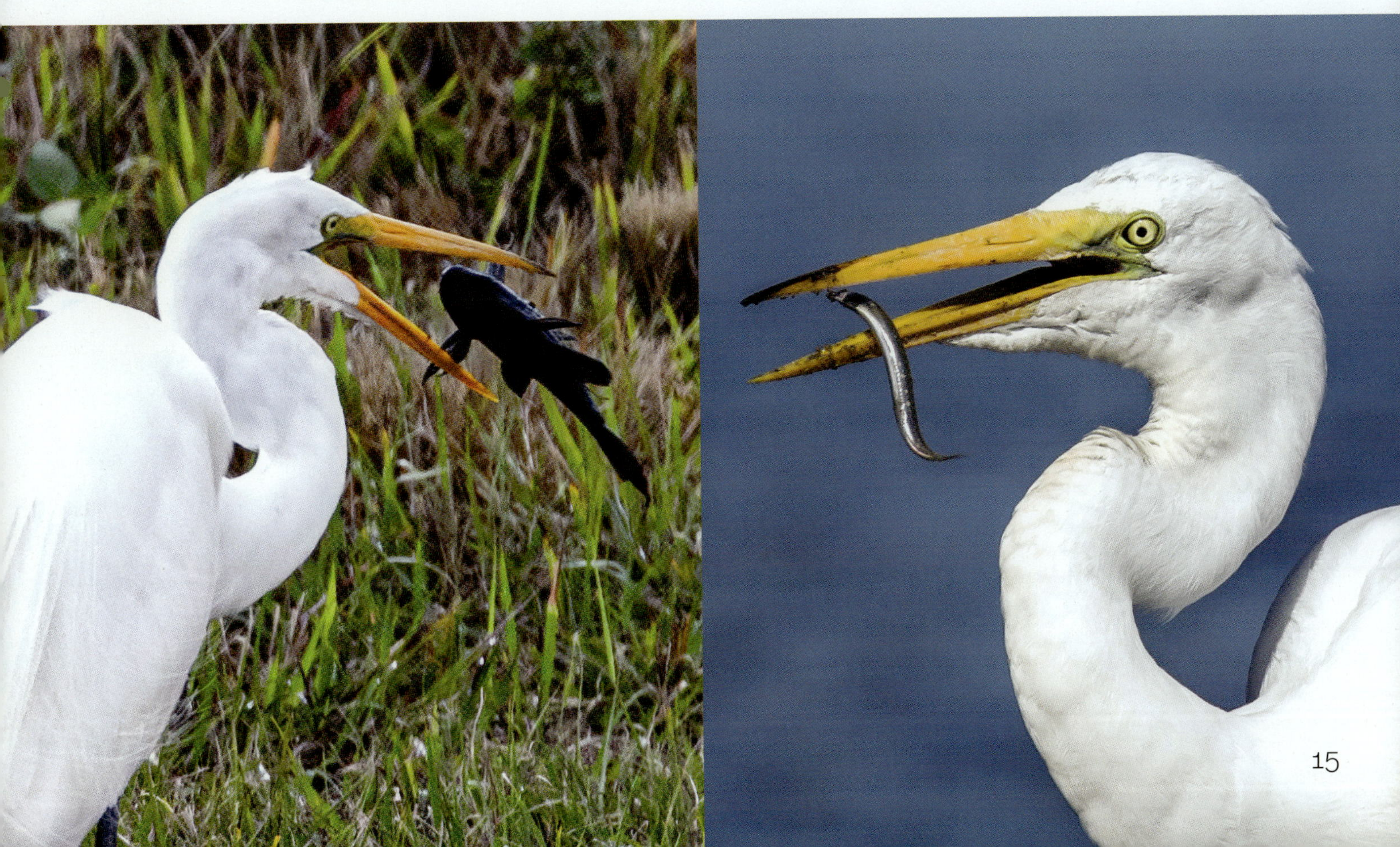

Snowy Egret

This common wading bird is about half the height of a Great Egret. Look for its brilliant white feathers, black bill, and bright yellow feet, which are sometimes called "golden slippers." Ornithologists think that the yellow feet help stir up prey as they forage through shallow water. I've seen a Snowy fly low over a pond, dipping its feet into the water as it goes along, possibly trying to frighten fish out into the open.

During breeding season, Snowy and Great Egrets develop beautiful white plumes on their backs and throats. In the late 1880s, these spectacular birds were hunted to near-extinction because the plumes, called aigrettes, were used to decorate ladies' hats. In 1886, an ounce of feathers was worth $32, twice the value of gold at the time. In less than nine months, more than 130,000 birds were killed in that year alone. Eventually, two Boston women, Harriet Hemenway and her cousin Mina Hall, started a boycott of the fashionable hats of the day, and the hunting stopped. Their efforts led to the creation of the National Audubon Society and later the passing of the Migratory Bird Treaty Act of 1918, which made it illegal to hunt birds for the market or to transport birds or bird feathers across state lines.

Although populations have rebounded, and you can see egrets fishing in many suburban ponds, these beautiful birds are still in danger due to wetland habitat loss caused by development and pollution.

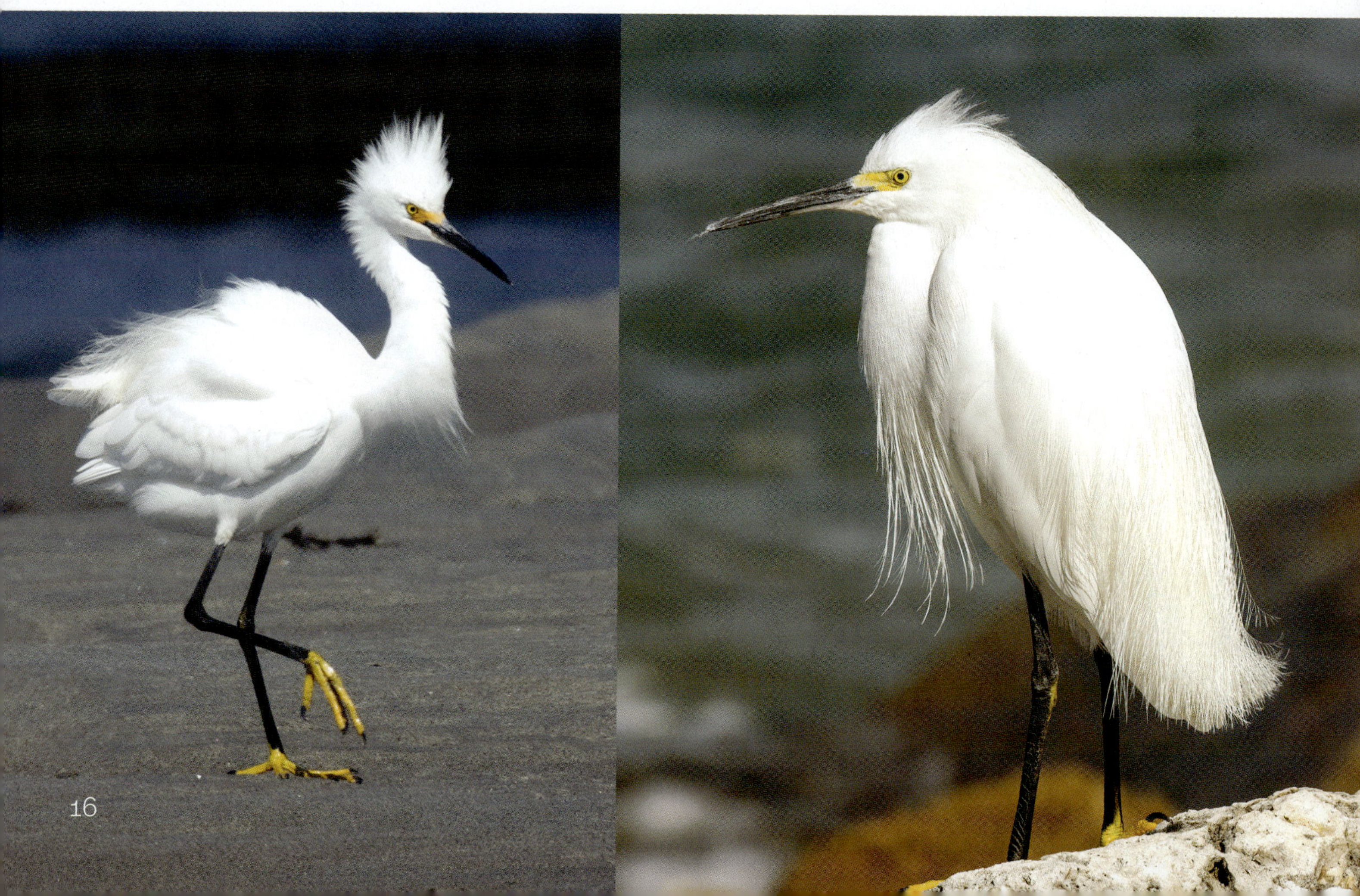

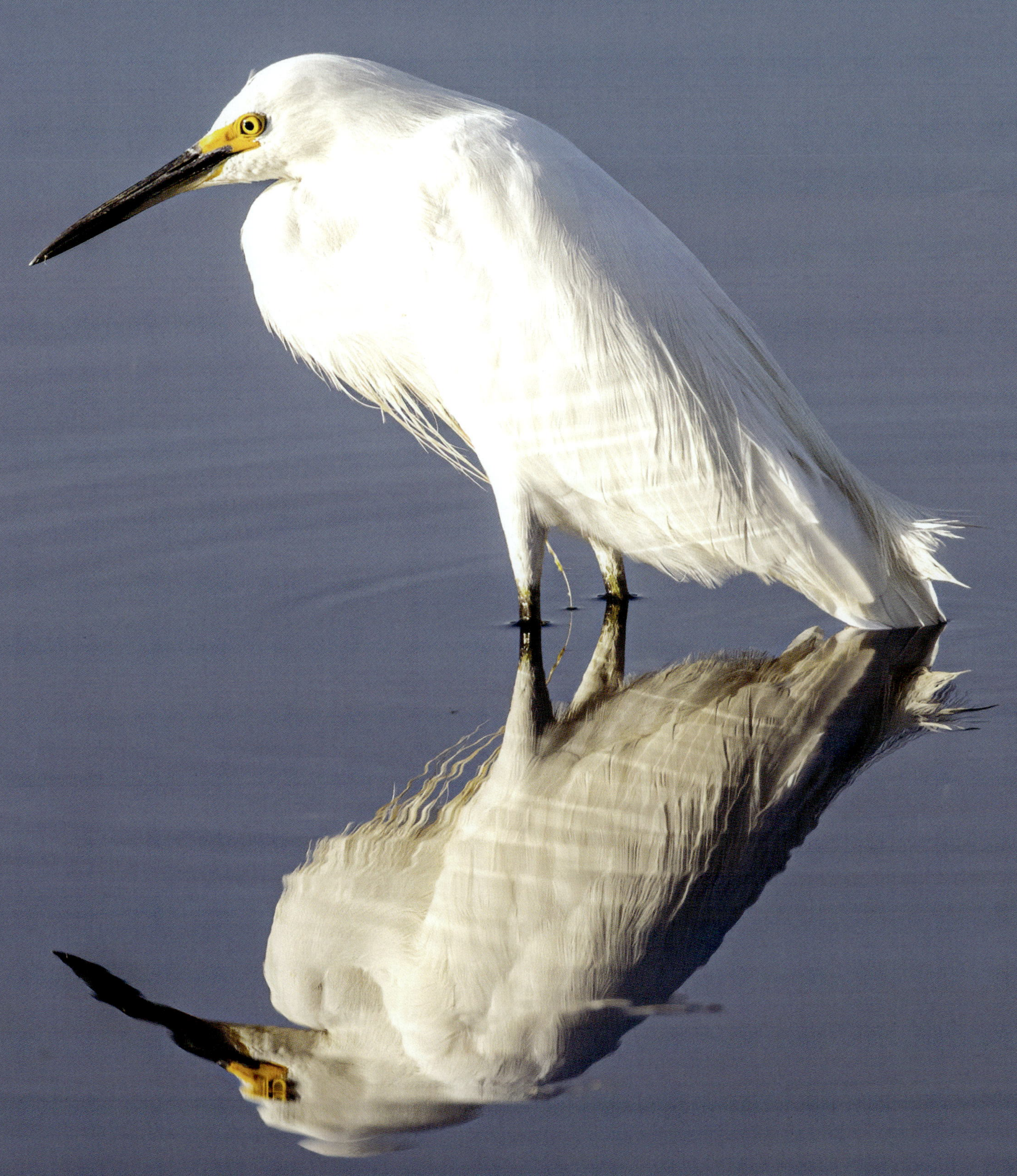

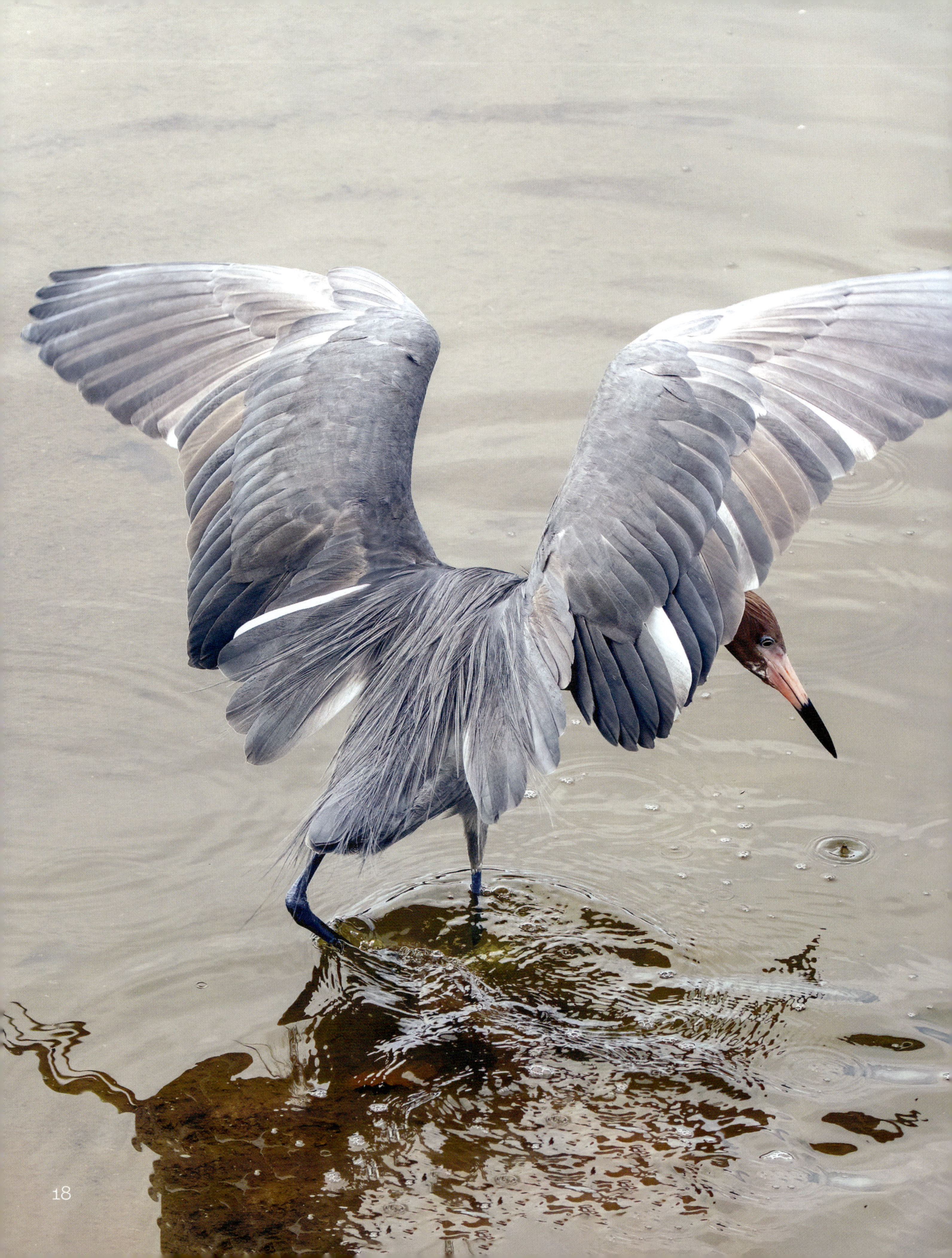

Reddish Egret

In the South Oslo Riverfront Conservation area in Vero Beach, there is a good chance of spotting a Reddish Egret. Walk to the lookout point, and you'll most likely see them fishing in the estuary. They are so focused on catching fish they often fail to notice a birdwatcher, providing an excellent opportunity for photography.

The body of a Reddish Egret is blue-gray, with a reddish head and neck, and a pink bill with a black tip. They are found in brackish water, and in contrast to the delicate stalking manner used by other egrets, they dash about the shallow water in search of fish. The movement of their wings as they are raised in the air produces a shadow that seems to attract nearby fish. Plume hunters wiped out their population until there were almost none left. They have made a slow recovery, and it is estimated that there are 2,000 breeding pairs in Florida at this time.

There are two color morphs, dark and white, with the dark birds far more numerous. The bird on the left could be a pied morph, a cross between the white and blue forms. The white variant could be mistaken for a Snowy Egret, but it maintains the striking pink bill, making the identification easier for visiting birders.

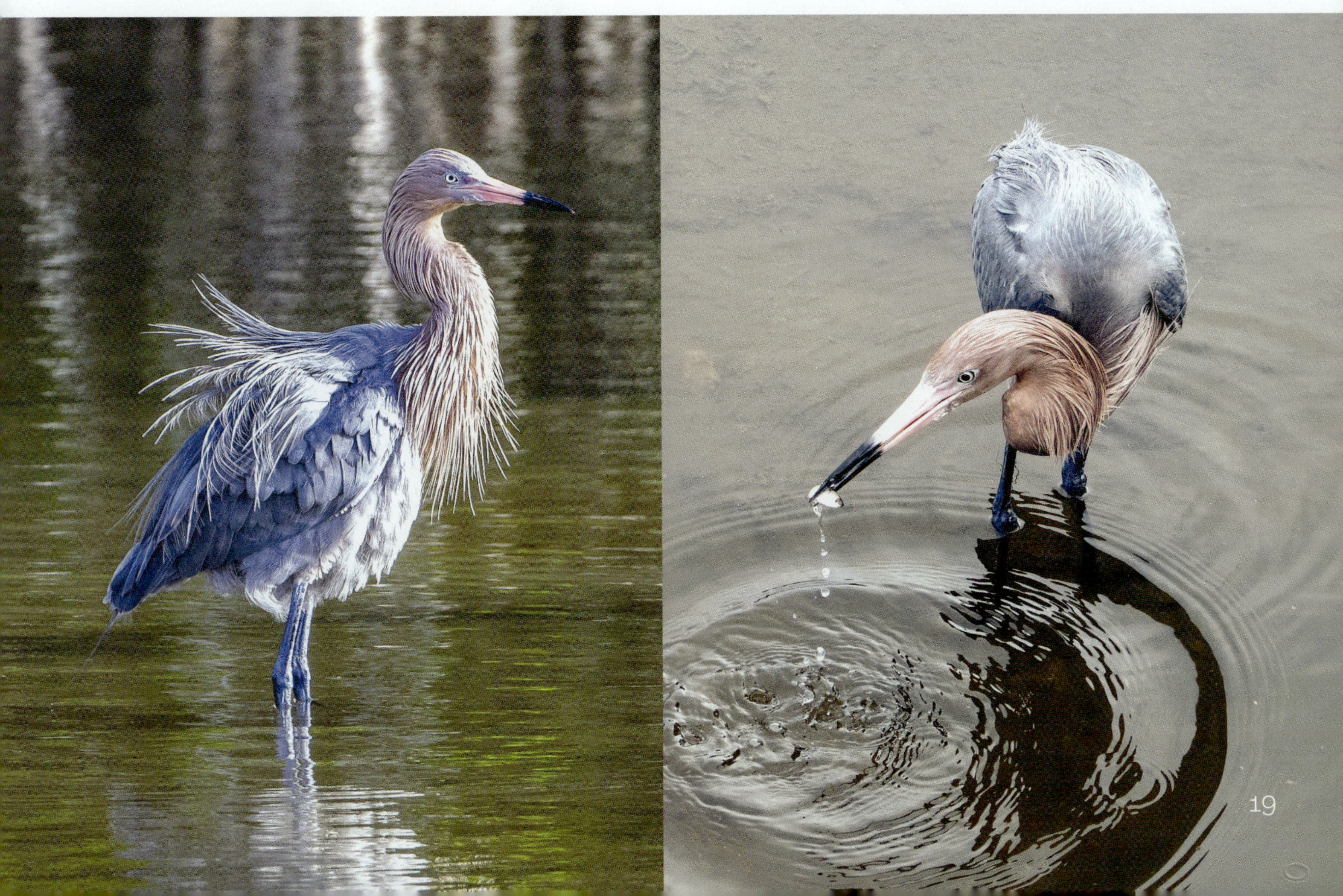

Cattle Egret

One of the most interesting aspects of birdwatching is discovering the myriad ways in which birds have adapted their behavior to thrive in various ecosystems. In Florida, small groups of Cattle Egrets can often be spotted following behind highway mowers or congregating in cattle pastures. Originally found in southern Europe and North Africa, Cattle Egrets made their living by following herds of browsing herbivores. They are related to herons, but they abandoned their aquatic lifestyle when humans introduced domesticated animals and improved the quality of their habitat. They have made one of the most effective range expansions of any bird, and they are now widespread around the world. They migrated from Africa to South America and by 1953 had settled in North America. Large herbivores or farmers' tractors attract them because they feed on the insects and frogs that are agitated by the movement. One of the most popular activities is riding on a cow's back, which provides a smooth ride and access to an endless supply of tasty bugs.

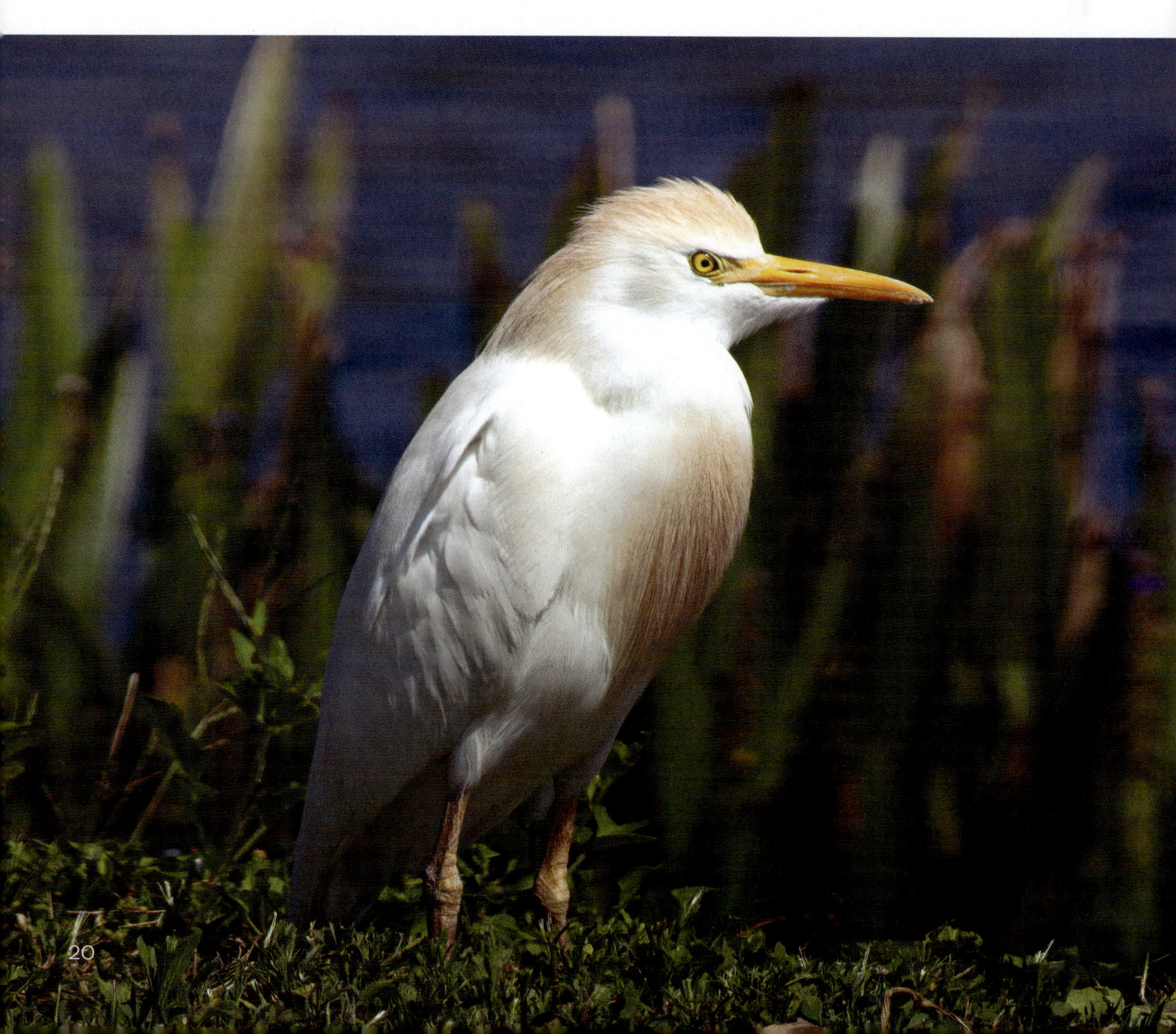

During most of the year, the adult's plumage is a bland white with no markings and a simple yellow beak. During the breeding season, the adult develops orange plumes on the breast and head, and the bill and legs become a deep orange-red.

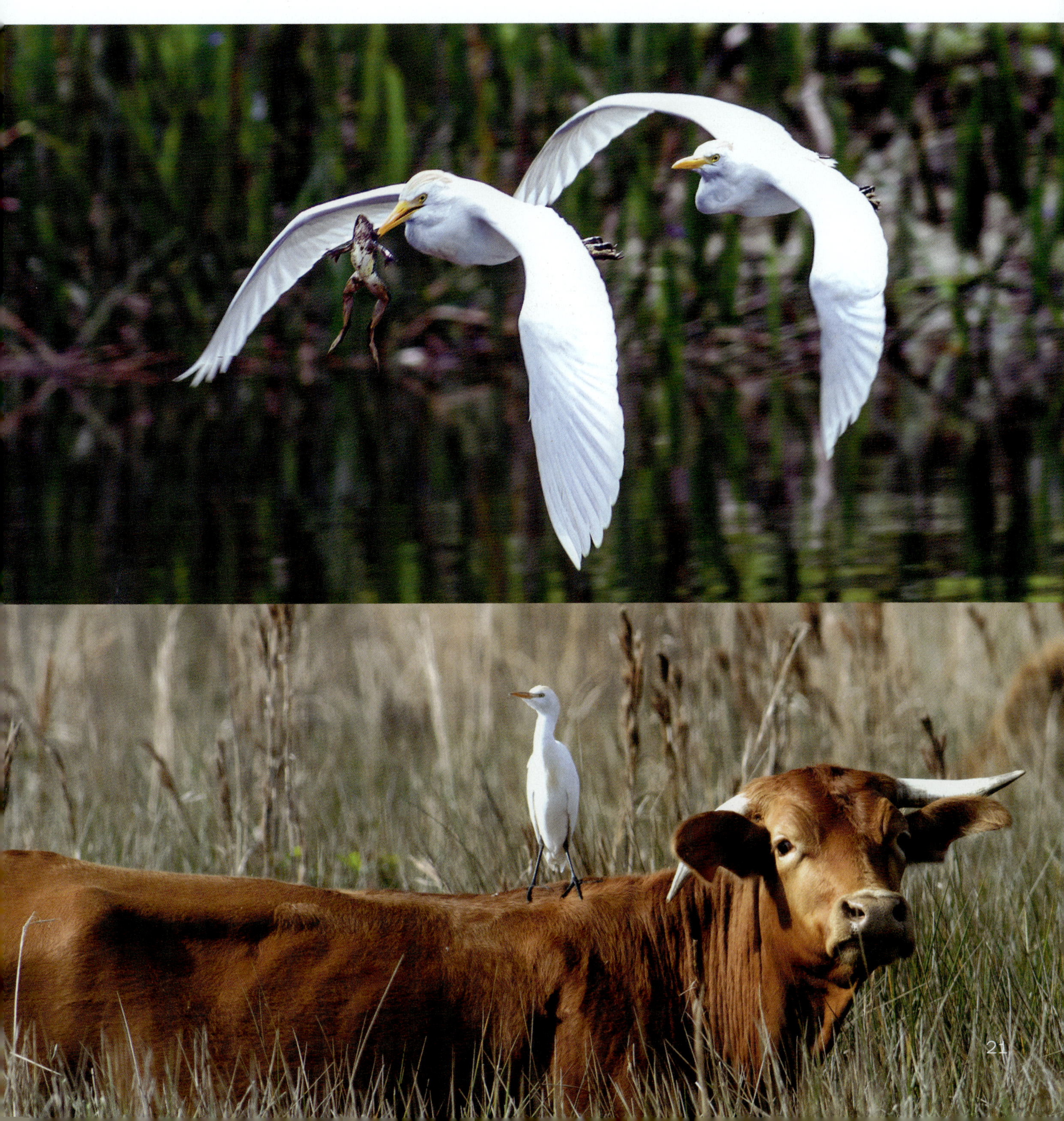

Roseate Spoonbill

The local favorite is the Roseate Spoonbill. Everyone notices and comments on these hot-pink birds. Spoonbills catch minnows and small crustaceans by swishing their large, partially opened spatula-shaped bill in the sediment to create turbulence and stir up prey. The bill contains special nerve endings that snap the jaw shut as it contacts prey. They get their coral-pink color from the carotenoid pigments found in the crustaceans they eat. Although immature birds are pale pink, breeding adults have deep red shoulder patches and a greenish tinge to their heads.

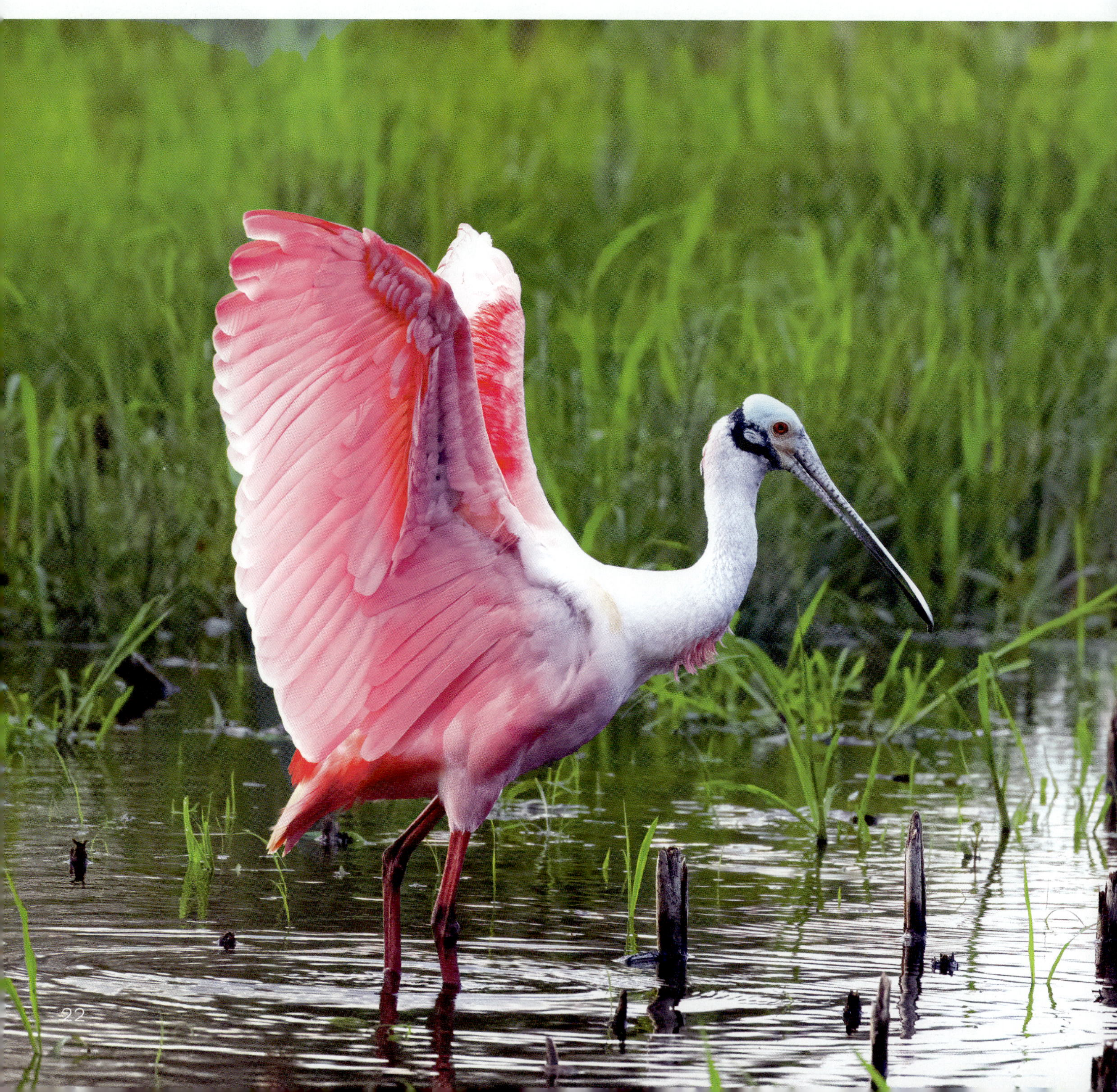

Roseate Spoonbills are found throughout South America, but the North America populations are restricted to South Florida, southwest Louisiana, and coastal Texas. Historically, this bird suffered because of its splendid plumage. Roseate Spoonbill wing and tail feathers were made into fans and described by Audubon as a regular article of trade in St. Augustine, Florida. Fortunately, the Migratory Bird Treaty Act of 1918 outlawed such commerce, but they are still considered a Species of Special Concern in Florida.

To keep predators away from their young, spoonbills nest on islands with dense vegetation. During the breeding season, the large rookery at Stick Marsh in Fellsmere attracts regional spoonbills and many bird photographers.

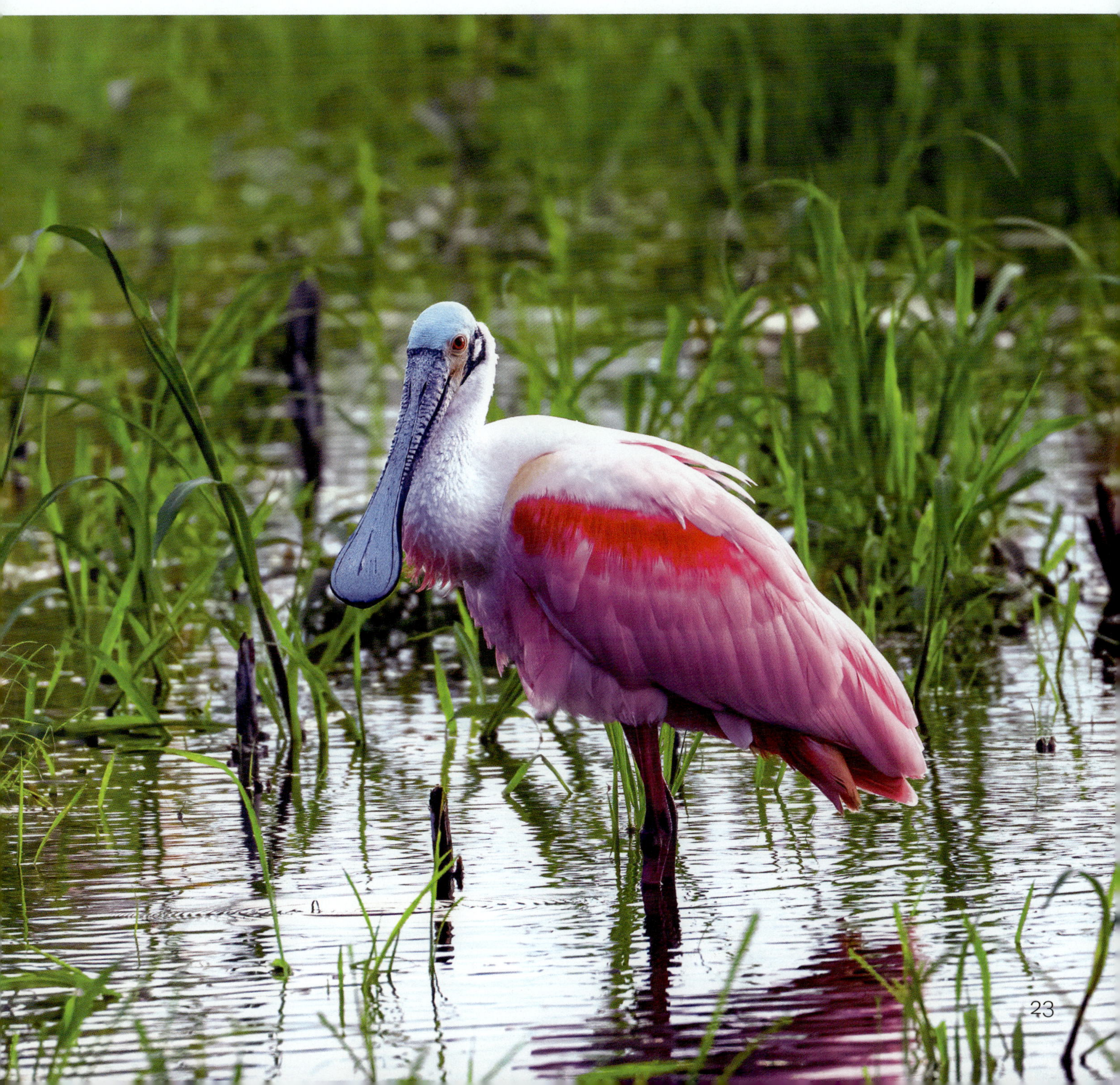

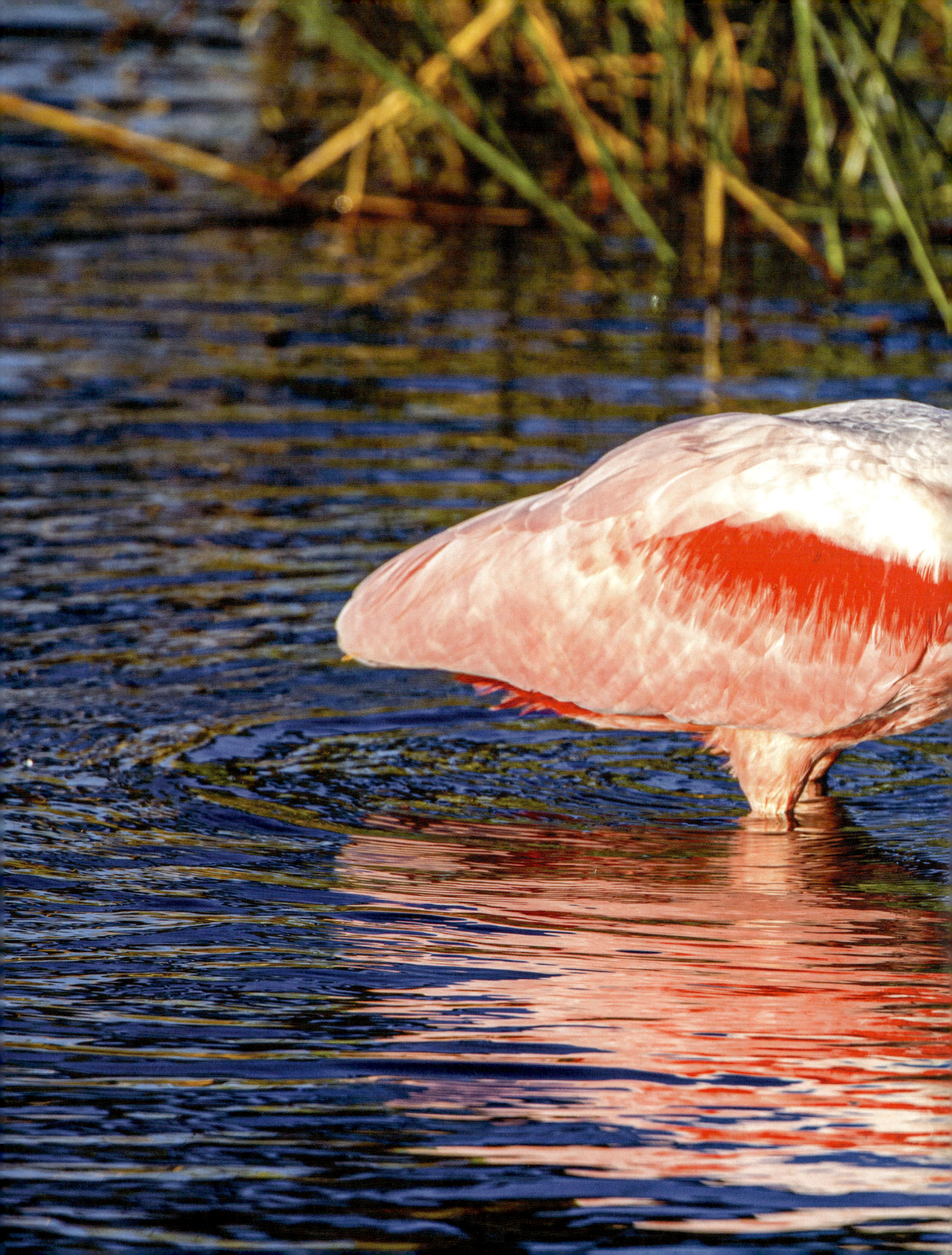

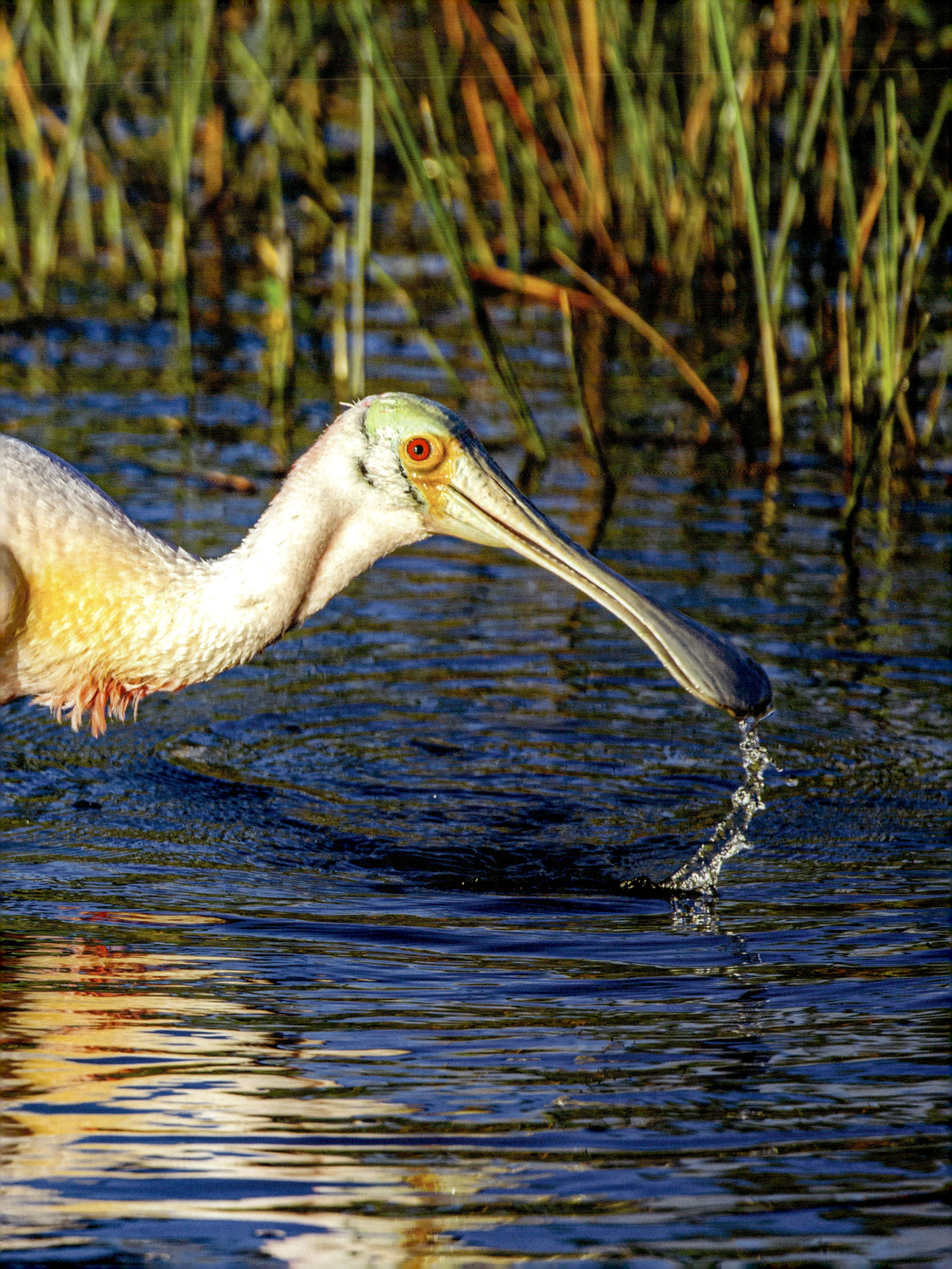

Wood Stork

This is the only member of the stork family found in North America. Breeding populations in South Florida have dropped significantly since the 1970s due to habitat loss and water-management practices. Storks rely on low water levels to concentrate fish, which they use to feed their voracious nestlings. Wetland restoration projects in the Everglades have taken this into account, and populations are slowly increasing.

Even though they are big and awkward on land, it is beautiful to watch them soar up to 2,000 feet in the air with white pelicans and vultures on a warm day. They can glide for miles, sometimes performing aerobatics and even flying upside down.

Biologists have confirmed that modern birds are related to dinosaurs, and the stork, in my opinion, is living proof of this relationship.

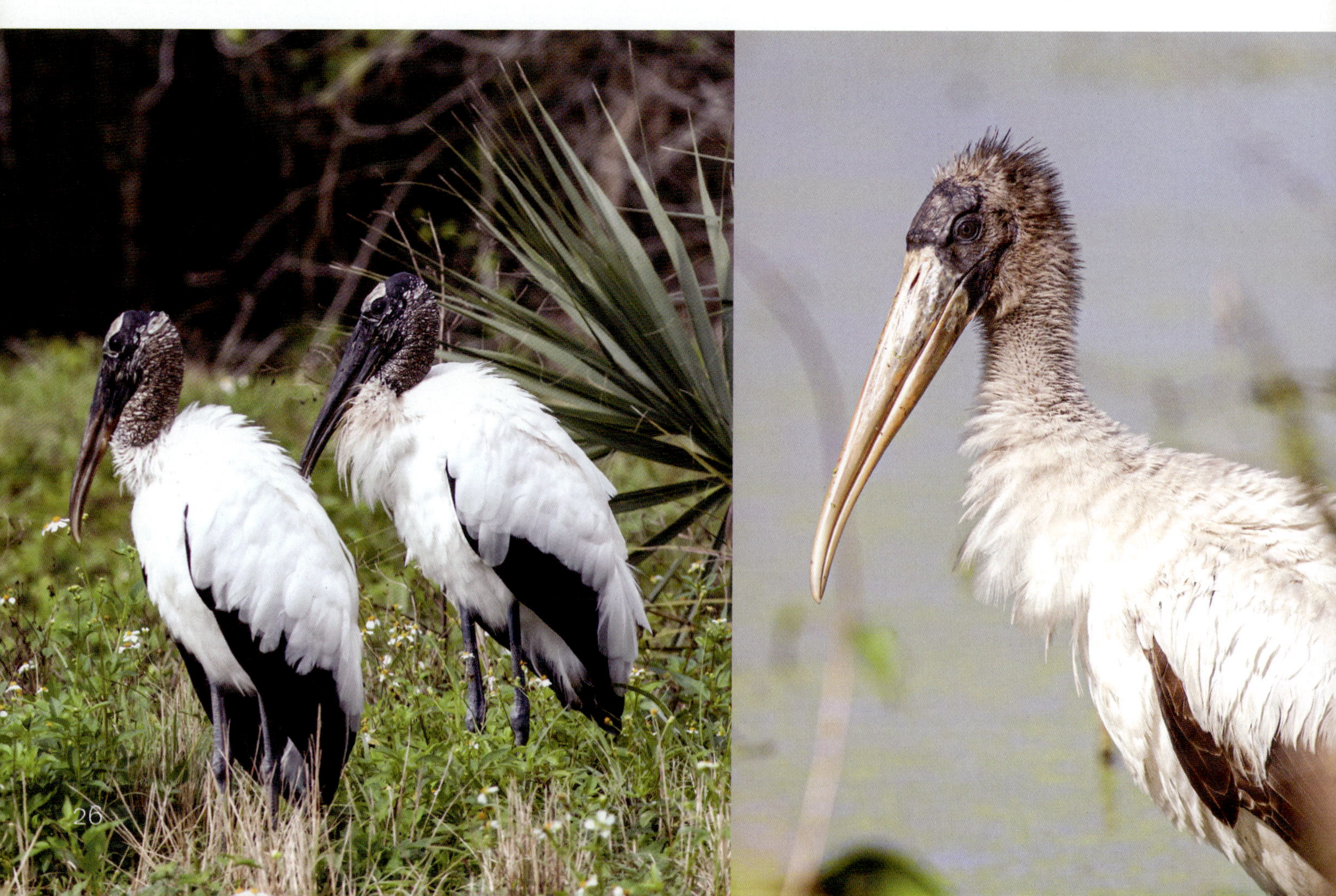

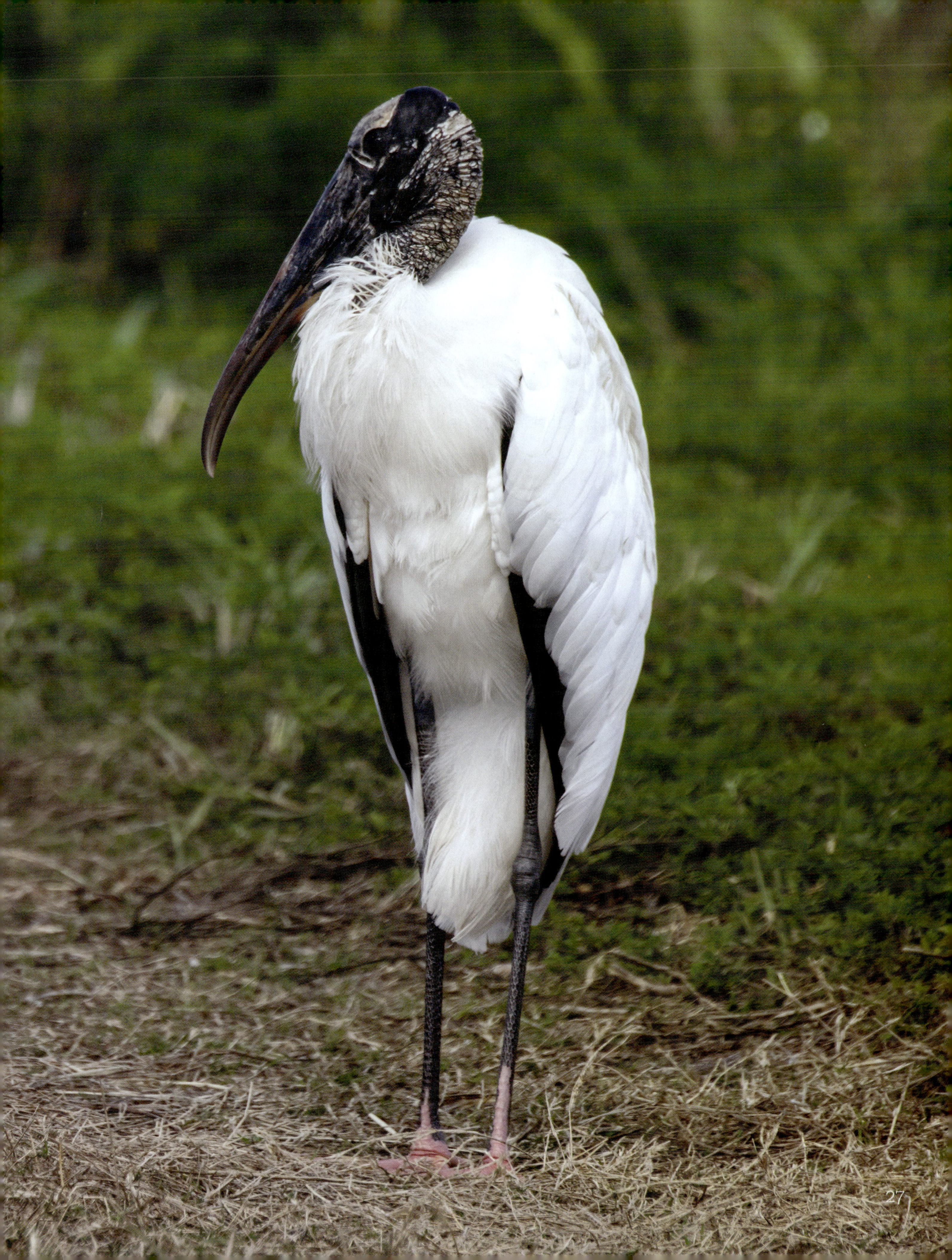

White Ibis

Unlike many wading birds that have been negatively impacted by human activity, White Ibis flocks are common daily visitors, probing for grubs and insects as they forage through shallow wetlands, lawns, parks, and golf courses. The striking pure-white plumage with black wing tips contrasts sharply with the long, curved, orange-red bill. They molt into fresh feathers prior to mating season, and the facial skin, bill, and feet turn a striking deep red, accentuating a bright blue iris. For the first year, a young White Ibis is a dull brown color, and they were once thought to be a separate species. That error has now been corrected, but this can be confusing for a northern birdwatcher studying these birds for the first time.

A White Ibis is an ideal subject for a beginner bird photographer to practice proper exposure in the Florida sun. To get detail in a white bird's plumage, everything has to be perfect, and if the highlights are overexposed, or "blown out," as we say, there is no saving the image in post-processing on the computer.

White Ibis nest in large rookeries, often on mangrove islands, which provide night-time protection from predators. The rookeries change location every year and are famous for their ability to withstand hurricane-force winds. At our location we are treated to hundreds of ibis returning to roost for the night and then they are "off to work" every morning at sunrise.

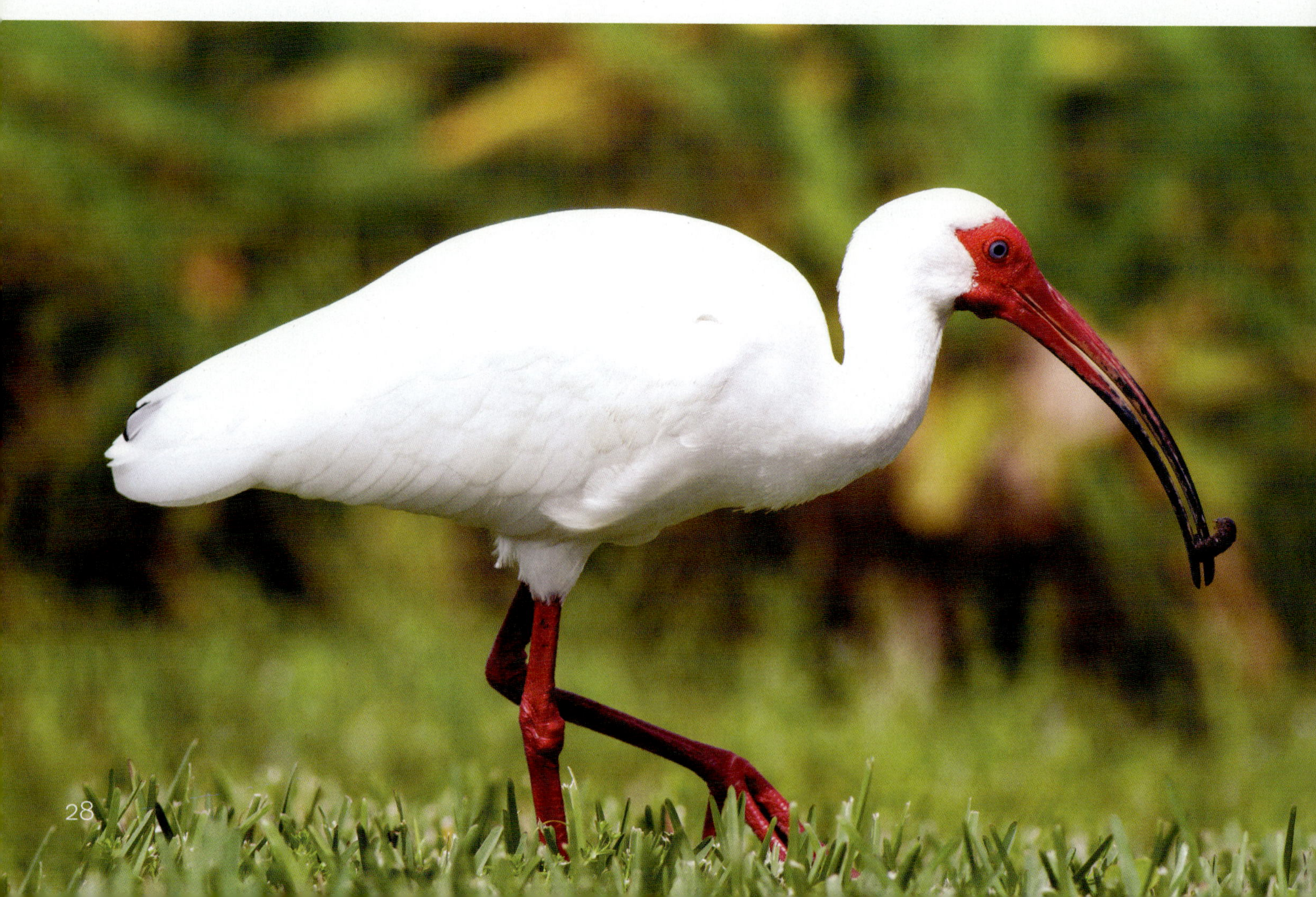

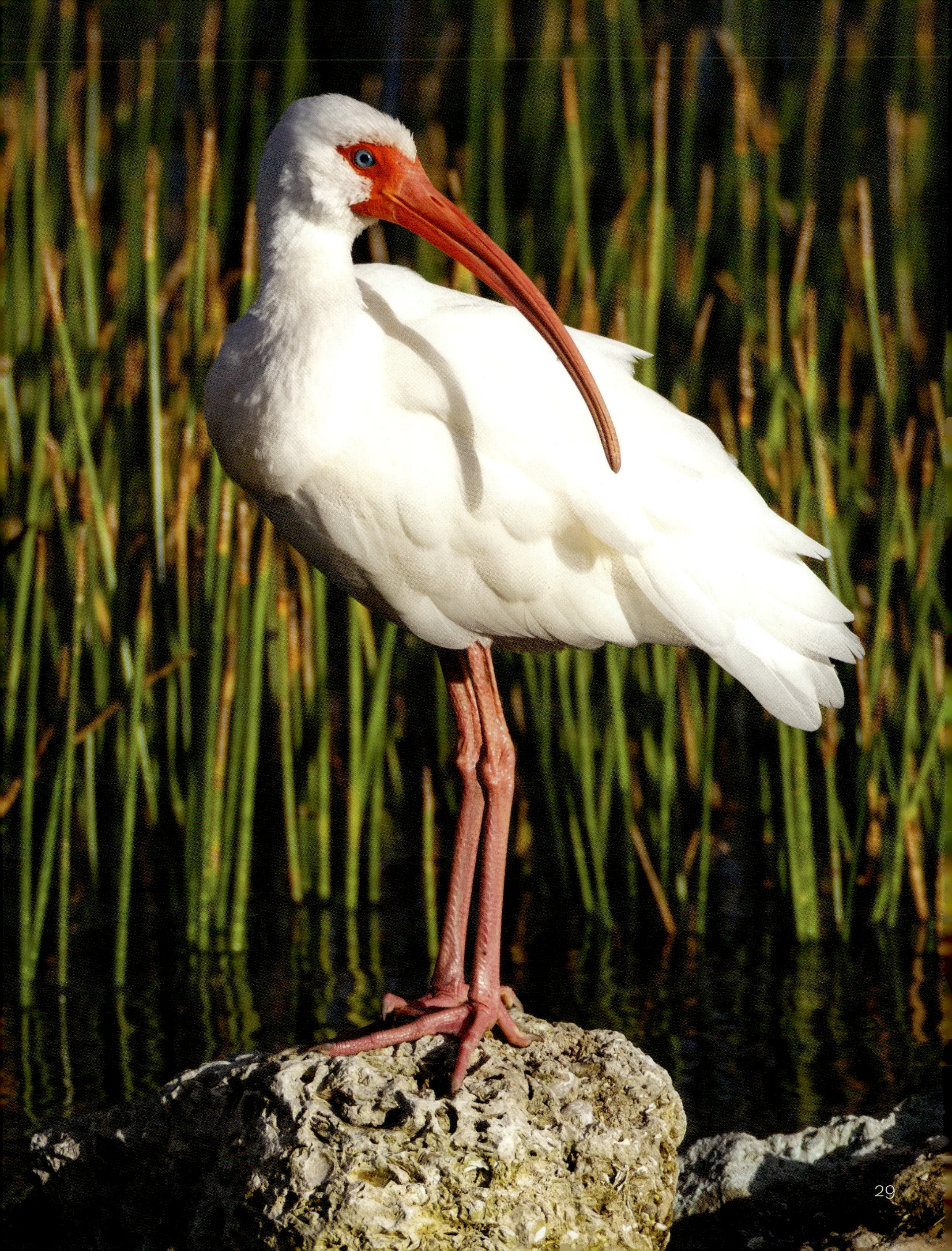

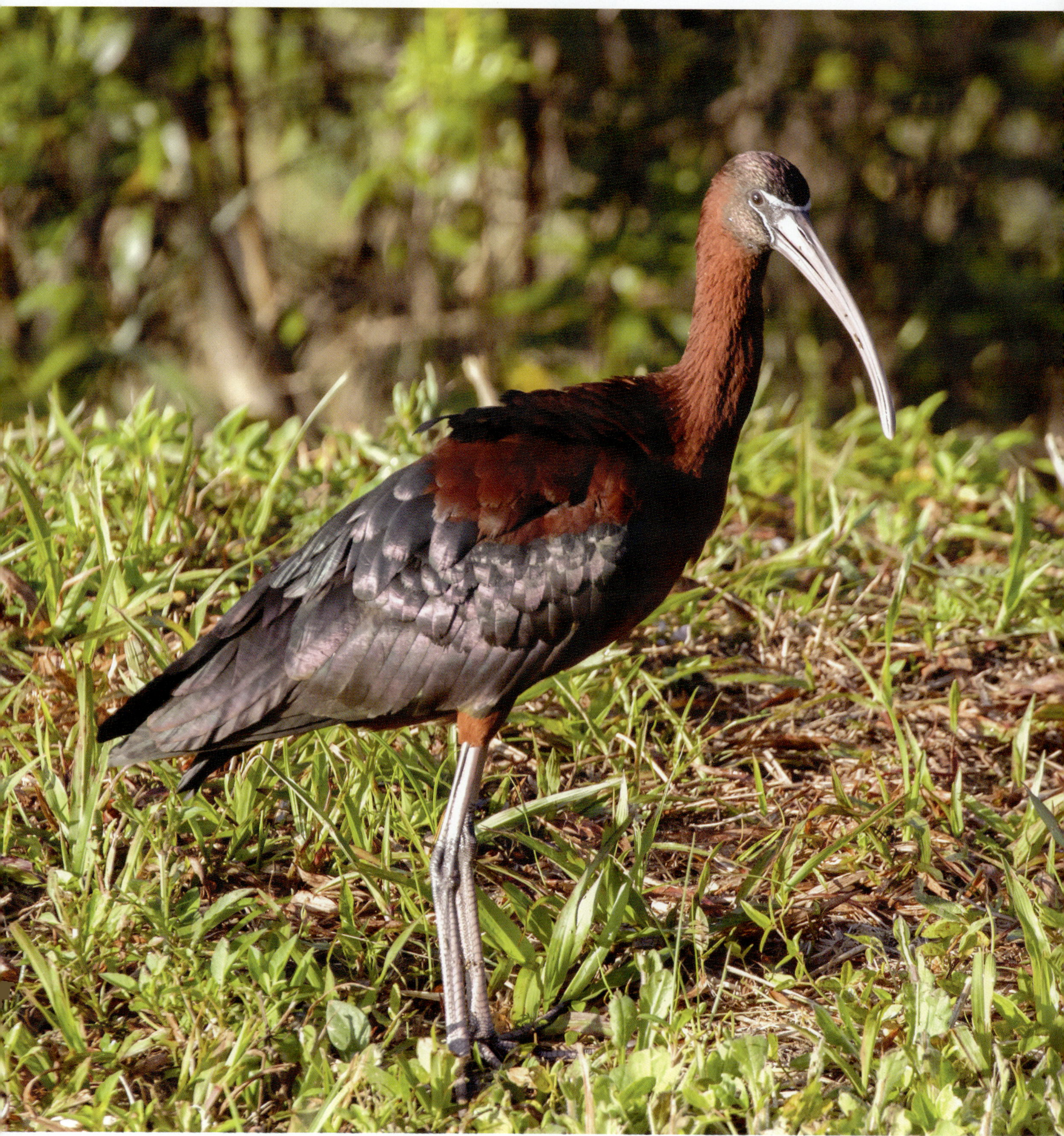

Glossy Ibis

The Glossy Ibis is similar to the White Ibis in size and structure, but its iridescent brown, emerald, bronze, and violet plumage makes this wader unmistakable. The first European explorers in Florida noted White Ibises in the 1700s, but the Glossy Ibis probably arrived from Africa by way of the Caribbean Islands around 150 years ago and was quite scarce in Florida until the 1930s.

They also prefer swamps and shallow wetlands, where they feed in small groups on crayfish, crabs, snails and snakes. However, unlike the White Ibis, they will disperse as far north as Maine after breeding. In August 2022, a flock of immature White Ibis was discovered in a marsh in Wells, Maine. This is a rare occurrence, and it is the first time in thirty years White Ibis have been recorded that far north.

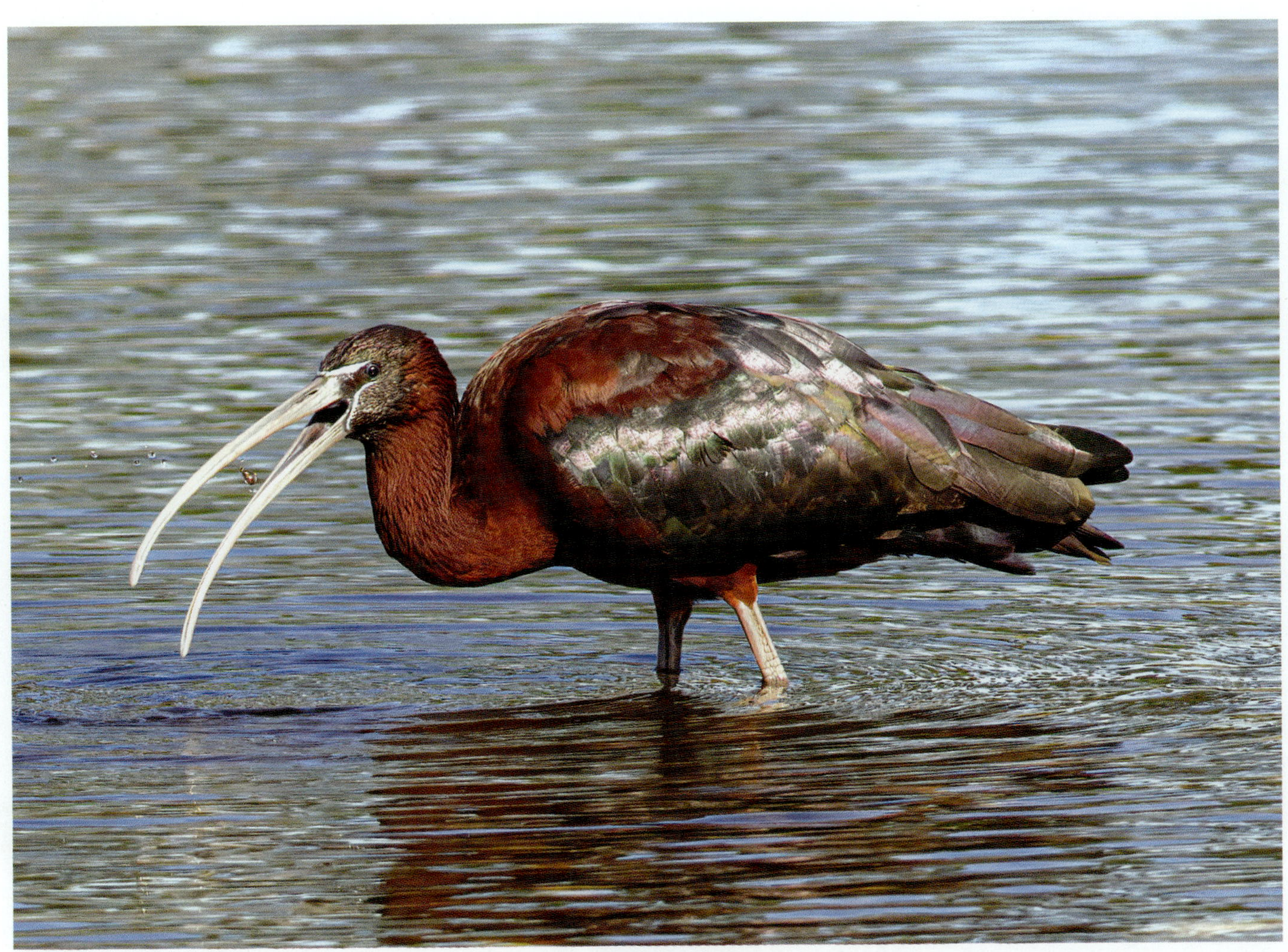

Limpkin

A Limpkin is an inconspicuous brown bird with white markings that give it a streaked appearance. The name comes from the peculiar gait described as "limping." Limpkin were hunted to near extinction in Florida by the beginning of the twentieth century, and they are slowly making a comeback. They are usually seen along the edges of ponds searching for apple snails, their favorite food, but they will also eat insects, worms, and mussels. This is a South and Central American bird. Florida and southern Georgia, where snails and freshwater mussels are found, is the northernmost part of their range. Management of non-native vegetation like hyacinths and cattails in foraging areas is important for Limpkin survival.

Limpkins are known for their loud wails or screams at dawn and dusk and sometimes through the night, as males defend their territories. Fortunately for all insomniacs, the noise stops once the breeding season is over.

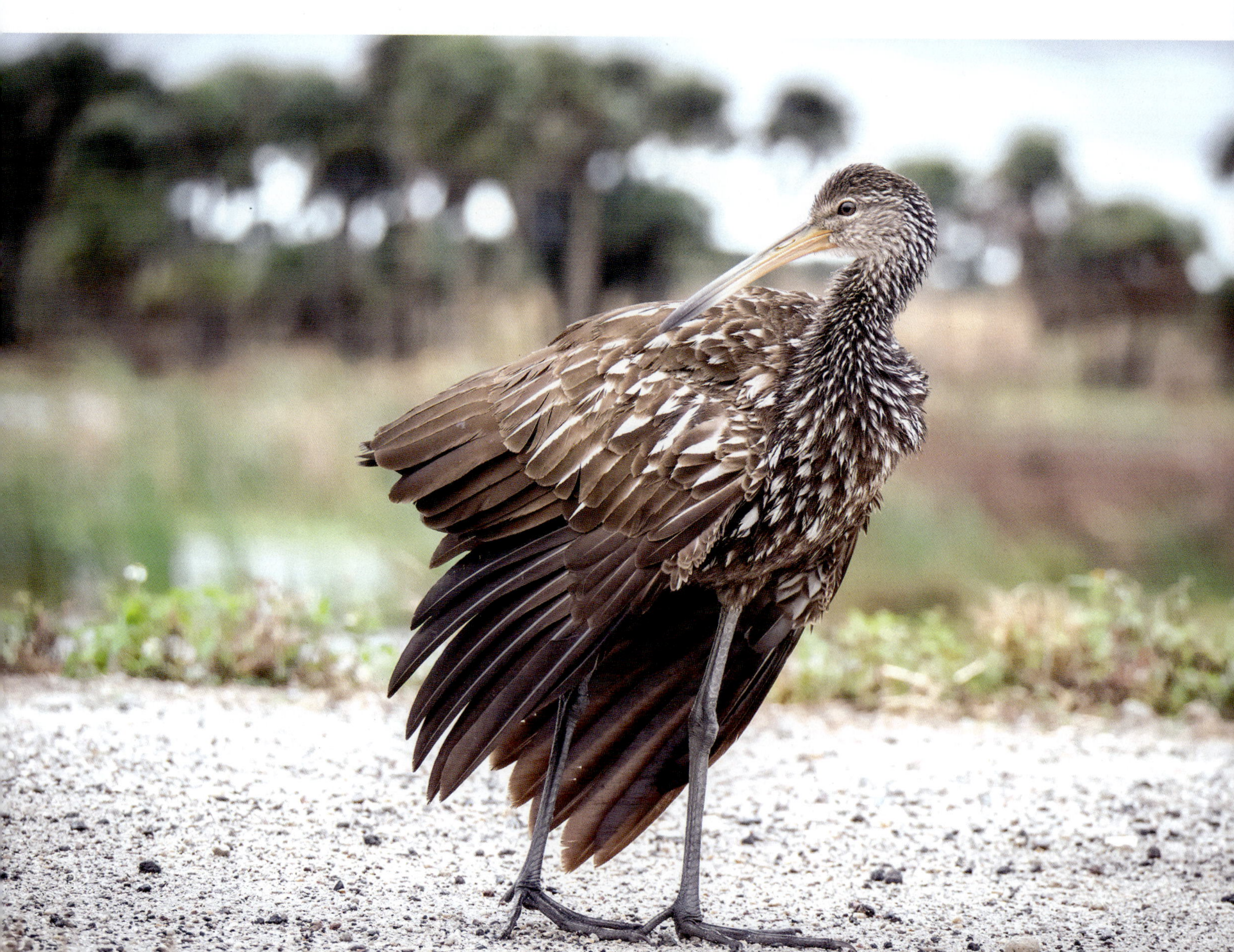

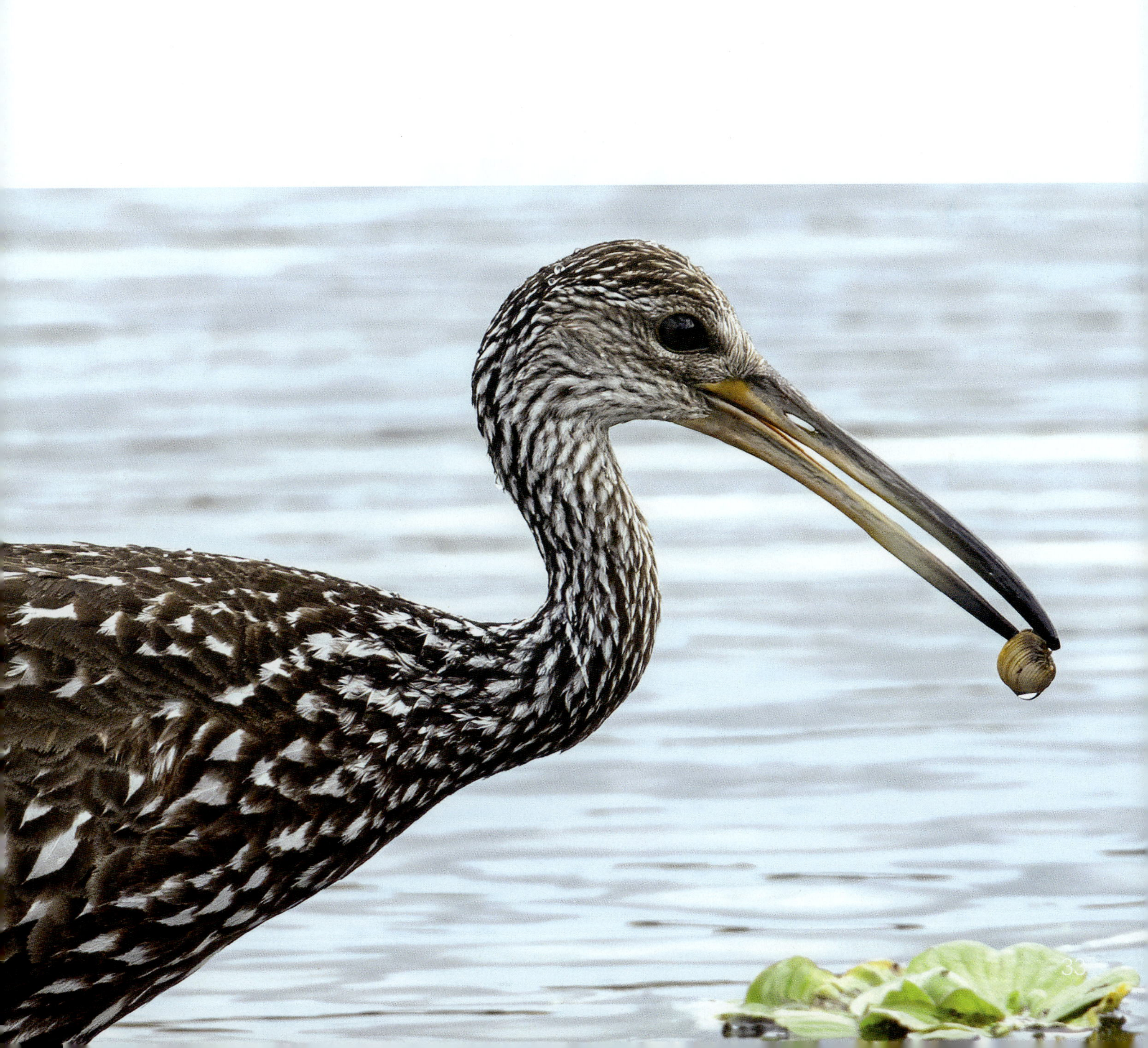

Sandhill Crane

When Audubon first encountered the Sandhill Crane in Florida, he mistook it for a juvenile Whooping Crane, but today we know it is a distinct species. It is considered to be the oldest surviving bird species on earth, and fossils dating back 2.5 million years have been found in Florida. As a northern birder, I was aware that Sandhill Cranes migrate to the wetlands and cornfields of western Maine in early spring, but I did not realize that Florida has its own subspecies of nonmigratory birds that nest here. They can be seen in pastures, walking along the roadside, in parking lots, or on a golf course.

We have a resident pair where we live, and everyone keeps an eye on their nest, waiting anxiously for the appearance of the new "colts," as young cranes are called. This year's nest was flooded after three days of heavy rain, but the pair has found a better location and is building a new nest.

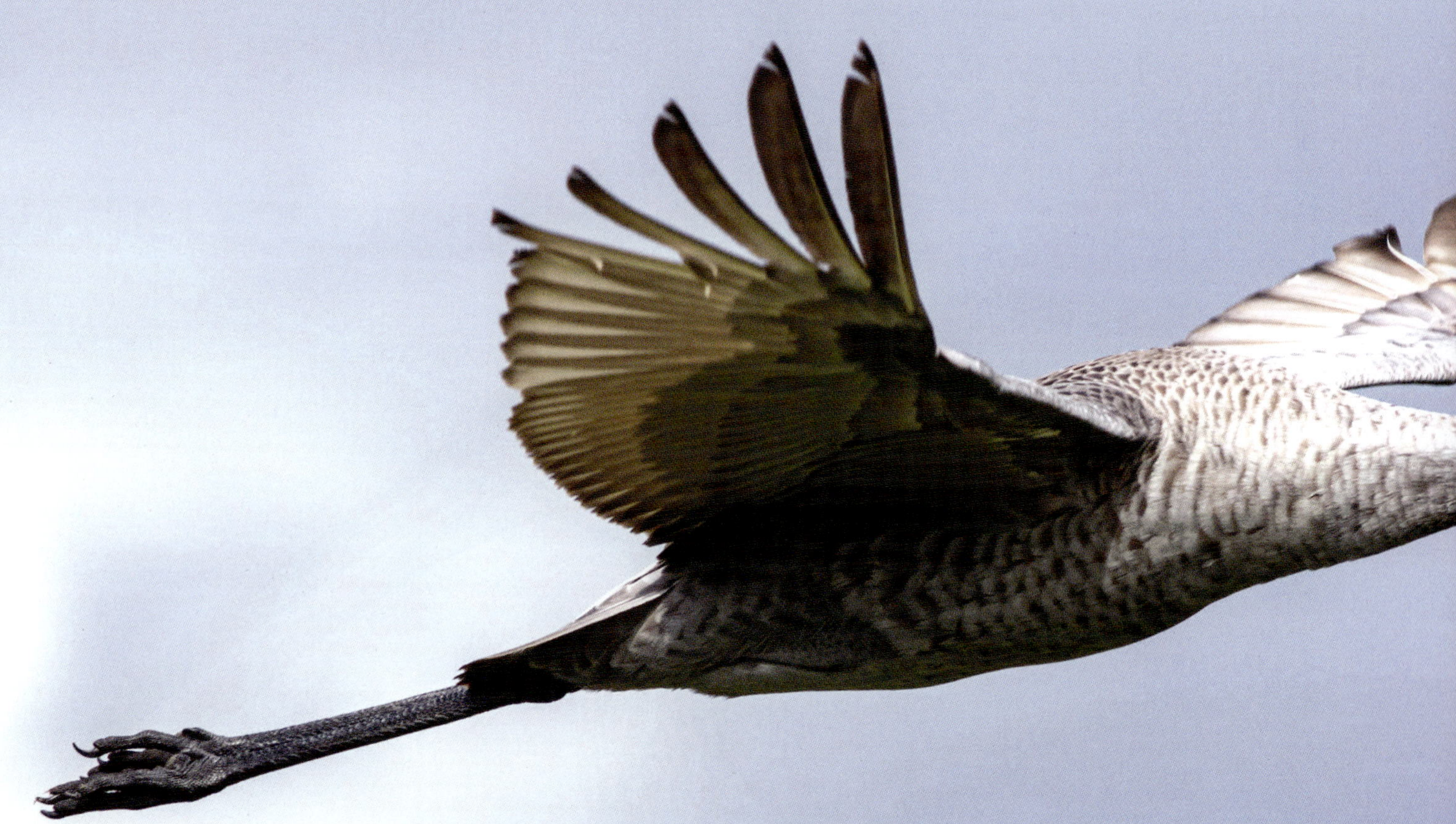

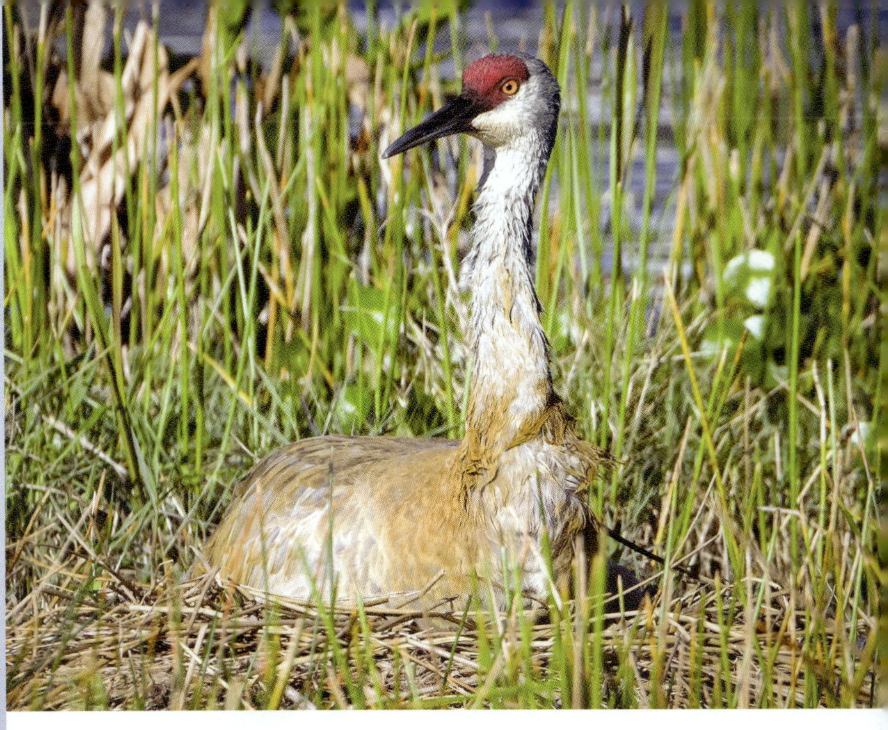

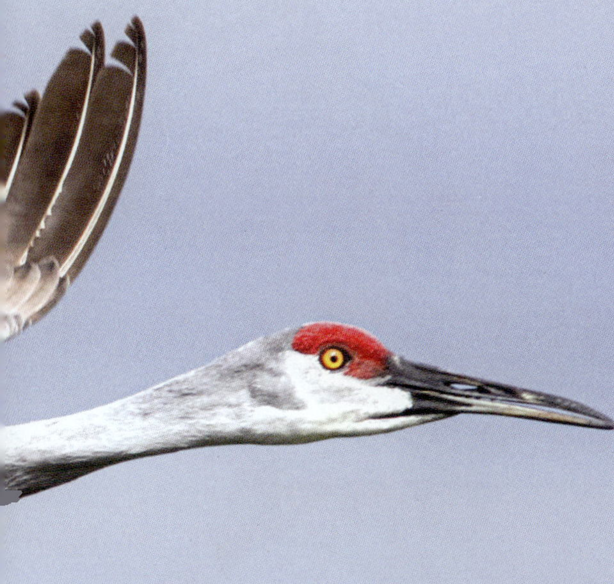

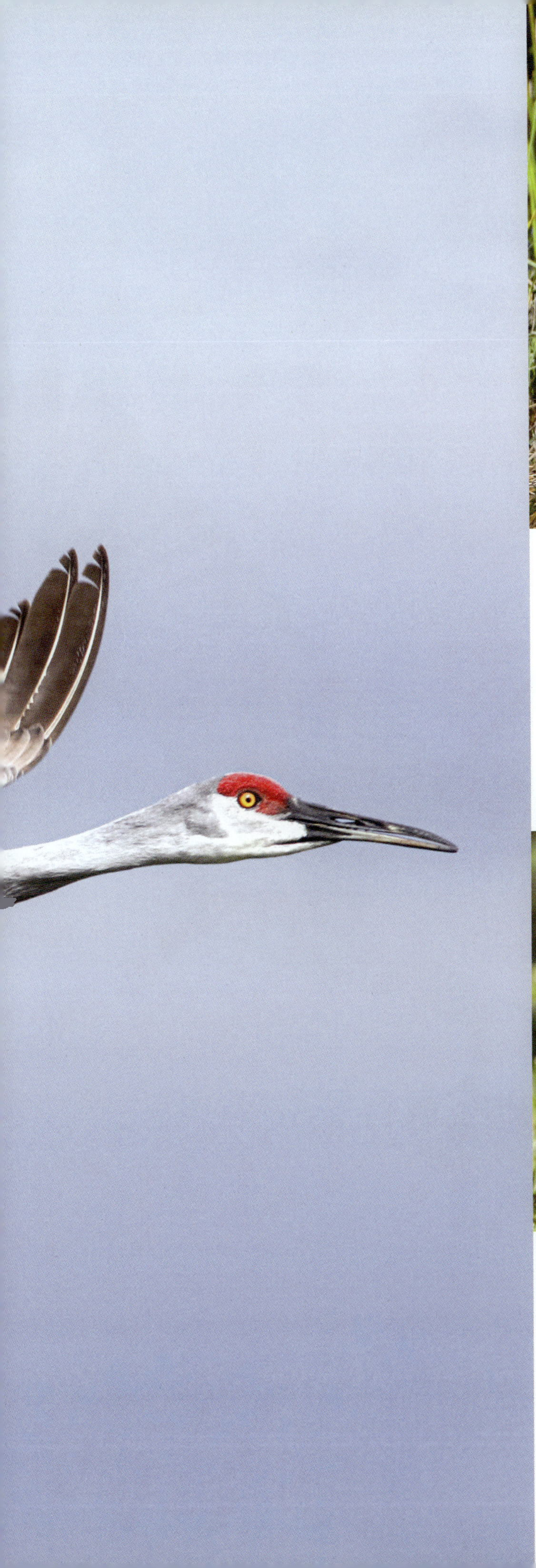

Cranes stand four-feet tall and have a six-foot wingspan. Their plumage is gray with a sharp red crown. They get their bronze color by rubbing iron-rich, red soil into their feathers while preening.

Crane pairs will remain together for years and perform a complex dance as mating season arrives. They often make loud trumpeting calls while foraging or in flight.

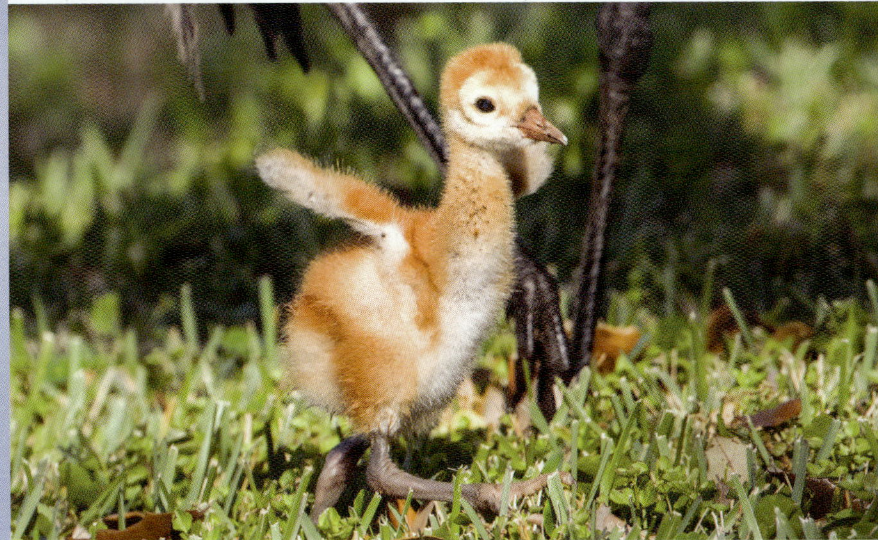

Colts leave the nest within twenty-four hours of hatching to follow their parents and learn how to search for grubs. The adults are unconcerned around humans, but will vigorously defend the youngsters if they are approached. Because cranes nest on the ground, they are vulnerable to predators such as raccoons and bobcats. Perhaps this is why they choose to nest so close to human activity in order to avoid danger.

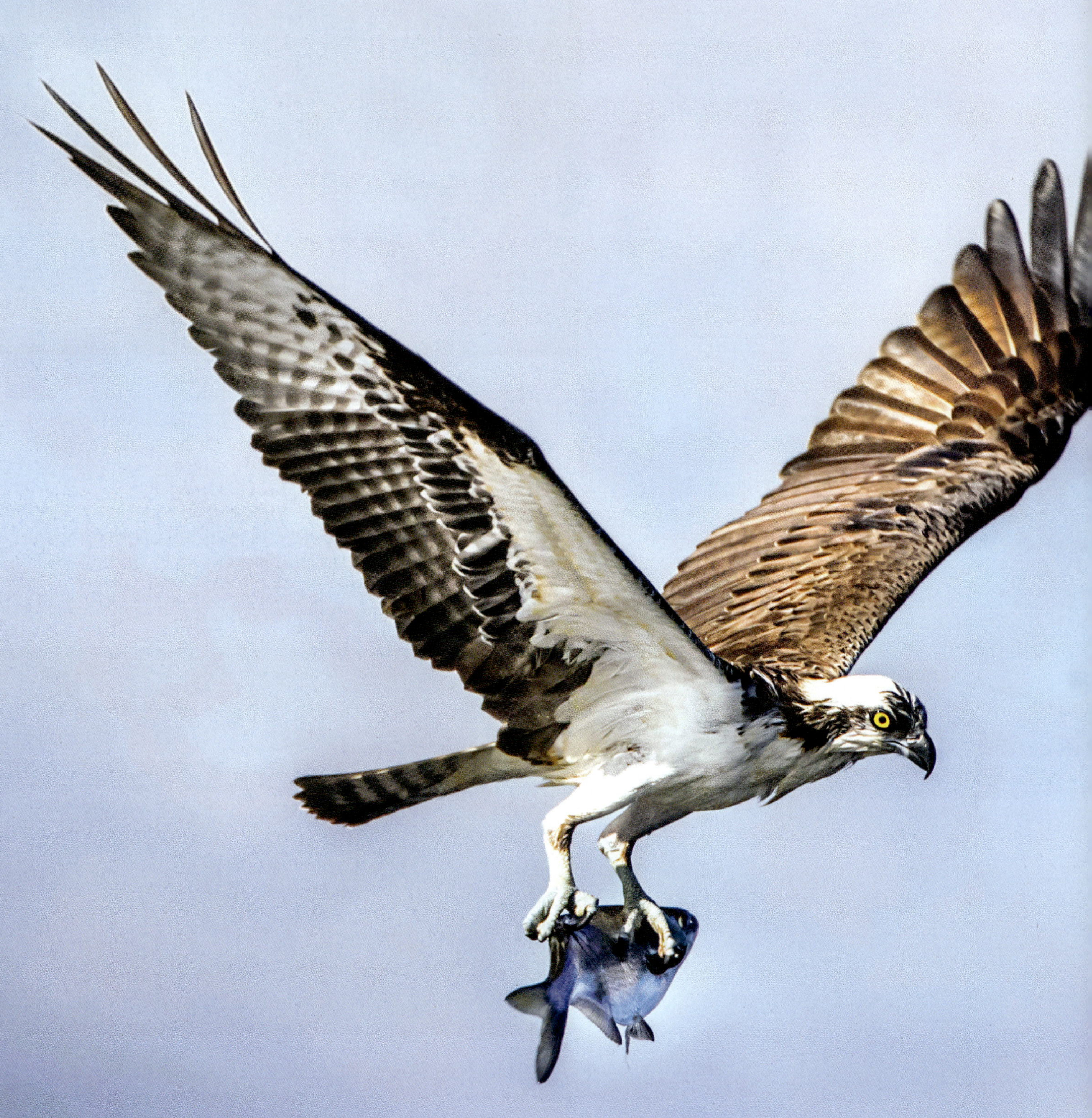

Raptors

Birdwatchers use the term "raptor" to describe large birds of prey such as eagles, hawks, falcons, vultures, osprey, and kites. Although there is no specific definition, raptors are known for a carnivorous diet. Raptors have large, hooked beaks, curved at the tip, and with sharp cutting edges to rip and teat their catch. Some birds have developed specialized adaptations like the Snail Kite. Their beak is long and narrow, designed for getting into a snail shell. Raptors also have exceptional eyesight, full color vision, and accurate depth perception that allows them to attack prey while in flight.

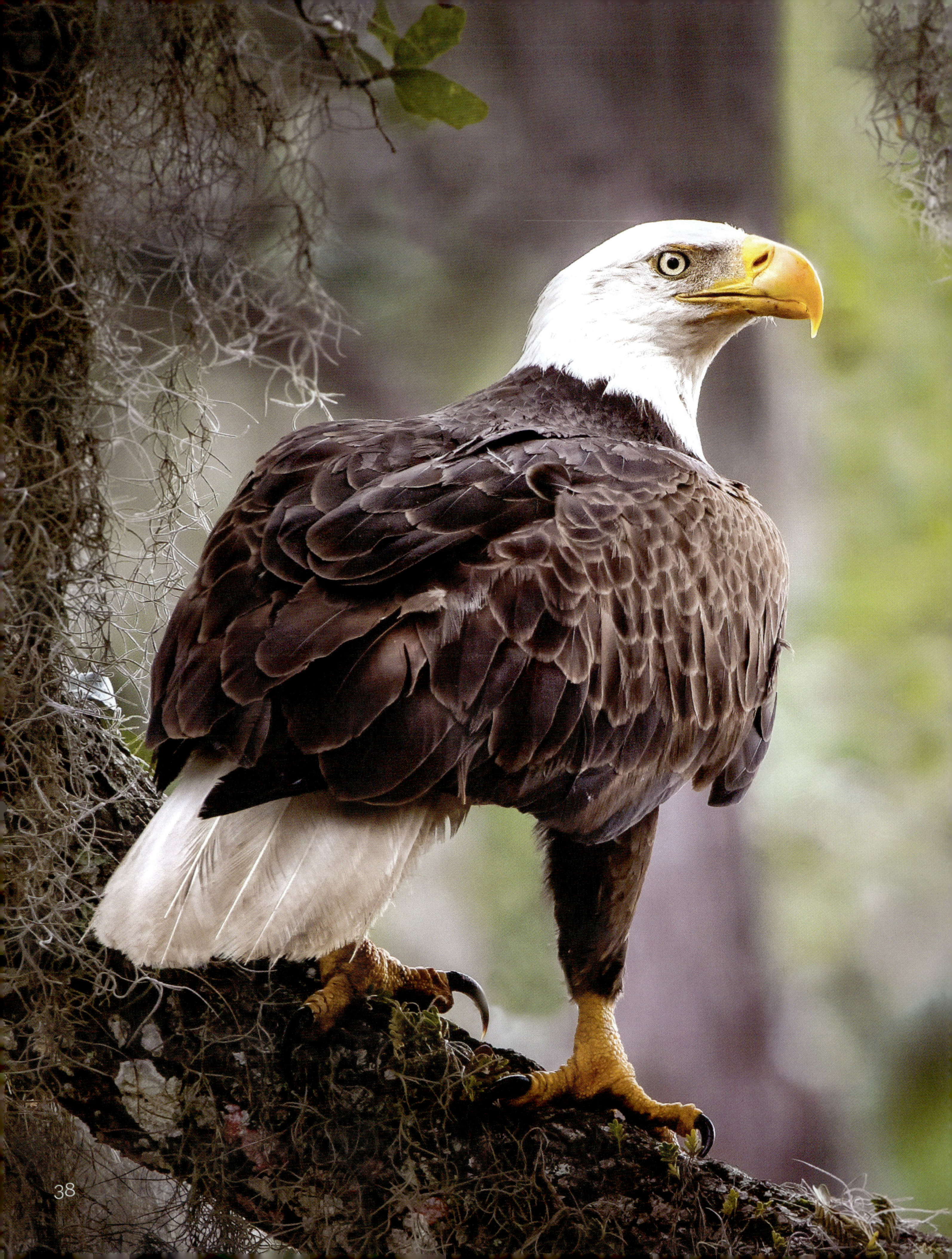

Bald Eagle

Everyone, birder or not, recognizes the huge and unmistakable Bald Eagle. Eagles are found throughout North America, and Florida is fortunate to have one of the largest concentrations of nesting eagles. These are large birds with a wingspan of seven feet and dramatic white head and tail. Because fish are their preferred food, they build enormous stick nests in solitary pine trees near a large body of water. The Florida population does not migrate, and mated pairs will use the nest year after year, raising one or two eaglets each nesting season. Young eagles have brownish-black feathers streaked with white and the white head and tail do not develop until they are five years old.

One quiet, foggy morning, a beautiful adult eagle flew across the road and perched ten feet from me. I was so excited I could barely get my gear together and get out of the car for this shot. This is now my favorite Bald Eagle photograph out of all the ones I've taken.

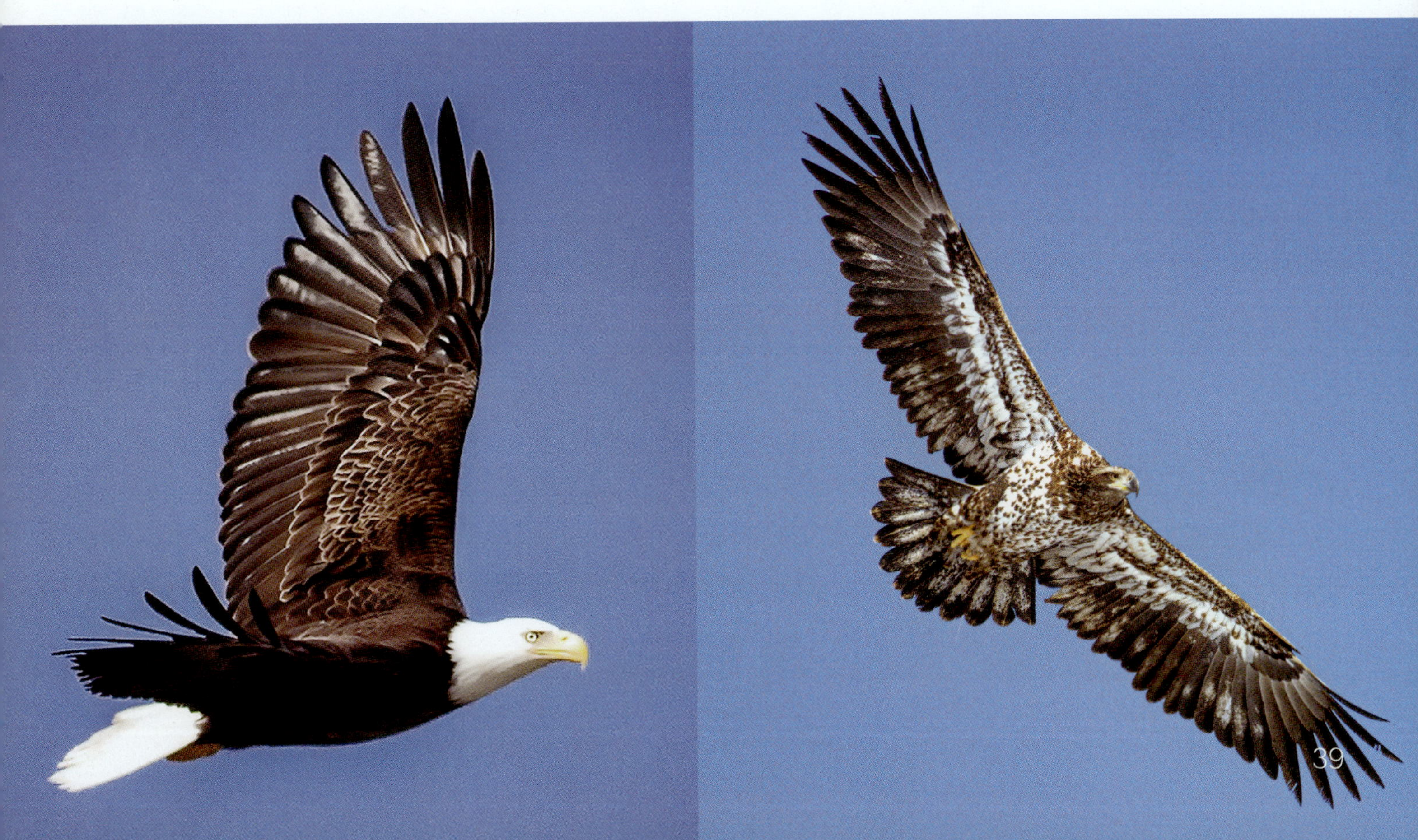

Osprey

Ospreys, like eagles, were severely harmed by the widespread use of DDT. First introduced for agricultural use in 1945, this chemical blocked calcium absorption in birds, causing eggshell thinning, breaking of the egg, and embryo loss. Because Ospreys only lay one to three eggs a year, this had a profound impact on their population. Thanks to the work of Rachel Carson and her 1962 book, ***Silent Spring***, DDT was banned in the United States in 1972. Eagle and Osprey populations have increased dramatically since then, and we have all become accustomed to Osprey nests on utility poles, channel markers, and man-made nesting platforms. Since Osprey are the only raptor to eat fish exclusively, they are still susceptible to mercury toxicity.

Osprey have amazing eyesight that allows them to dive on a fish, talons extended, from great heights. They are the only raptors that completely immerse themselves in the water when catching fish, shaking like a dog, drying off as they fly away. They have unique talons with a reversible outer toe that allows them to carry a fish headfirst, minimizing wind resistance. Osprey must defend their catch from larger birds of prey like eagles. The bird below is not about to give up its lunch easily.

Every bird photographer wants to get the iconic image of an Osprey hitting the water, talons outstretched, just as it captures a fish. On any given day at Sebastian Inlet State Park there is a row of bird photographers with big lenses hoping to get that perfect photo.

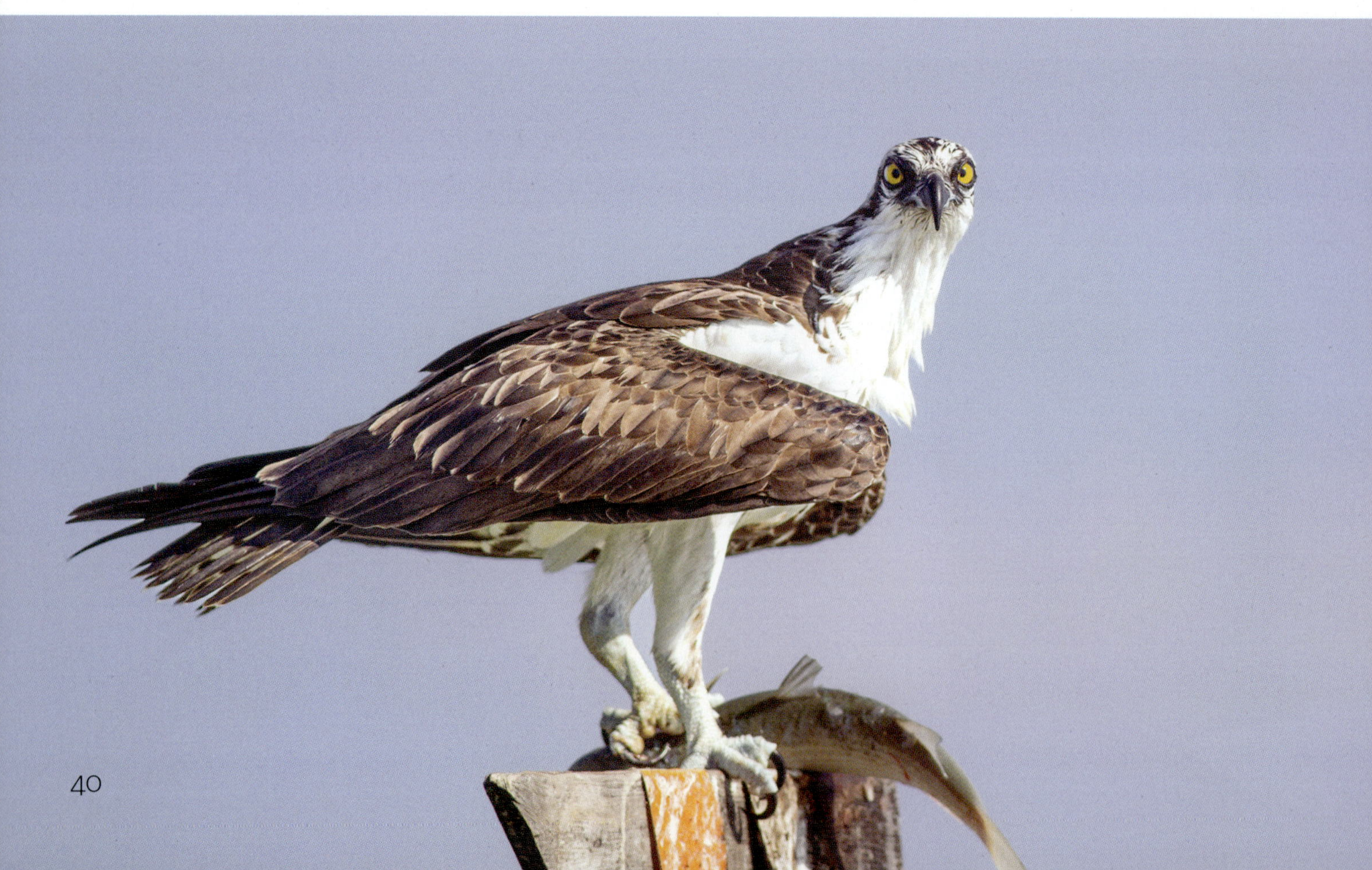

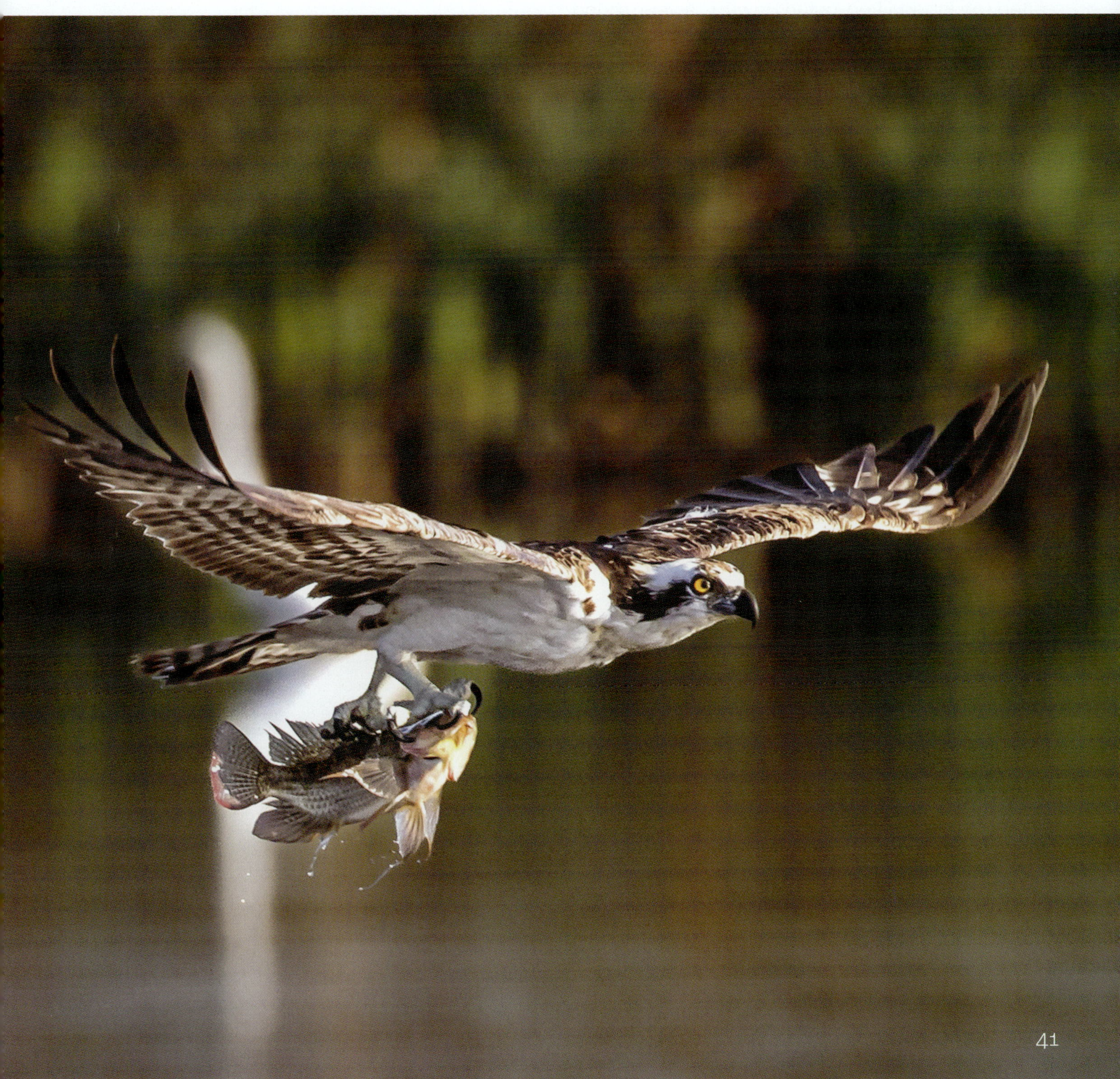

Red-tailed Hawk

This bulky raptor occurs all across North America and extends its range into the Caribbean Islands and Central America. A soaring hawk displaying a brick-red tail is easily identified as a Red-tail but young hawks are more difficult to identify. An immature hawk takes two years to develop adult plumage and the classic red tail.

Red-tails prefer woodland habitat but are found all over Florida. In fact, one of the many subspecies, called the Florida Red-tailed Hawk, is a year-round resident. They prefer to hunt small mammals and rodents, but they are generalists and will eat whatever is available.

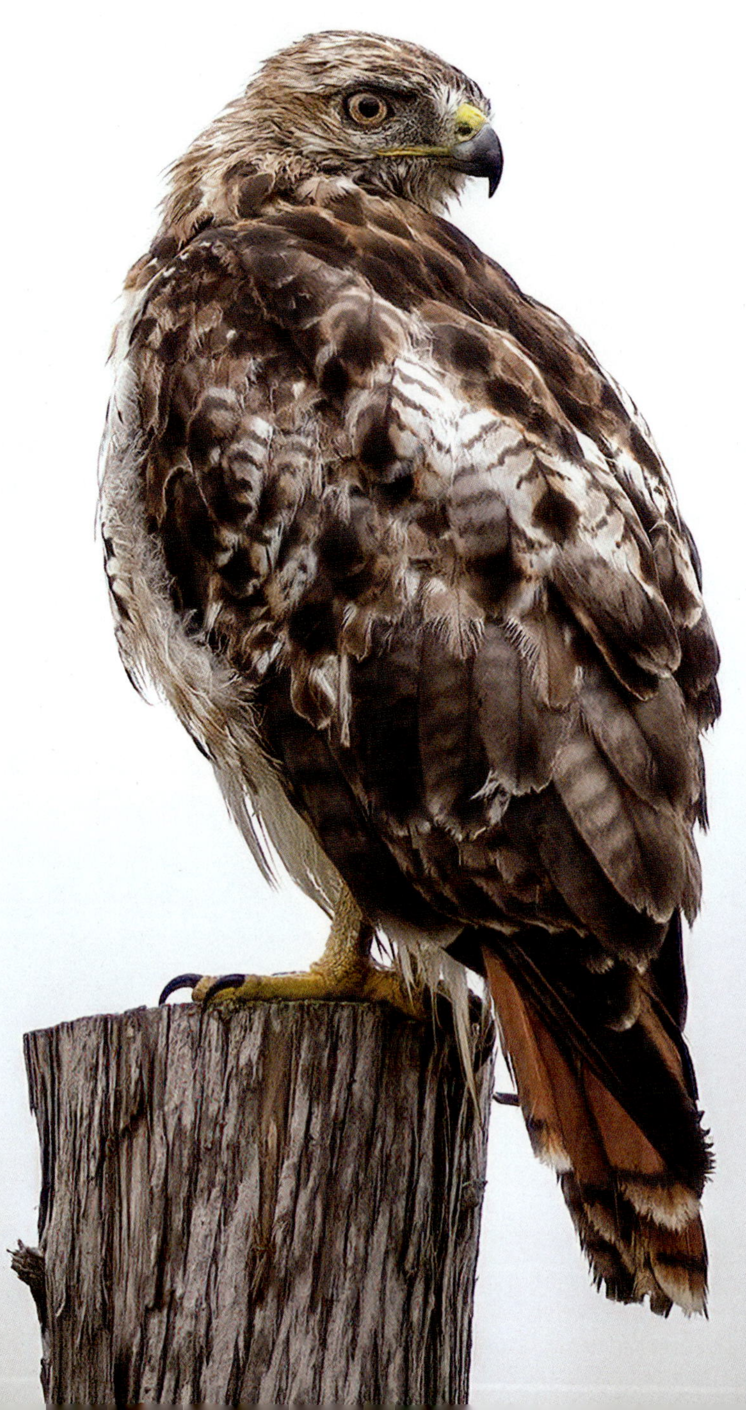

Cooper's Hawk

Cooper's Hawks and their smaller, similar cousins, Sharp-shinned Hawks, are migratory in Florida and common winter birds in suburban neighborhoods and city parks. Cooper's Hawks are adapted to hunt small to medium-sized birds and mammals, and they are known for their agile flight and quick reflexes. They use their keen eyesight and strong legs and talons to capture and kill their prey. Cooper's Hawks will often perch and wait for prey to pass by, and then strike quickly and decisively. They will also sometimes pursue prey on the ground, running or hopping through the underbrush to catch their quarry. They love to raid bird feeders.

The hawk in the photo has a blue-gray back, reddish-orange front and large square head with a black cap, so I am fairly confident calling it a Cooper's. Cooper's and Sharpies can be difficult to distinguish in the field, even for the most accomplished hawk watcher.

This hawk was named in honor of William Cooper, an early-nineteenth-century American biologist best known for his study of seashells.

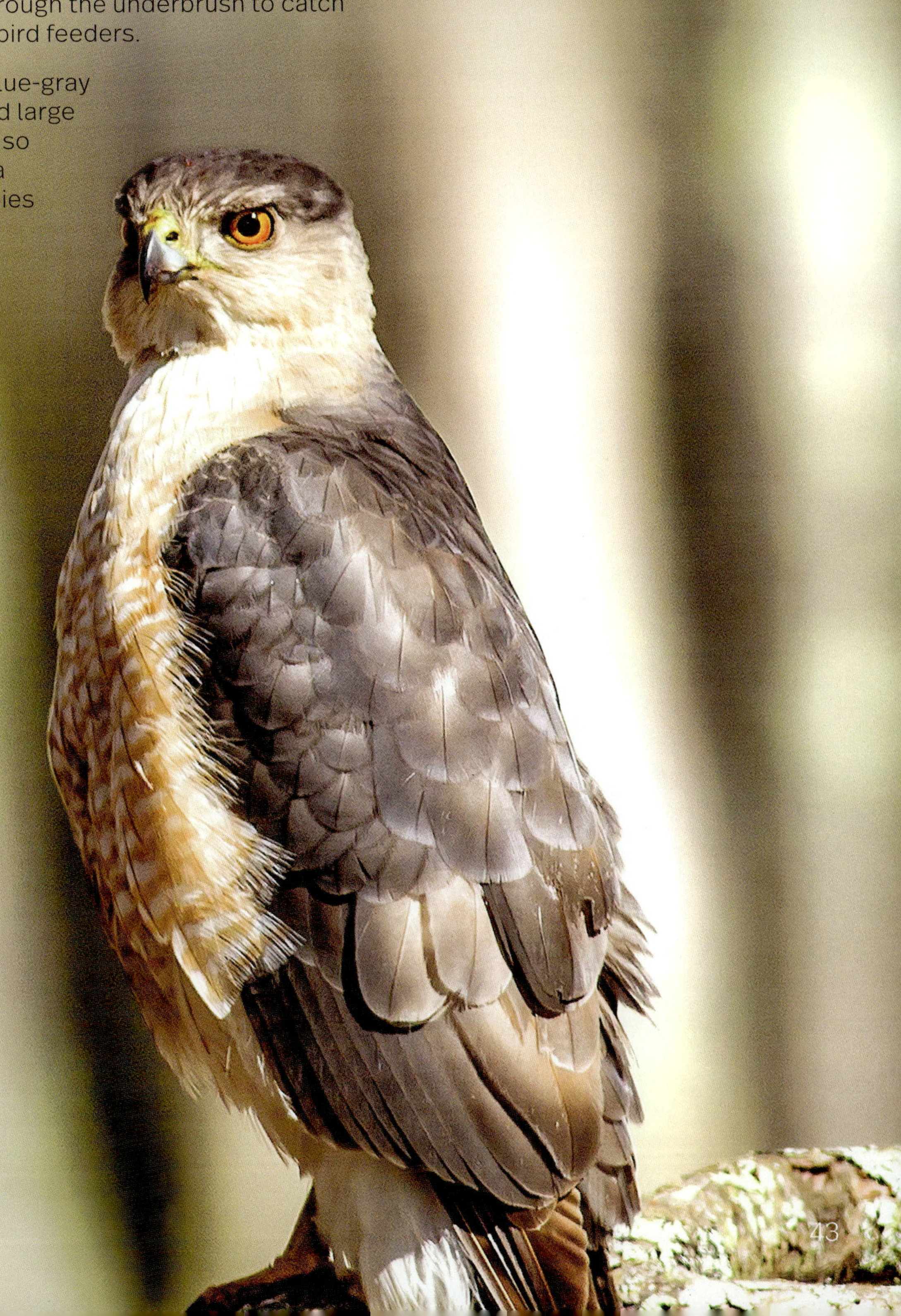

Red-shouldered Hawk

This is a hawk found in Florida's wet woodlands and cypress hammocks. The piercing cry is unmistakable and a common sound on any bird walk in a wooded area. They are often seen in backyards and parks. They can be quite tame and unperturbed by human photographers. This handsome bird was perched on a snag and allowed me to walk within ten feet to get a photo. The Florida subspecies has a more pale coloration of the head and breast than other varieties.

Red-shouldered hawk mated pairs often nest in the same place year after year.

In the breeding season, they build nests in tall trees, and both male and female hawks take part in incubating the eggs and raising the young. After the young fledge, the family group will hunt together, with the parents teaching the young how to capture prey. They live on small mammals, reptiles, insects and occasionally will take a small bird.

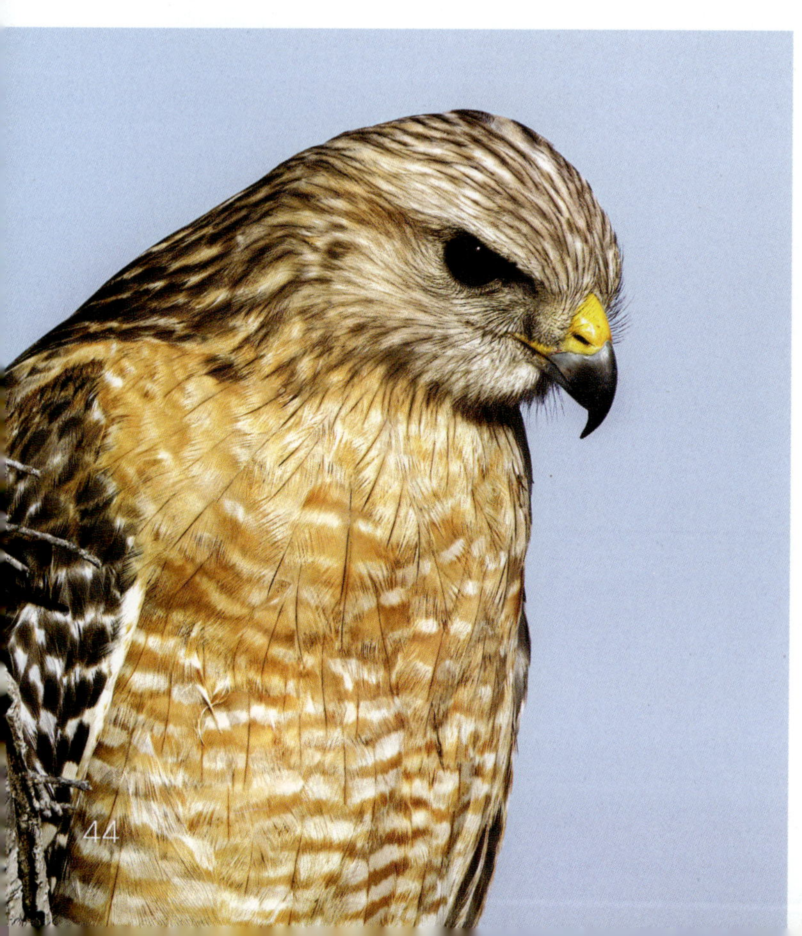

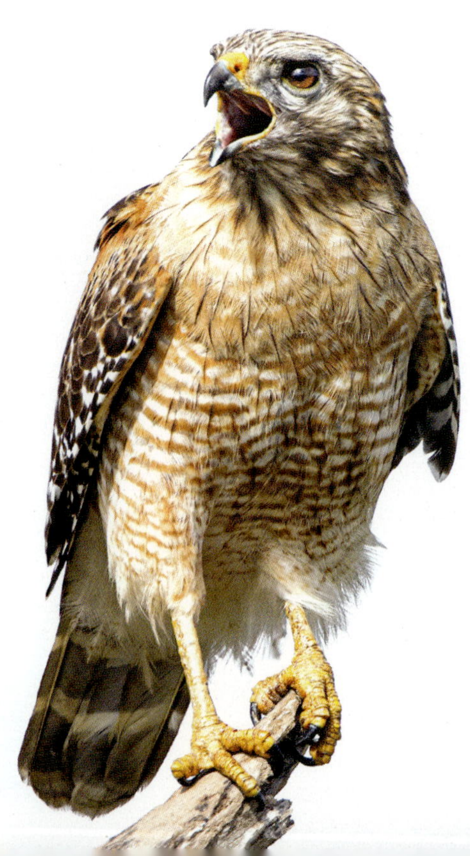

Like many hawk species, an immature Red-shouldered has different plumage than the adult. Audubon mistakingly called young birds the Winter Hawk and included a plate with that name in his original portfolio. The image was removed from later editions after the error was discovered.

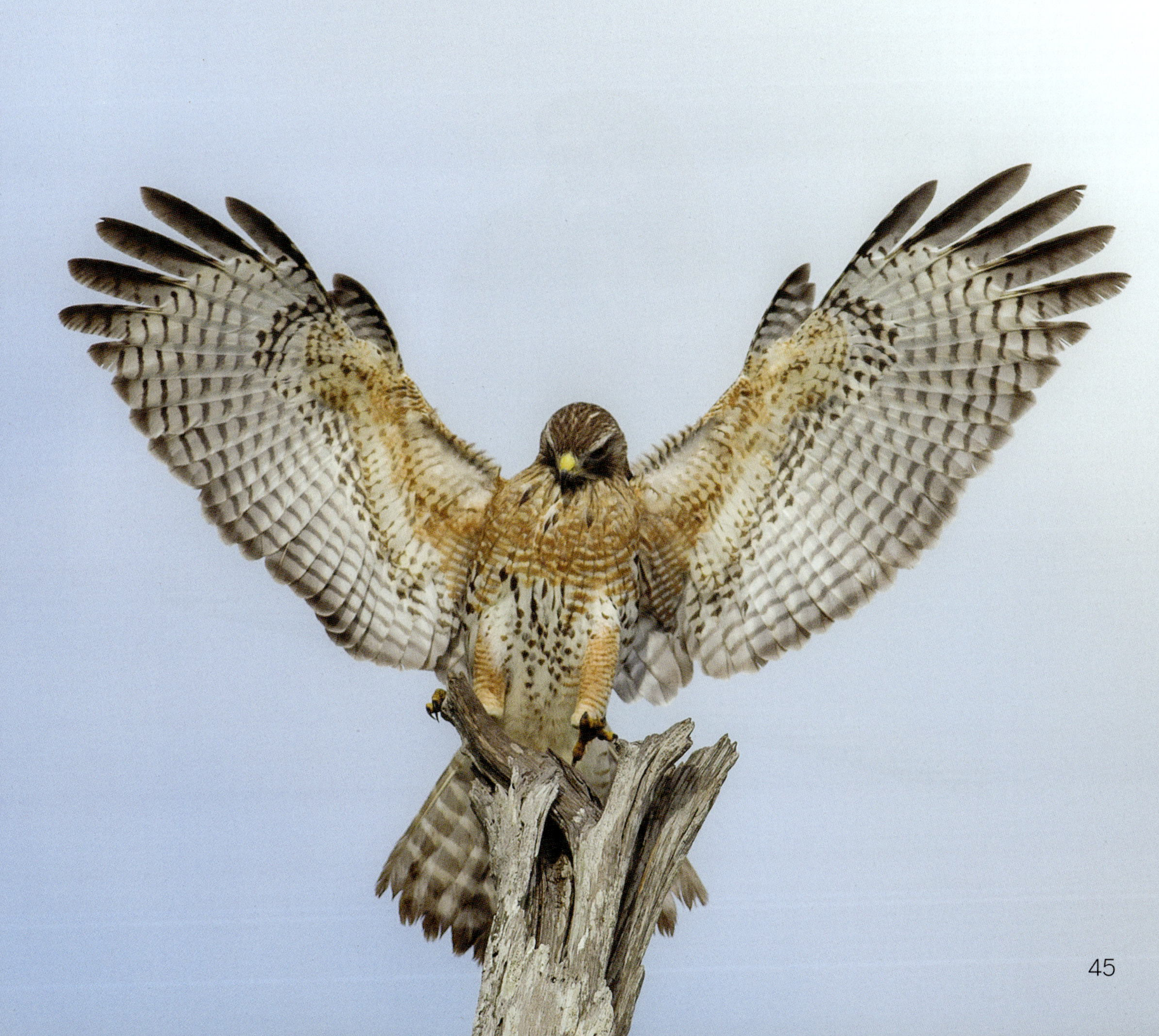

Short-tailed Hawk

Coming from the north, this was a new hawk species for me to add to my life list. The range of this tropical species barely makes it into North America, but there are a few resident birds known to nest in Florida. Short-tails hunt birds by soaring high and then diving to attack their prey. Birdwatchers frequently miss them because they fly in mixed flocks with other raptors and vultures. In contrast to vultures, they have compact bodies and short, round tails with a distinctive white patch on the rump.

The first one I saw and photographed was soaring over the cattle pastures next to Fort Drum Marsh Conservation Area on Route 60 west of Vero Beach. On another day, I was fortunate to spot one perched on a utility wire along Route A1A on Orchid Island, and it stayed long enough for me to get a photograph.

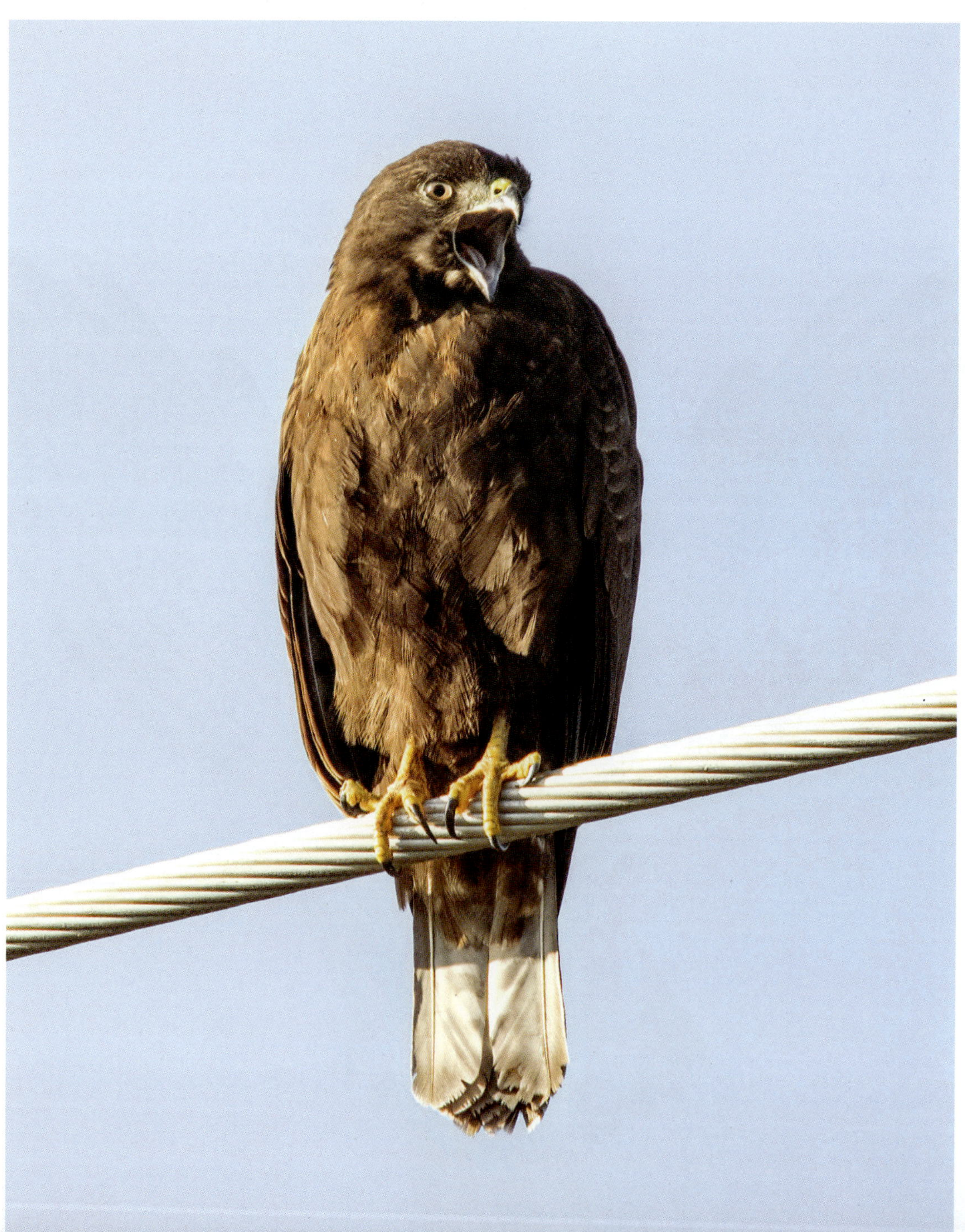

Broad-winged Hawk

Broad-winged hawks are famous fall migrants that travel in huge numbers along the mountain ridges of eastern North America on the way to wintering grounds in South and Central America. They prefer deep woodlands so are seldom seen except during migration.

Look for the broad white band in the tail as they soar overhead. Large raptors are able to separate their primary wing feathers into "fingers" as they hunt, allowing them to fly at slow speeds without stalling.

Broad-winged Hawks breed in northern Florida, but we only see them in South Florida during the winter.

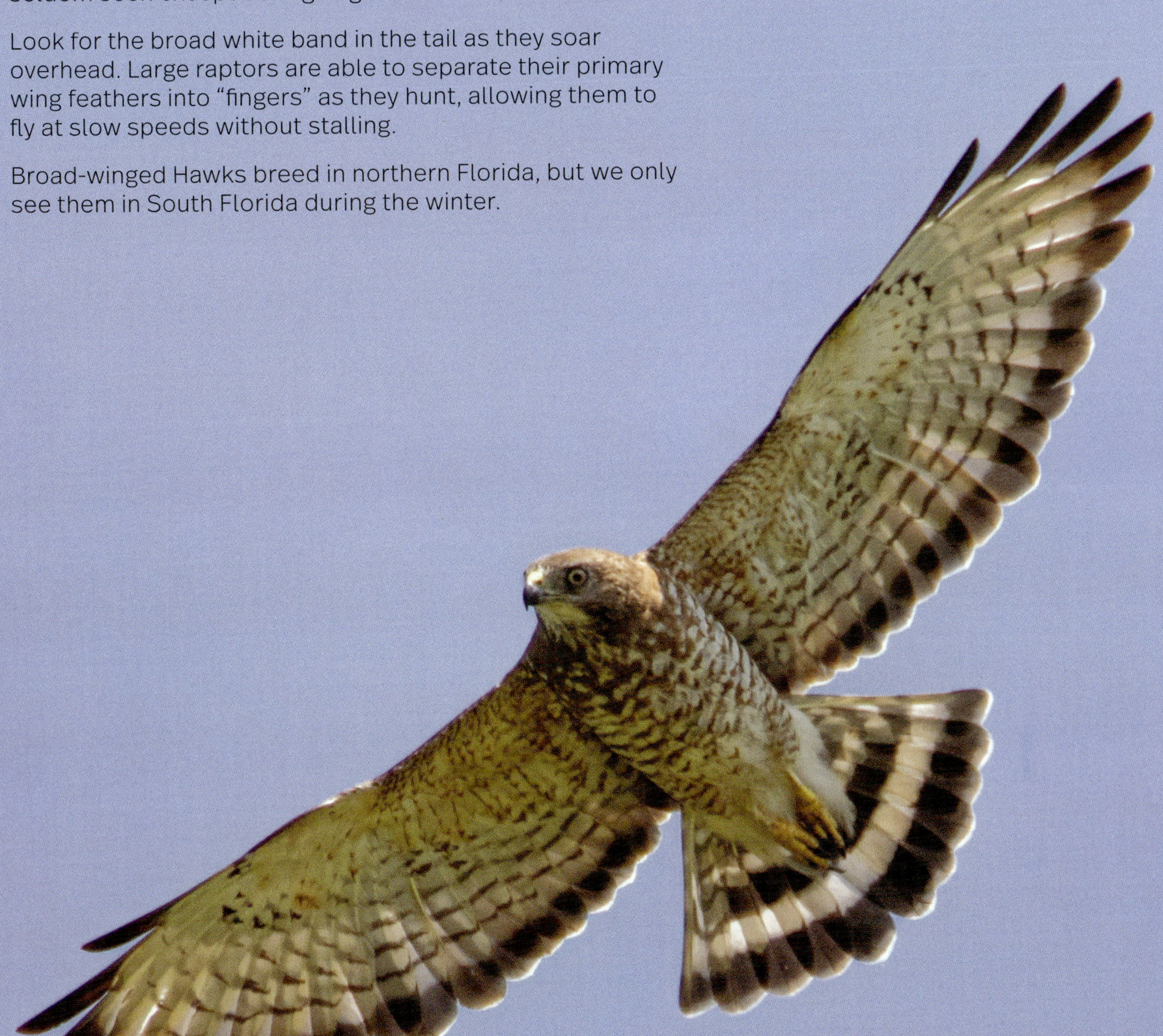

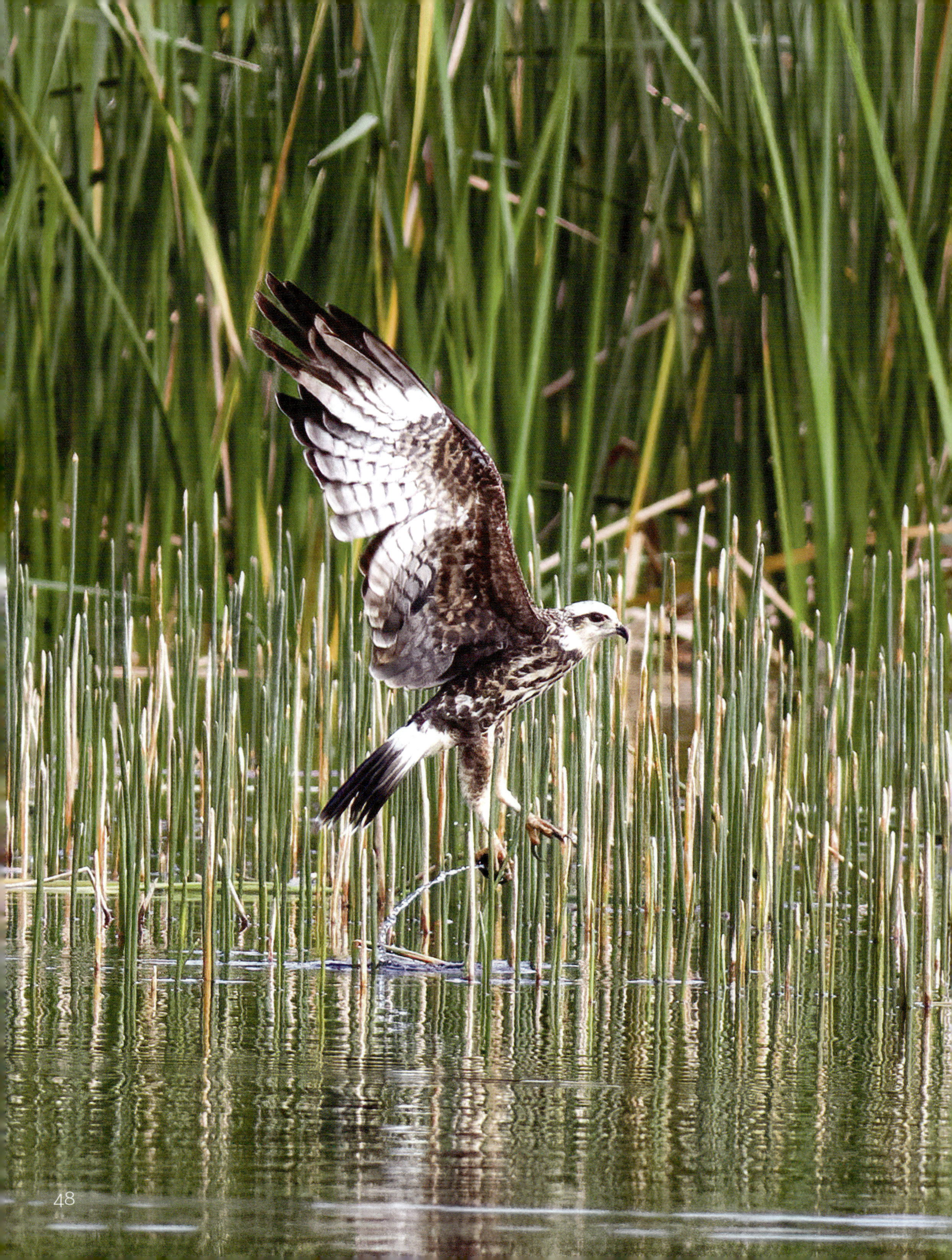

Snail Kite

Snail Kites are one of Florida's most unusual and fascinating birds. They are also known as Everglades Kites and feed almost entirely on freshwater Florida apple snails. The birds glide over a wetland, plucking a snail from a grass stem, then land to extract the snail with a specially adapted, hooked bill. They also have specialized feathers on their chest to help hold the slippery snails.

Evolutionary changes gave kites the special bill they require to be successful, but at considerable price due to their limited food options. Kites became endangered because of the loss of snails due to water-management practices. Non-native snails accidentally introduced from the aquarium trade have provided a new source of snails, and the kite population seems to be increasing.

The males are dark gray with orange legs and an orange, black-tipped bill, and females are brown with white streaking and a prominent white "eyebrow." In February, they can be seen performing aerial courtship displays at the Loxahatchee National Wildlife Refuge in Palm Beach County.

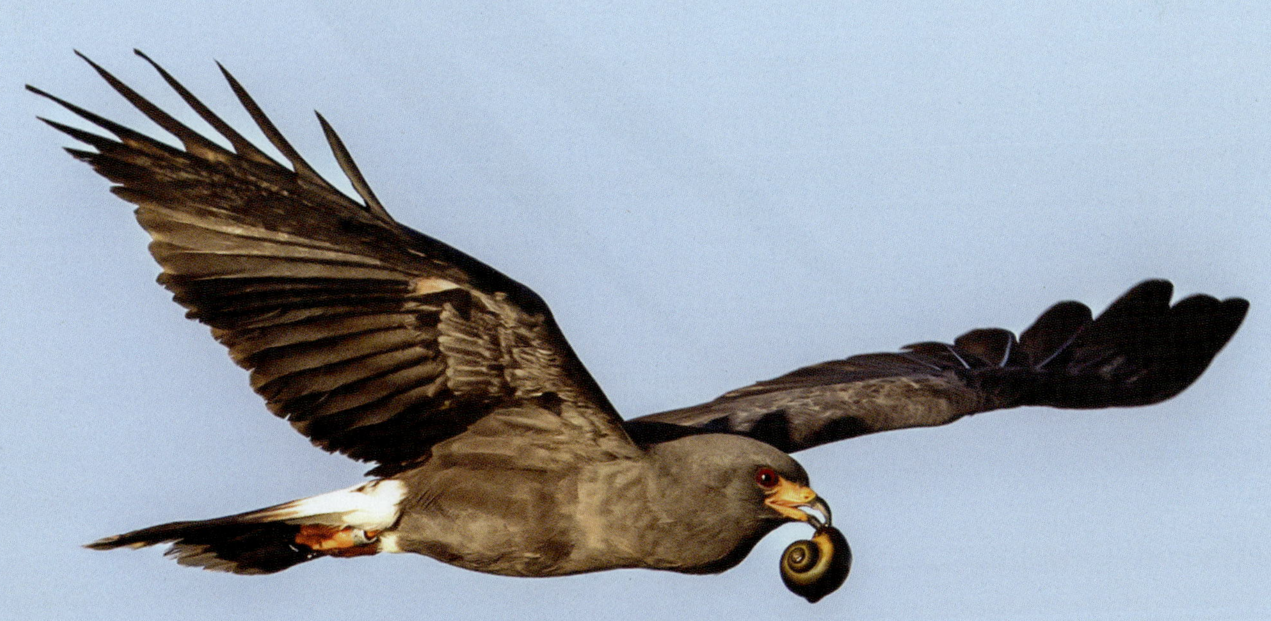

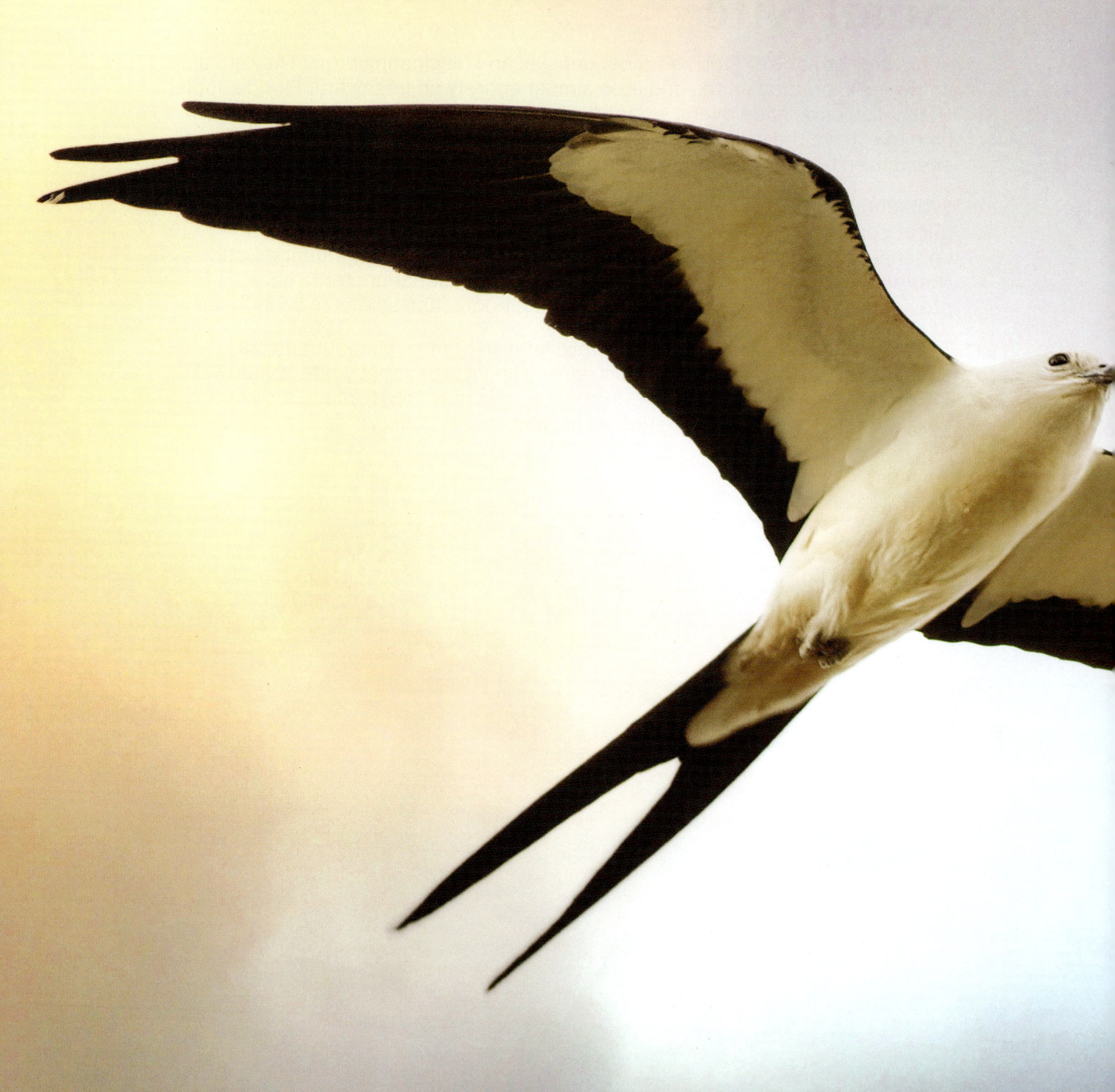

Swallow-tailed Kite

One of the highlights of the season for a northern birdwatcher is the return of Swallow-tailed Kites to Florida from their winter home in South America. These fabulous fliers were once found throughout the Southeast, but the majority of their breeding range is now confined to Florida and the Gulf Coast. In late summer thousands of birds congregate in communal roosts near Lake Okeechobee before embarking on a five-thousand-mile trip across the Gulf of Mexico to the Yucatán Peninsula, then over the Andes into the grasslands of central Brazil. The best time to see them is in late July, when they are one of the first birds to migrate south for the winter.

I always look forward to their return in early March, and it seems the windier day, the better. They have a four-foot wingspan and can fly for hours with hardly a wingbeat. They are described as "buoyant" because they twist and turn in the air to swoop down and catch insects and dragonflies, often plucking lizards and tree frogs from leaves and tree branches while in flight.

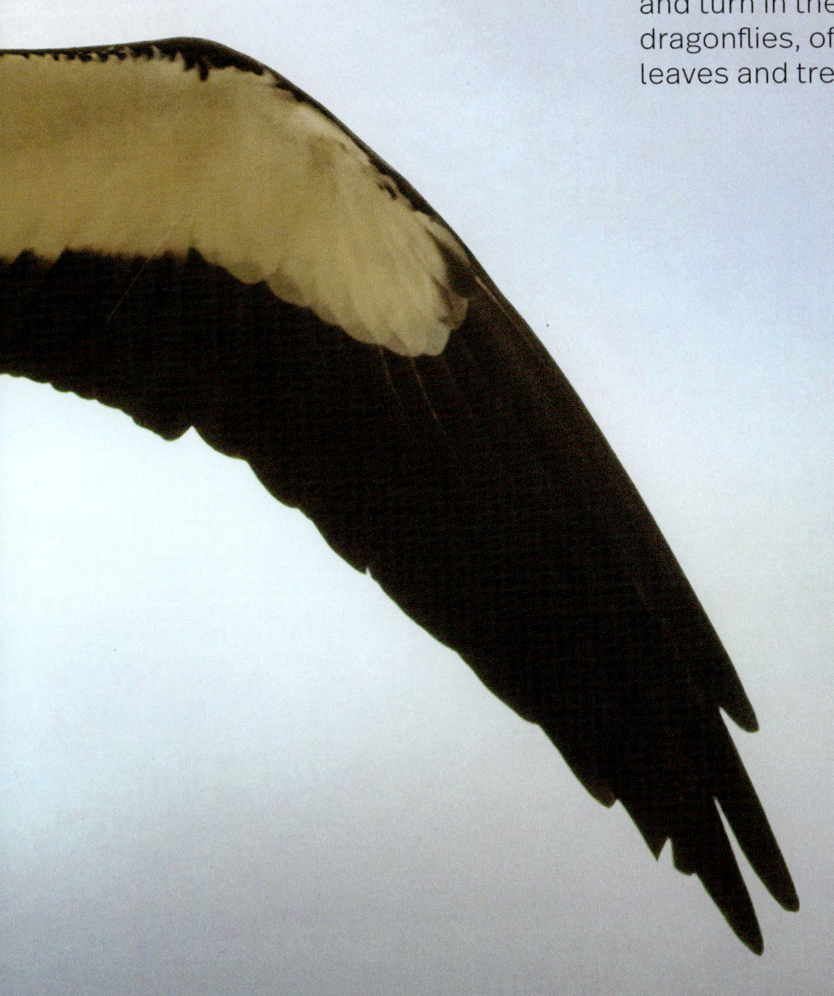

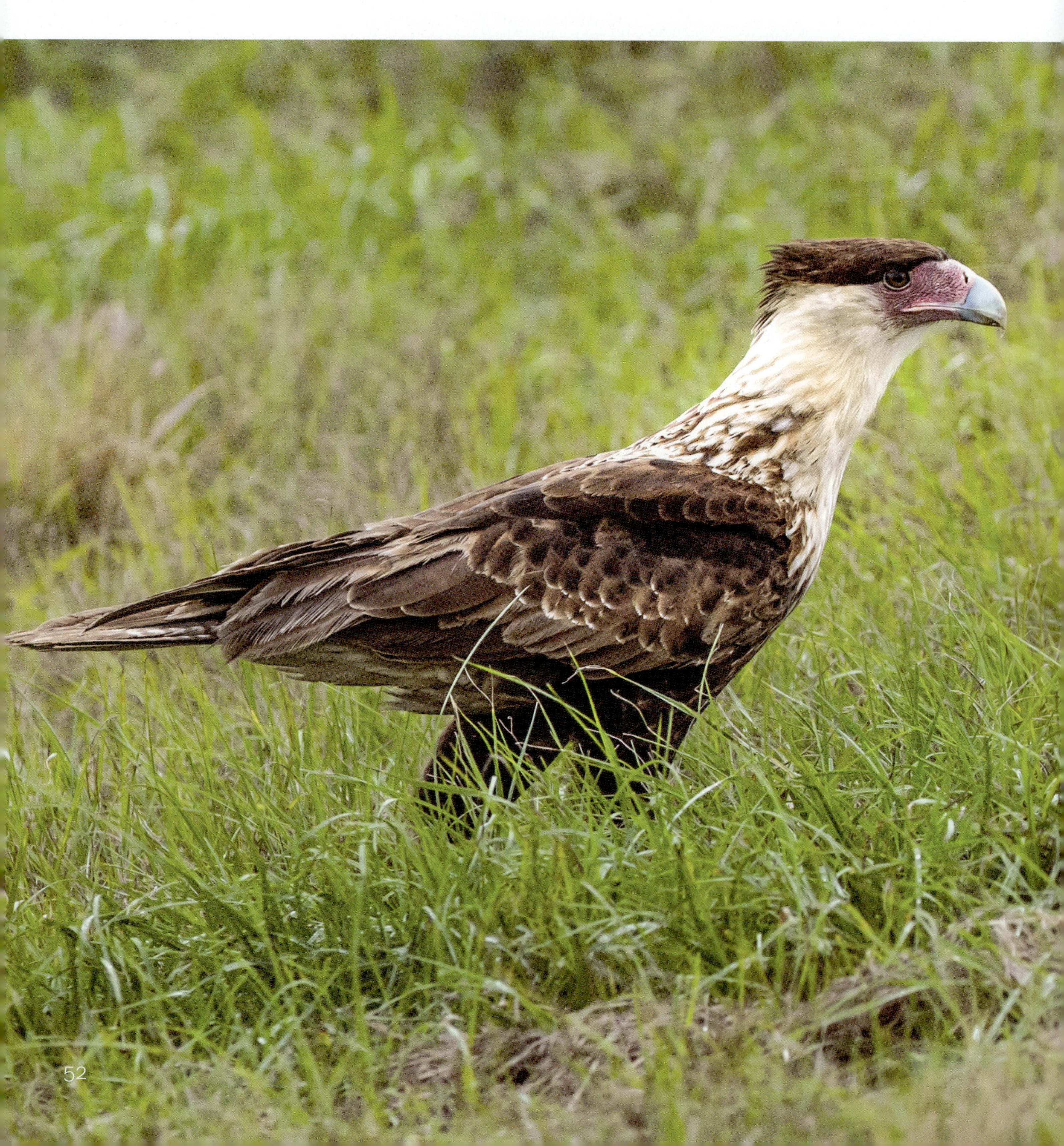

Northern Crested Caracara

Caracaras are large birds of prey that are about the size of a small eagle or large hawk. Many species are spread across South America, and when Darwin first encountered Caracaras in the Falkland Islands, he was at a loss as to how to classify them. Ornithologists now consider them a subfamily of falcons, but they behave more like vultures. They are frequently seen on the ground feeding on carrion in cattle pastures and along roadsides. Crested Caracaras are found from the southern tip of Argentina to the Andes mountains, but their primary range is in Mexico and south Texas, where they are known as the Northern Crested Caracara. Audubon discovered an isolated population in the savannas of central Florida in 1831 and they are known as Audubon's Crested Caracara in his honor. His painting of two hostile caracaras is one of his finest depictions of birds in action.

Caracara numbers in Florida have declined over the years due to habitat loss, illegal shooting. and traffic mortality but they have managed to hang on. Because there may be only 500 left, the Florida subspecies is protected under the Federal Endangered and Threatened Species Act.

Look for Caracaras perched on utility poles and hunting over pastures on Route 70 between Okeechobee and Arcadia, west of Fort Pierce. Finding and photographing one of these ancient descendants of the dinosaurs is worth the trip.

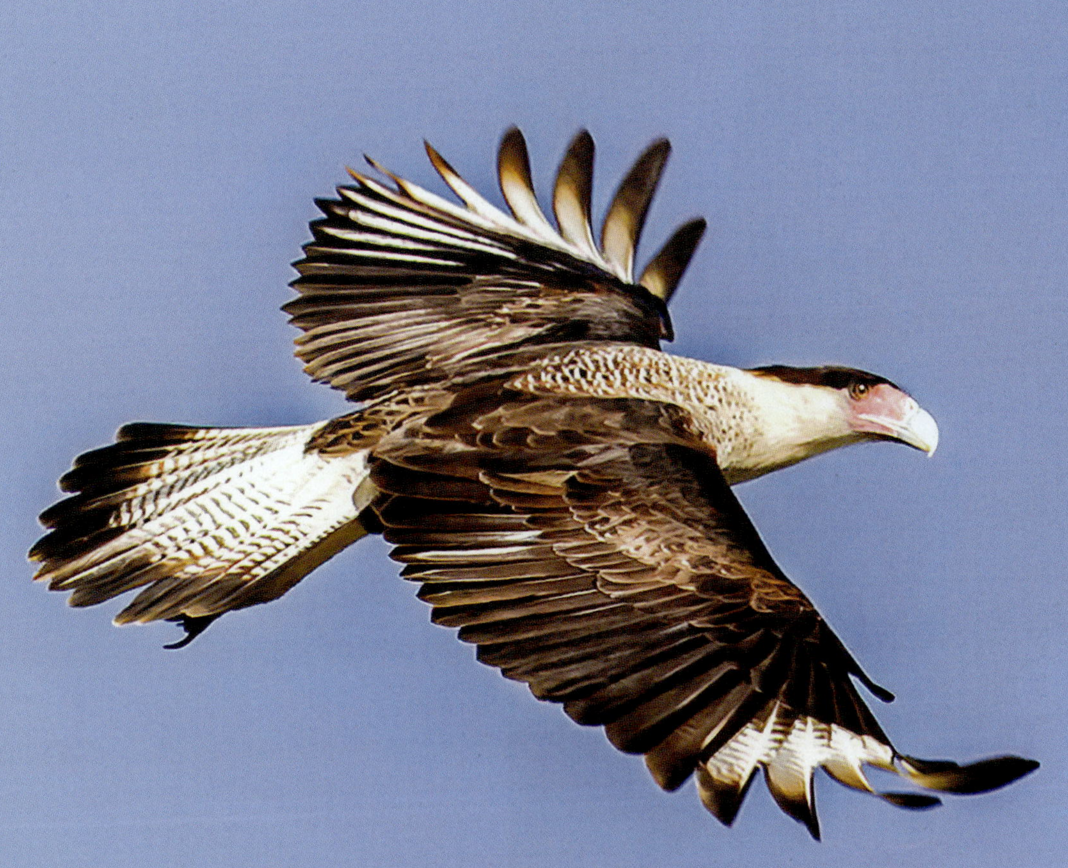

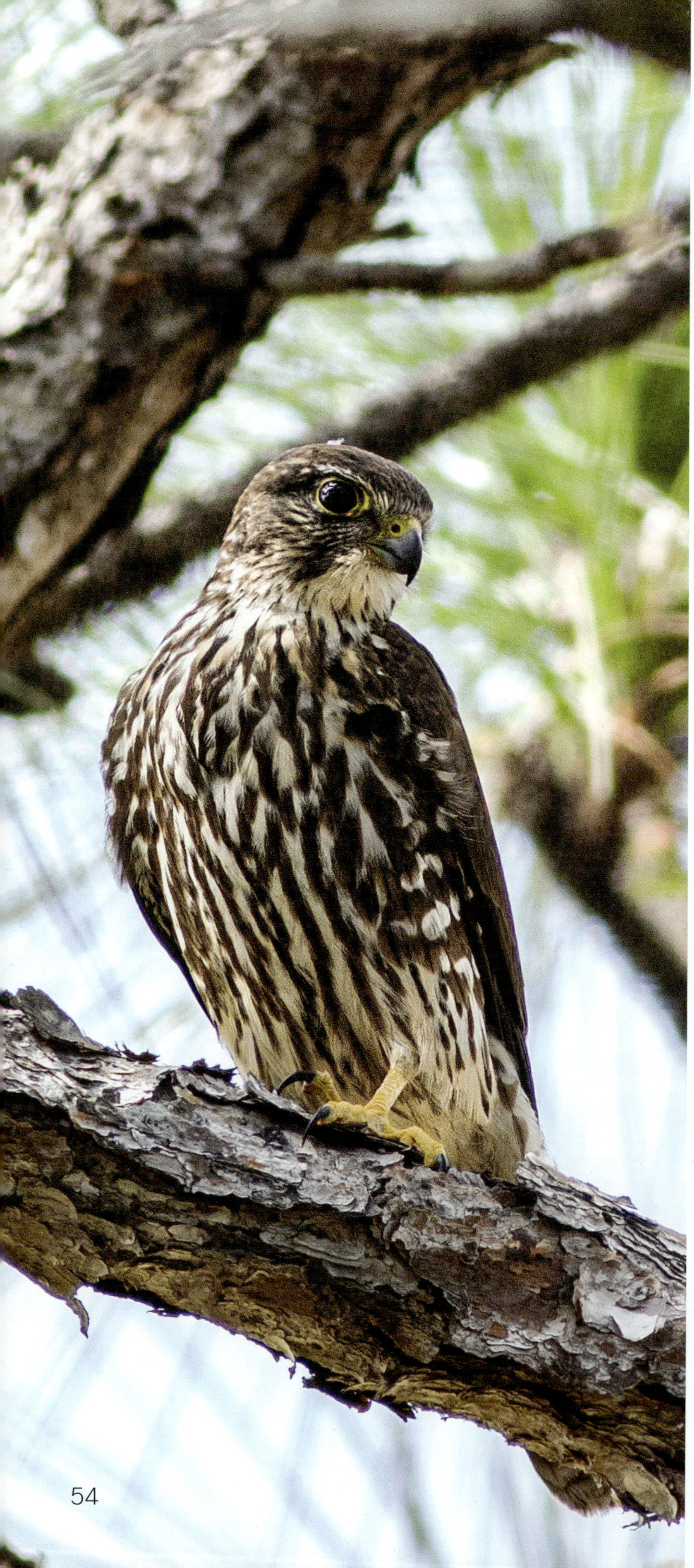

Merlin

These are aggressive predators that use swift surprise attacks to bring down songbirds and shorebirds. Merlin were originally called Pigeon Hawks, maybe because they terrorize pigeon flocks, flying horizontally at speeds up to thirty miles an hour. Merlin are only slightly larger than the similar American Kestrel but they appear heavier with sharply pointed wings and dark streaking on the breast and belly. They often appear to birdwatchers as a dark flash as a flock of birds goes up in alarm.

Lately they have become more common in urban areas, relying on large populations of House Sparrows as easy prey. They can be found anywhere, but I often see them patrolling the beaches as they hunt for sandpipers.

American Kestrel

The kestrel, the smallest local falcon, used to be called the Sparrow Hawk because of its small size, not because it captures sparrows. These birds are about the size of a robin, with a blue-gray head and wings and a reddish-brown back and tail. They hunt from perches or utility wires and can be seen hovering over a potential target along the roadside.

Grasshoppers are their favorite food, but they will eat any small rodent or bird they capture. Kestrels can see ultraviolet light, allowing them to track the urine trails left by voles, a favorite prey mammal.

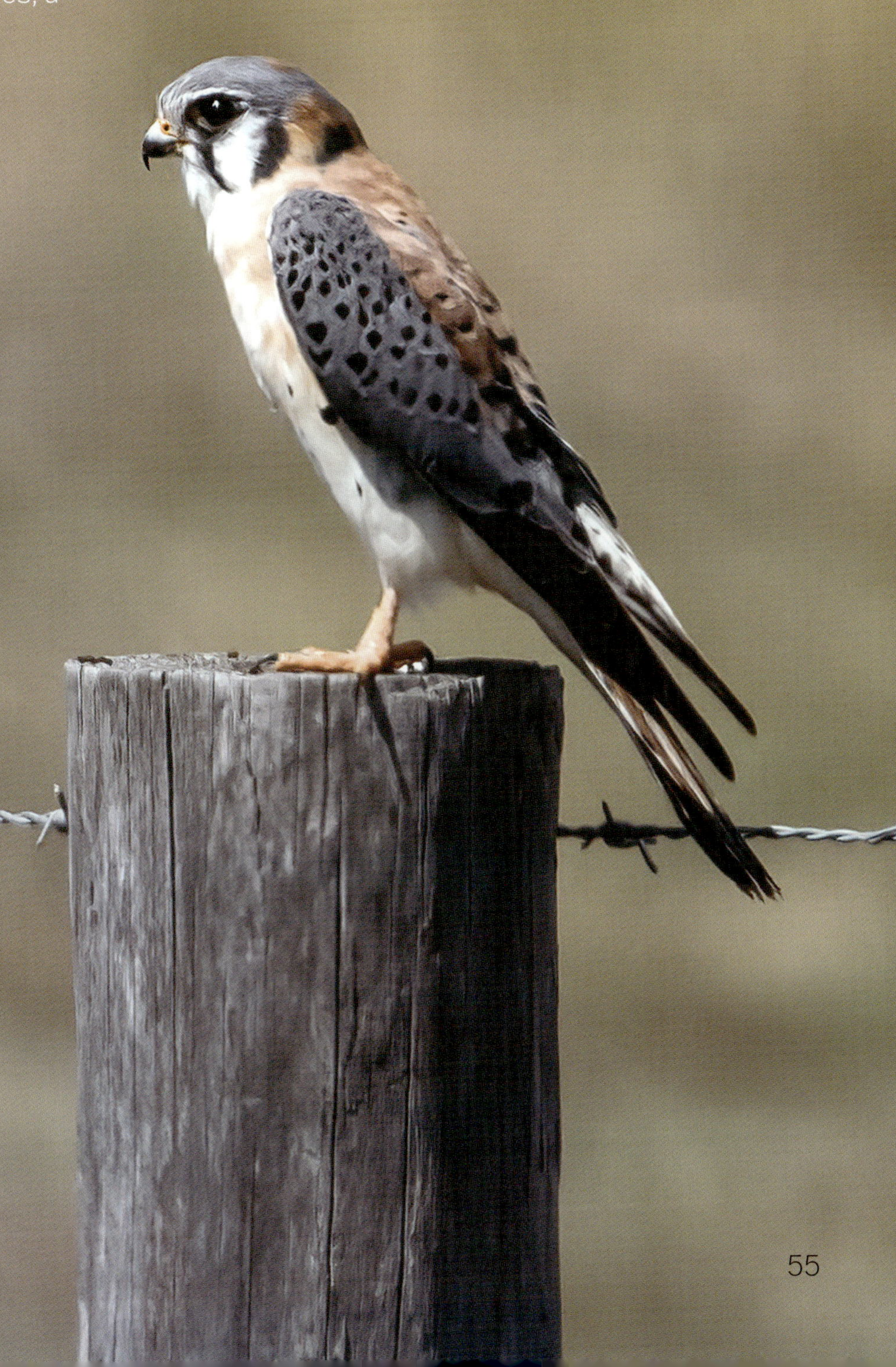

Turkey Vulture

A vulture is a bird of prey that feeds on carrion rather than live animals. They are characterized by a bald, featherless head. Turkey Vultures, according to ornithology research, can smell food from nearly a mile away. These large birds are quite common, often seen soaring high overhead as they scout for food. In flight, their wings are held in a distinctive V shape. While Turkey Vultures are regularly seen as far north as Maine, Black Vultures rarely venture that far.

Turkey Vultures are year-round residents in Florida, but numbers can increase dramatically as northern birds migrate south in the winter months. They can be a nuisance in urban areas where they roost because of their propensity to eat vinyl material such as roofing, insulation, and outdoor furniture.

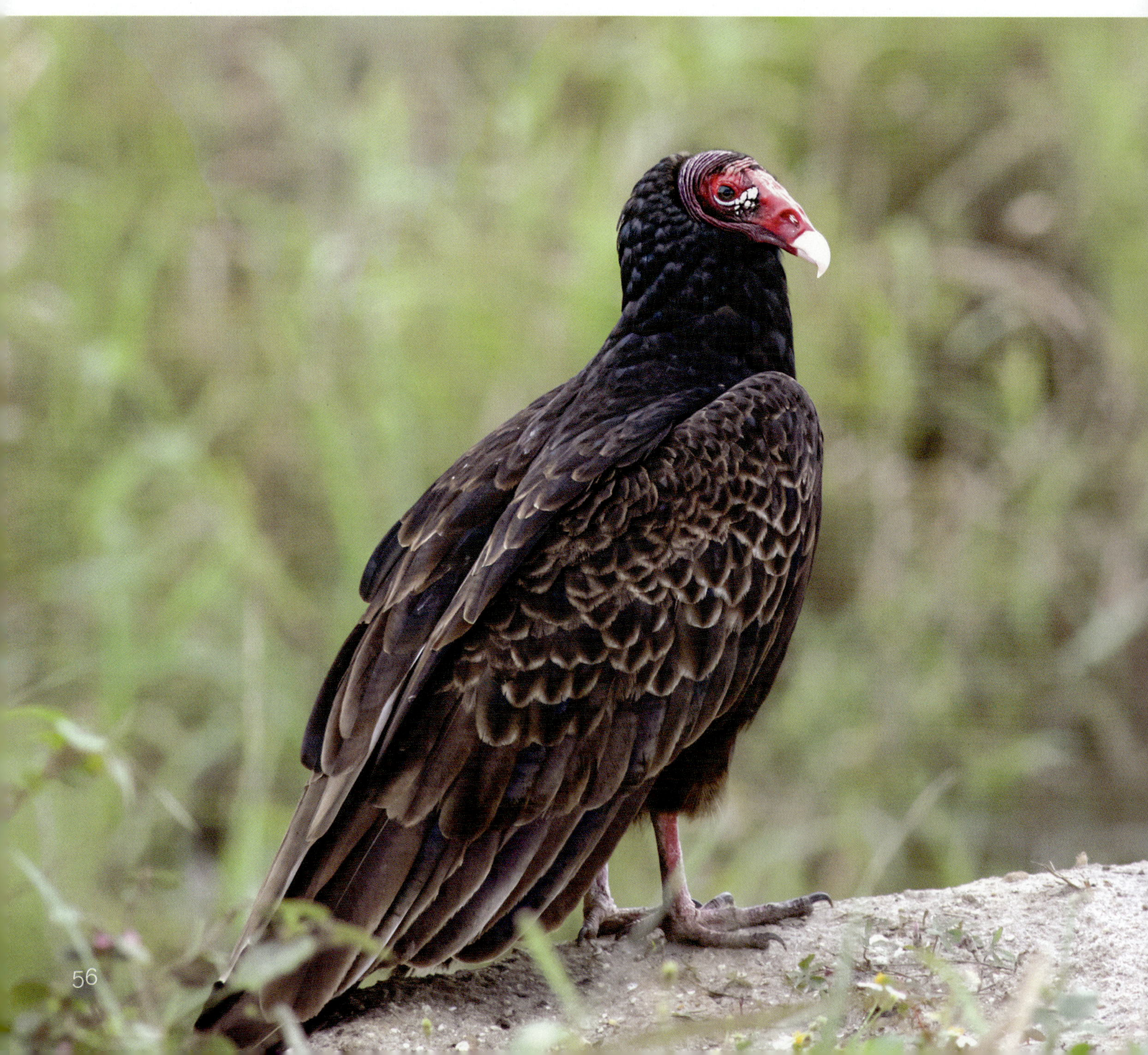

Black Vulture

Because Black Vultures cannot smell carrion, they associate with Turkey Vultures and follow them to carcasses. The more aggressive Black Vultures will often drive off the Turkey Vultures. In contrast to Turkey Vultures, Black Vultures have been known to kill newborn or weak animals. These vultures sometimes form large groups called kettles, soaring and circling, while riding the thermals over landfills and along highways. They can be differentiated from Turkey Vultures by their short tails and white wing-tips.

Vultures have extremely strong stomach acid, which allows them to eat bacteria-infected food that would be lethal to other animals. All vultures play an important role in the disposal of carrion that could be a breeding ground for diseases.

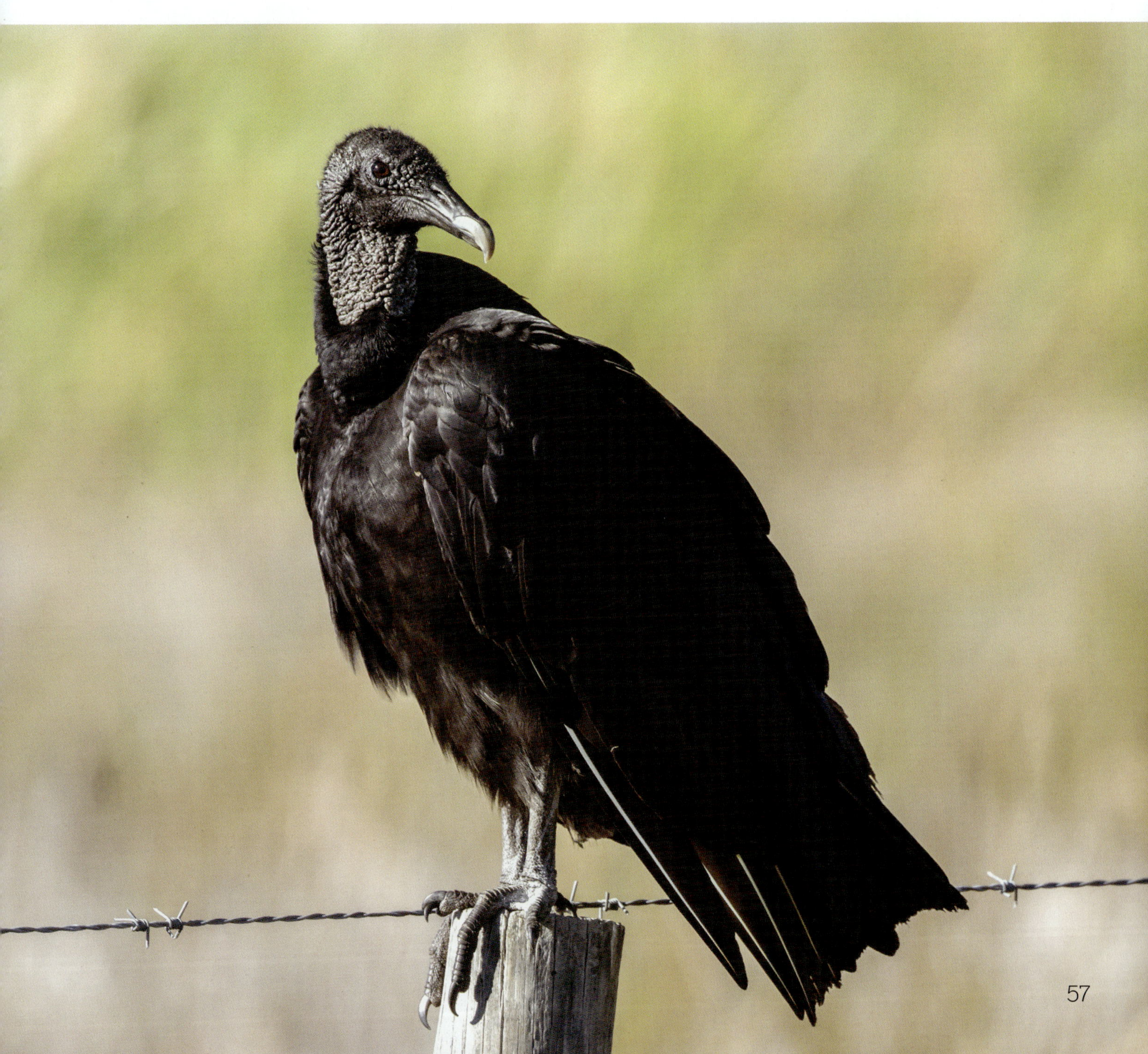

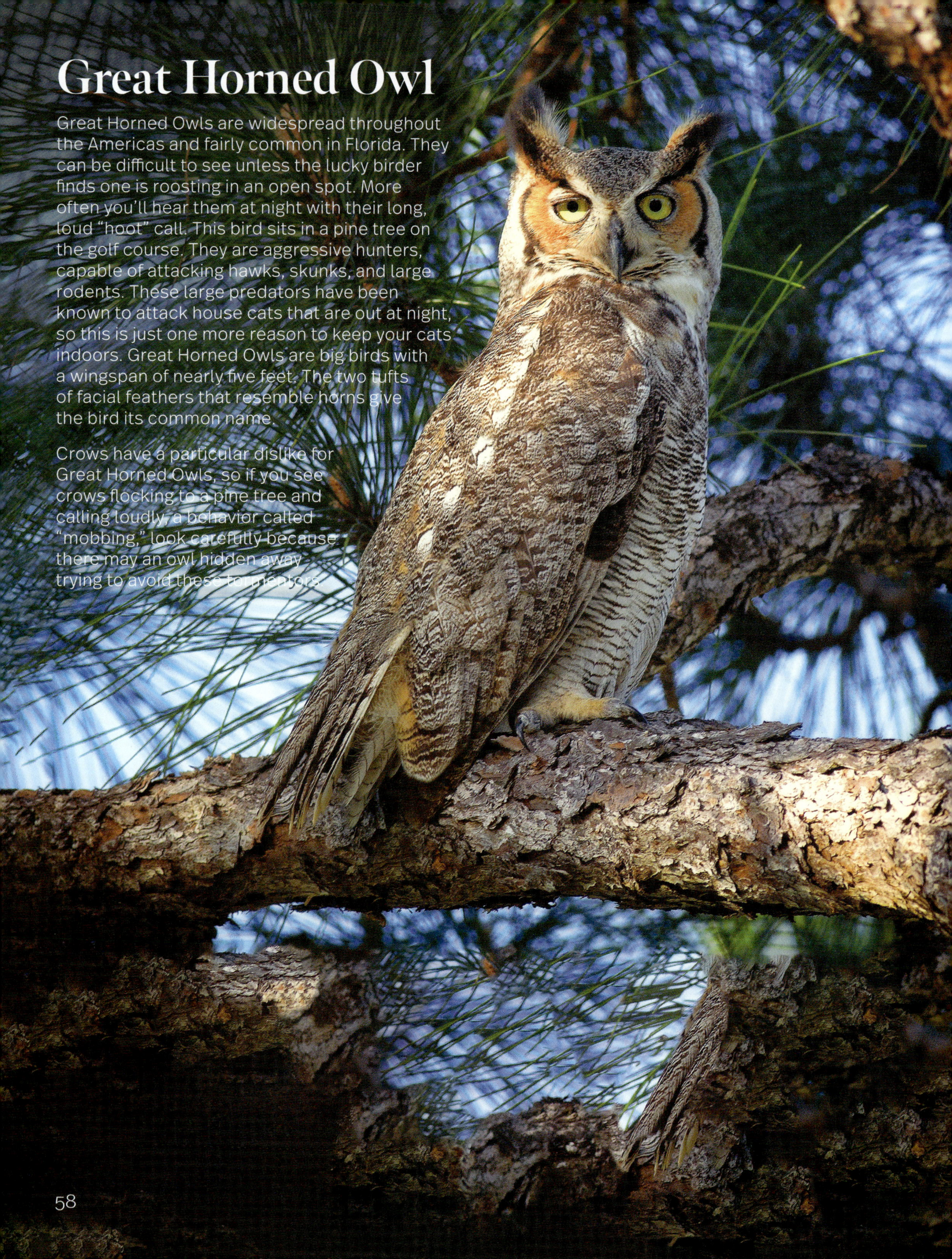

Great Horned Owl

Great Horned Owls are widespread throughout the Americas and fairly common in Florida. They can be difficult to see unless the lucky birder finds one is roosting in an open spot. More often you'll hear them at night with their long, loud "hoot" call. This bird sits in a pine tree on the golf course. They are aggressive hunters, capable of attacking hawks, skunks, and large rodents. These large predators have been known to attack house cats that are out at night, so this is just one more reason to keep your cats indoors. Great Horned Owls are big birds with a wingspan of nearly five feet. The two tufts of facial feathers that resemble horns give the bird its common name.

Crows have a particular dislike for Great Horned Owls, so if you see crows flocking to a pine tree and calling loudly, a behavior called "mobbing," look carefully because there may an owl hidden away trying to avoid these tormentors.

Barred Owl

When you are hiking through the Florida woods and hear a bird hoot "who-cooks-for-you," chances are excellent there's a Barred Owl calling from a nearby cypress hammock. They are territorial birds that mate for life and nest in tree cavities or sometimes take over a hawk's nest.

Since owls hunt at night they have specially adapted hearing and feathers that allow totally silent flight. Barred owls typically sit motionless on a branch, watching carefully until a squirrel, mouse, or frog makes a move. During the day, they roost, perfectly camouflaged, hidden against a tree trunk.

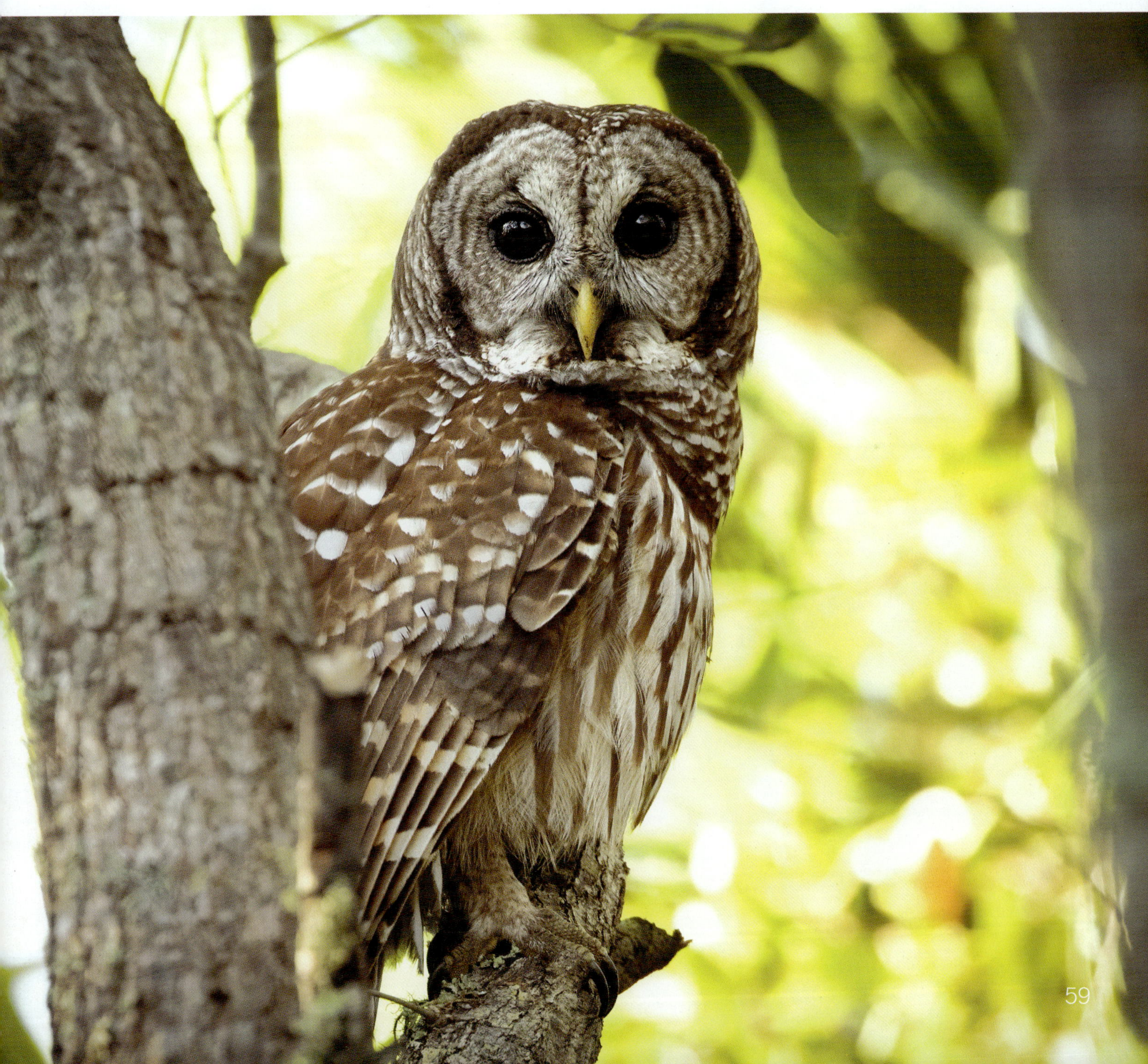

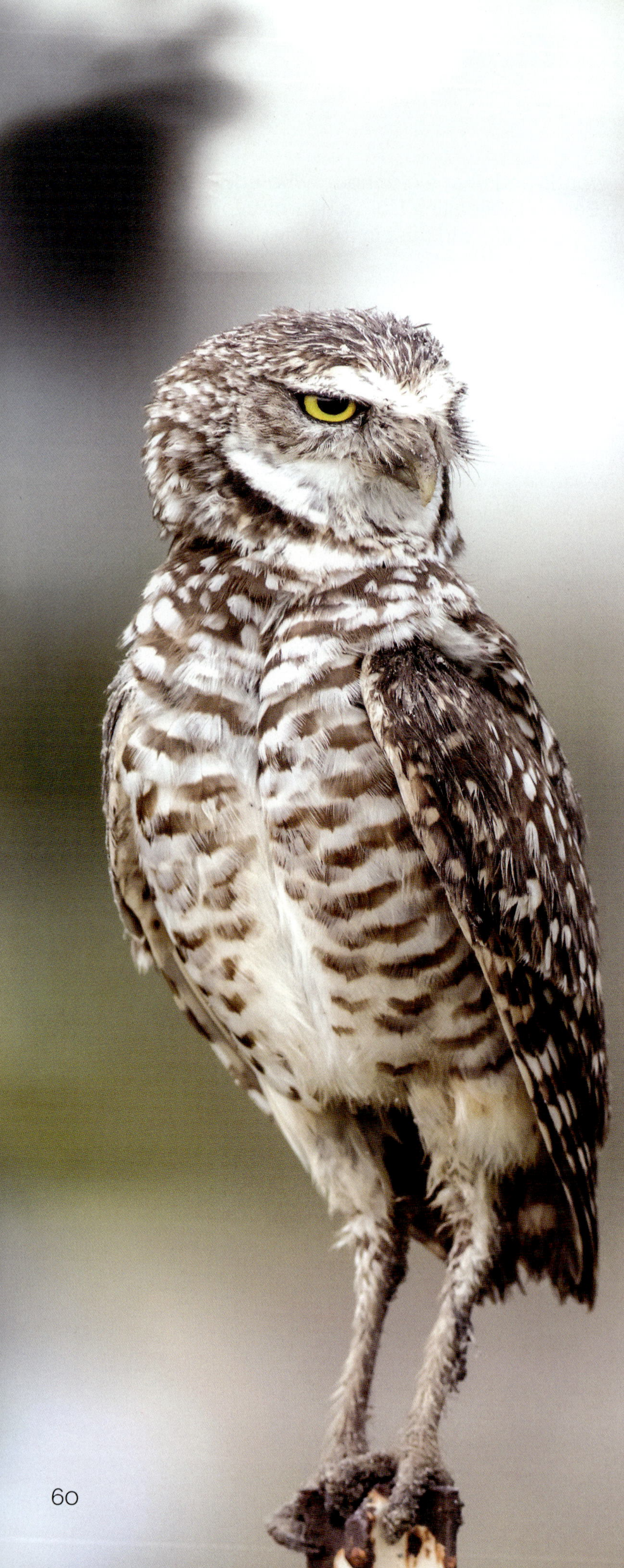

Burrowing Owl

Burrowing Owls are alert, inquisitive, and charming little owls that gravitate to open land throughout North and South America. Unlike other owls, they are active during the day and often nest in burrows previously created by groundhogs and prairie dogs. They are also tolerant of human activity. They are endangered and vigorously protected especially in the city of Cape Coral, where there are an estimated 1,000 nesting pairs spread out in vacant lots and city parks. Every year, in February, Cape Coral hosts a Burrowing Owl Festival.

I photographed this one in a colony on a playground near a soccer field in Fort Lauderdale.

Screech Owl

Screech-Owls are tiny, only six to ten inches tall, and actually known for their soft trilling call, rather than screeching. Normally an inhabitant of deep woods, screech-owls are adaptable to human environments and can be common in suburban areas. Ornithologists refer to the three color variations—gray, red, and brown—as morphs.

This is an example of a red morph that liked roosting in the eaves over our garage door.

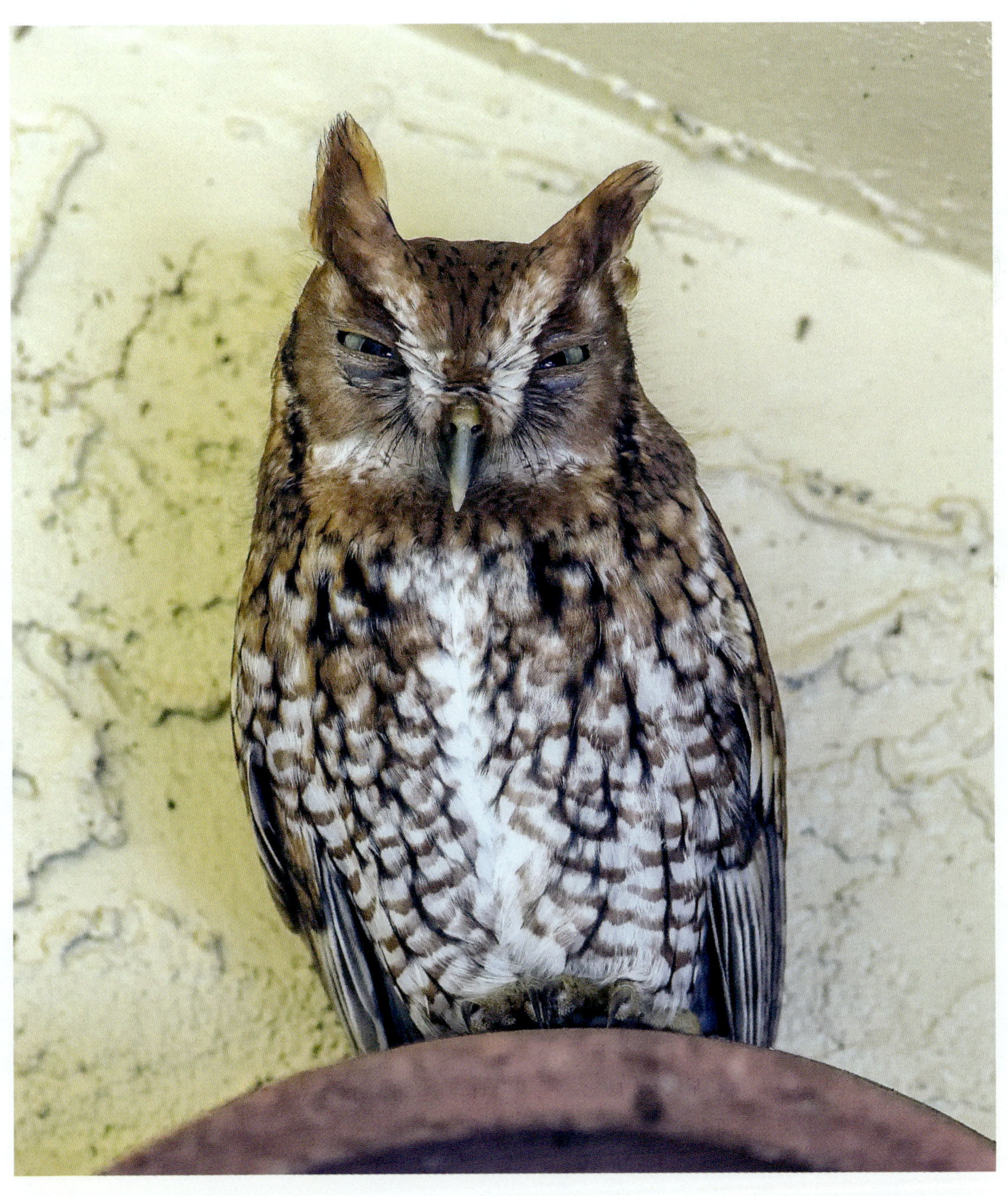

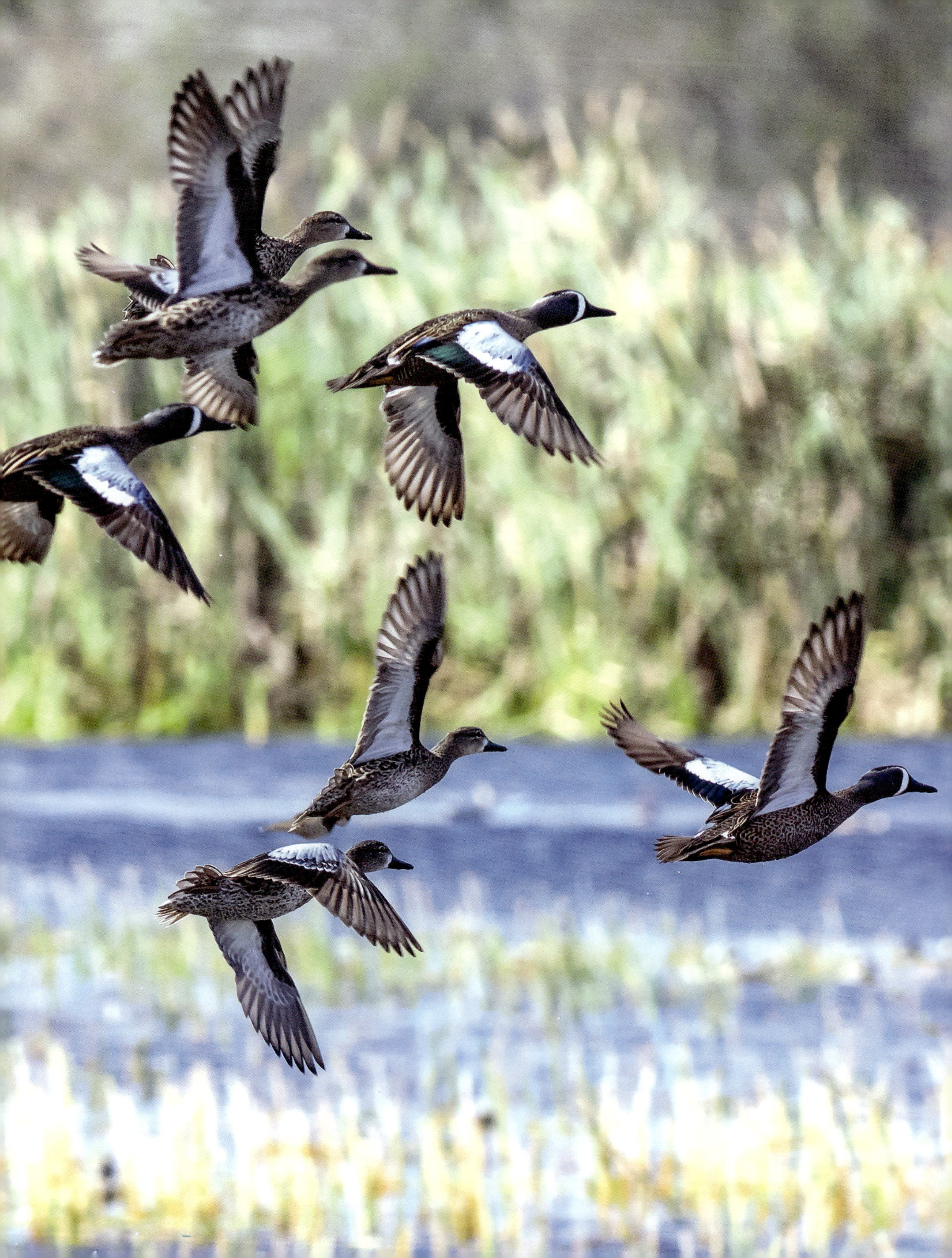

Waterfowl

To a birdwatcher, waterfowl are the birds such as ducks, geese and swans that spend most of their non-flying time on the water. These birds live in many different aquatic habitats including ponds, marshes, coastal estuaries, and shallow ocean bays. The preservation of wetlands is critical to the survival of waterfowl. Marshes and estuaries are not smelly, bug-infested swamps but rather among the most biologically productive habitats in the world. The term waterfowl is expanded by birders to include other aquatic birds like coots and gallinules.

In North America a variety of ducks and geese are hunted with strict seasons and bag limits. The Federal Duck Stamp Act of 1934 requires hunters to buy a special stamp in addition to a hunting license. This program has been very successful and has helped establish many waterfowl conservation areas. The 6,270 acre T.M. Goodwin Waterfowl Management Area in the Upper St. Johns River Basin near Fellsmere is shared by hunters, anglers, and birdwatchers alike. It is an an important wintering area for migrating waterfowl and a favorite place for bird photographers.

Mallard

Except in a few northern counties, wild Mallards typically spend the winter in Florida in small, dispersed flocks and are rarely seen in large numbers. During the Mottled Duck breeding season in Florida, the wild Mallards travel to northern nesting grounds, making interbreeding extremely rare.

According to the Florida Fish and Wildlife Conservation Commission, domestic Mallards are illegally released in significant numbers all around Florida. Each year, it is believed that feed stores sell more than 12,000 Mallard ducklings, many of which are later released. These birds are causing problems because they are not native to Florida.

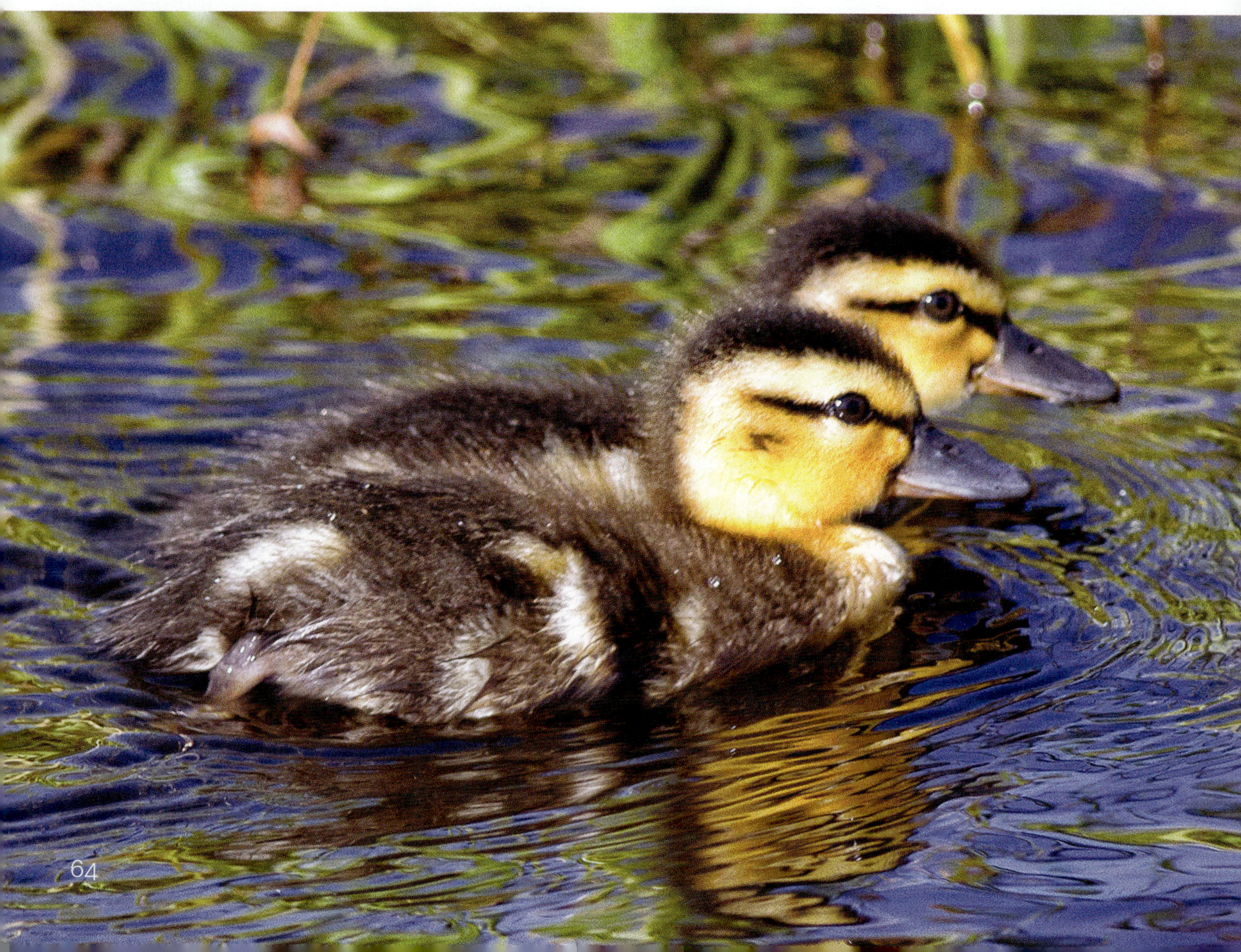

More mixed flocks are being seen in the wild by state biologists, who have noted that feral Mallards are mating with Mottled Ducks and hatching hybrid young as a result. In Florida, every Mallard released has the potential to worsen the hybridization issue. As a result, each year sees a decline in the number of pure-bred Florida Mottled Ducks. Complete hybridization could lead to the extinction of the Florida Mottled Duck due to the species' limited breeding population (which is believed to be between 30,000 and 40,000).

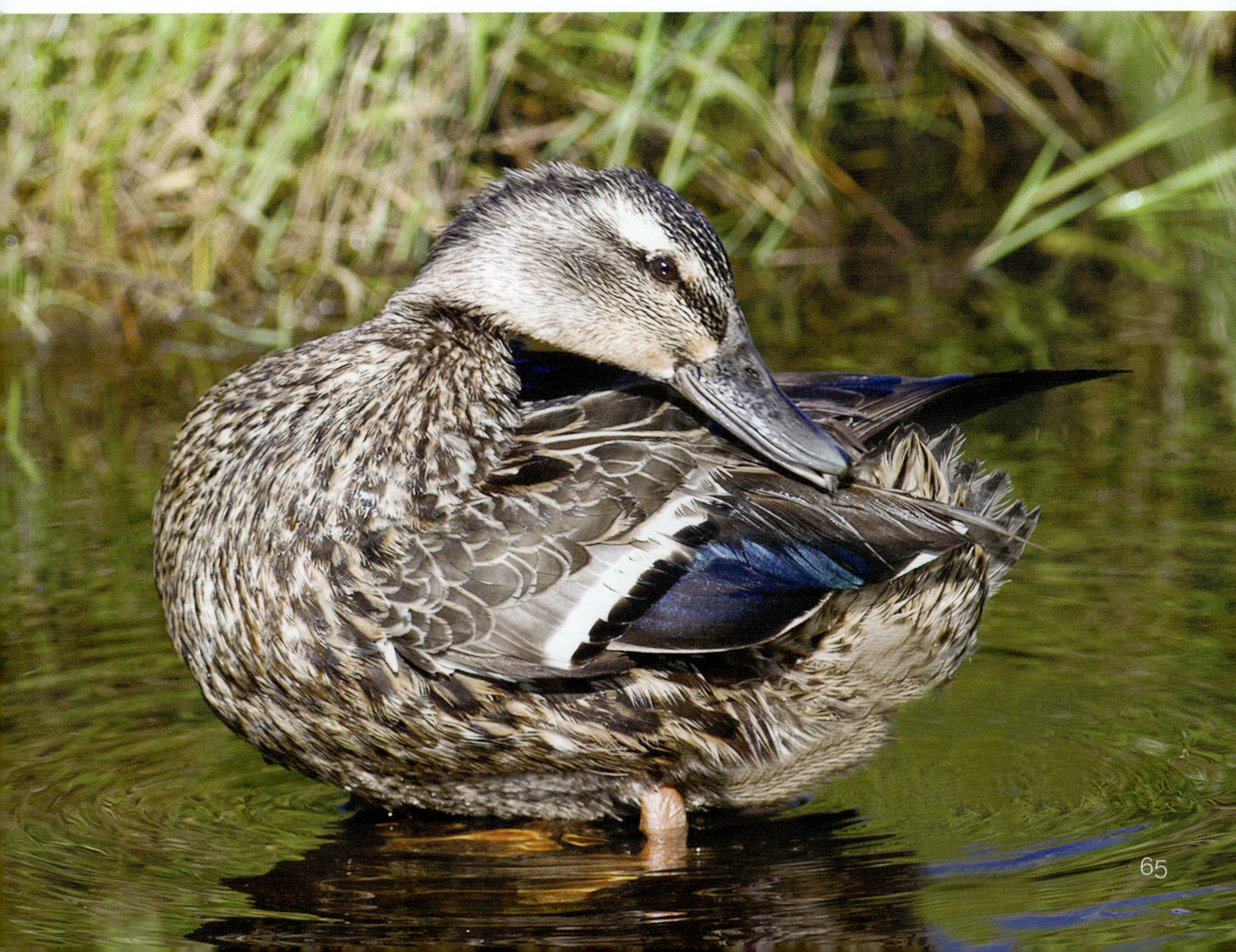

Florida Mottled Duck

This small brown duck has adapted to living in southern ponds and marshes and does not migrate. There are two subspecies: the Gulf Coast Mottled Duck and the Florida Mottled Duck found in south-central Florida. They share ancestry with the more common Mallard and American Black Duck. Unfortunately, over the past fifty years, their numbers have decreased by 80 percent.

The majority of ducks a birdwatcher encounters in Florida are migratory, spending their winters in an ice-free environment, with the exception of the Mottled Duck, domesticated Mallards, and a tiny colony of Wood Ducks in northern Florida. Mottled Ducks are classified as dabbling ducks because they graze on plants and crustaceans in shallow water while feeding with their heads underwater and tails pointing up.

Northern Shoveler

Northern Shovelers are found in large numbers throughout northern Europe, Asia, and across most of North America. This duck uses its large, specially adapted bill to filter out tiny invertebrates and plant material from the surface of a pond. Their unique spoon-shaped bill is a wonderful evolutionary adaptation allowing shovelers great success competing for food with other ducks.

Breeding males have the same plumage as Mallards, with an iridescent green head and neck, white breast, and cinnamon-brown flanks. Mated pairs form long-lasting bonds in the winter, and they remain together all summer. In Florida, they are found on fresh or brackish water but never in salt water. Sewage treatment ponds are a favorite resting place. After spending the winter in Florida, they will migrate to prairie lakes in the northern states and Canada to raise their young.

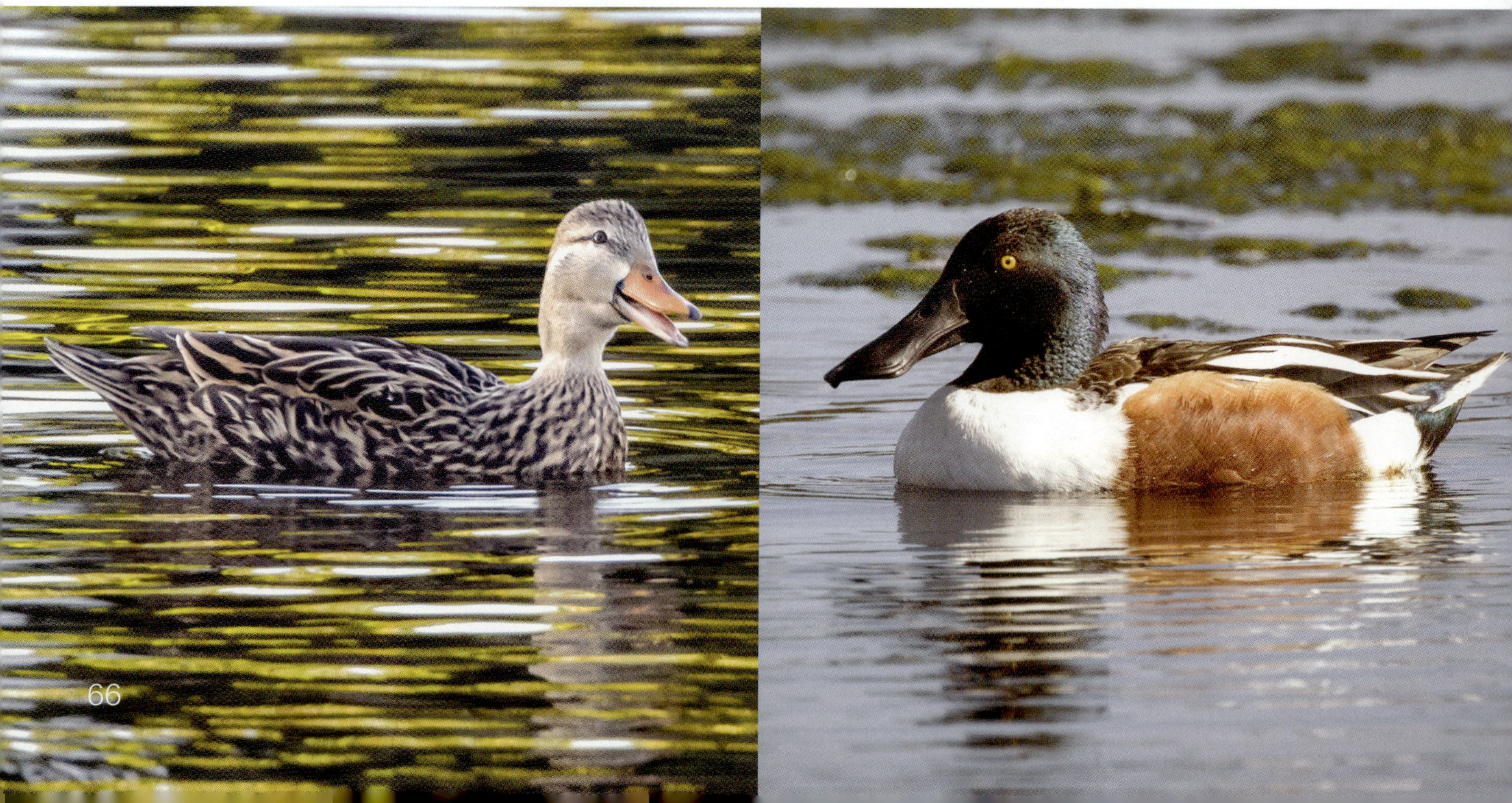

Lesser Scaup

Scaup get their odd name from "scalp," the Scottish word for clams, oysters and mussels, their favorite foods. A Lesser Scaup is nearly impossible to distinguish from the related Greater Scaup, but they are the more numerous of the two species. Scaup are classified as diving ducks because they dive underwater to find their food. While still the most common diving duck in North America, their numbers have dropped markedly since the 1990s for unknown reasons. The most likely explanation is the major loss of wetland habitat in the prairie pothole region of boreal Canada where they breed. In Florida, they can be found in large rafts of hundreds of birds and are common in the Indian River Lagoon along the east coast.

Wood Duck

These beautiful ducks can be year-round residents in North Florida, but migratory ducks also spend the winter here. Woodie males are the most beautiful of our ducks with an ornate green crest, green head with white stripes and a red eye. Females are dull brown with a crest and a large white eye patch. Nearly extinct after years of habitat loss and hunting pressure, Wood Ducks have made a comeback thanks to preservation of woodlands and the placement of nest boxes on public waters throughout the state.

Wood Ducks are found in ponds and cypress swamps because they nest in tree cavities to protect their young from predators like foxes and raccoons. They have evolved claws on their webbed feet that allow them to perch in trees. I have even seen them occupying a woodpecker nest hole in a broken-off palm tree. Females are known to lay their eggs in another hen's nest if they are unsuccessful finding a nest of their own.

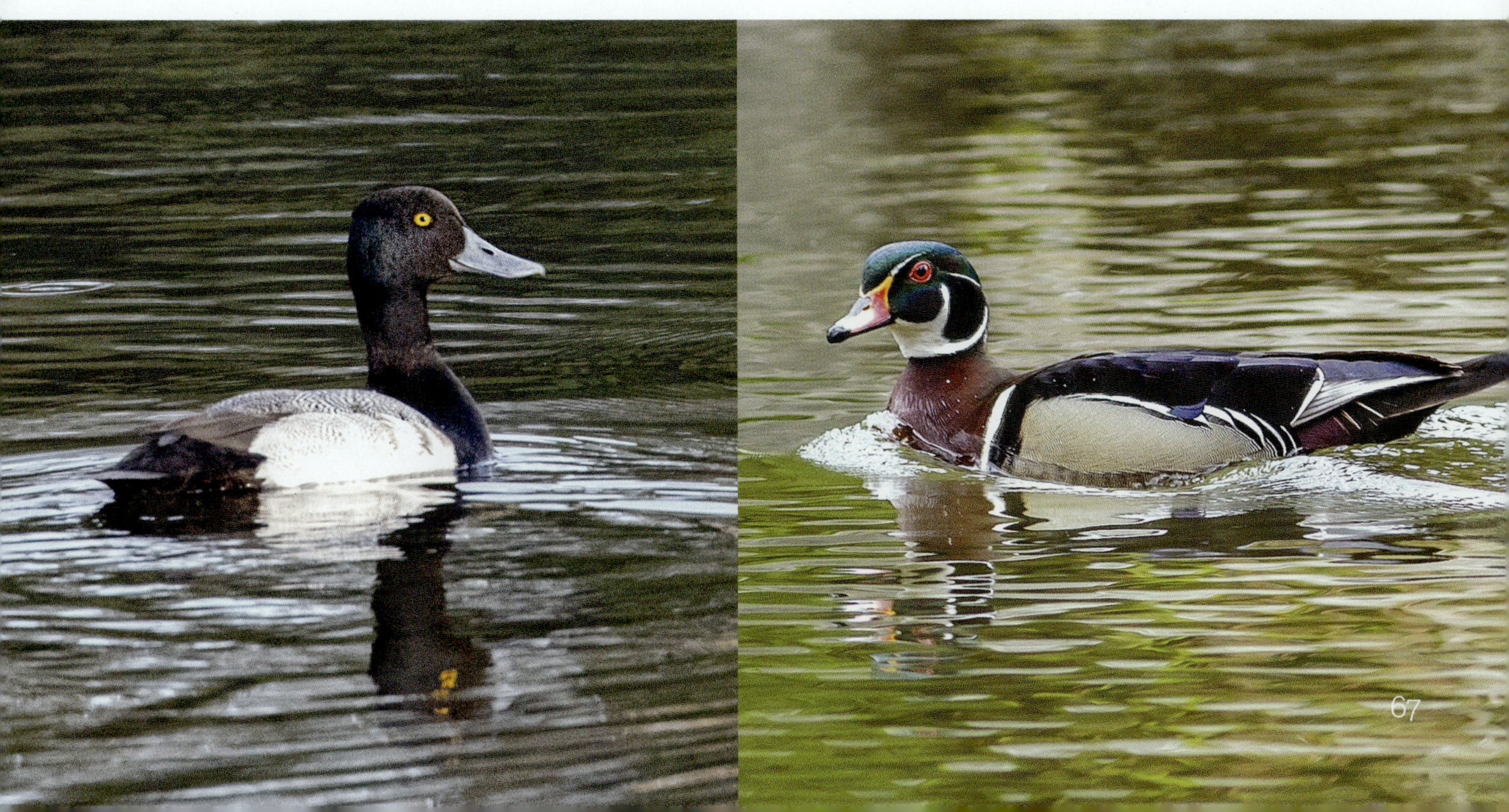

Ring-necked Duck

Ring-necked Ducks have a dark reddish-brown ring around their neck that is impossible to see except in perfect light. They resemble a Scaup because of their black head and whitish-gray flanks, but the white ring at the tip of their bill sets them apart. This is an excellent example of how many birds were named by biologists studying specimens in the lab rather than by observers in the field.

Ring-necks never gather in large flocks and are typically found in mixed groups with other duck species. They are classified as diving ducks and live on mollusks, crustaceans, and aquatic plants. These ducks are long-distance migrants, flying from western boreal forests to spend the winter in a large area across southern North America and into central Mexico. In Brevard County, the T.M. Goodwin Waterfowl Management Area near Fellsmere is a great place to look for them along with many other varieties of waterfowl.

American Wigeon

Wigeons have a creamy white patch on their forehead, which is why hunters refer to them as "baldpates." Their eyes are surrounded by a green border, and their bills are blue-gray with black tips. These ducks, which can be found in enormous flocks from California to the Gulf Coast during the winter, are among the most common dabbling ducks in all of North America. Because they are primarily vegetarians, they may live in any open marsh or wetland and sometimes visit parks and golf courses to graze on the grass.

A flock of American Wigeons may occasionally contain a related Eurasian Wigeon, so birders always pay close attention to make sure they are not missing a rare sight. In my experience, wigeons were never abundant on Florida's east coast, but in 2022 a sizable flock wintered on Centennial Pond at the Pelican Island National Wildlife Refuge.

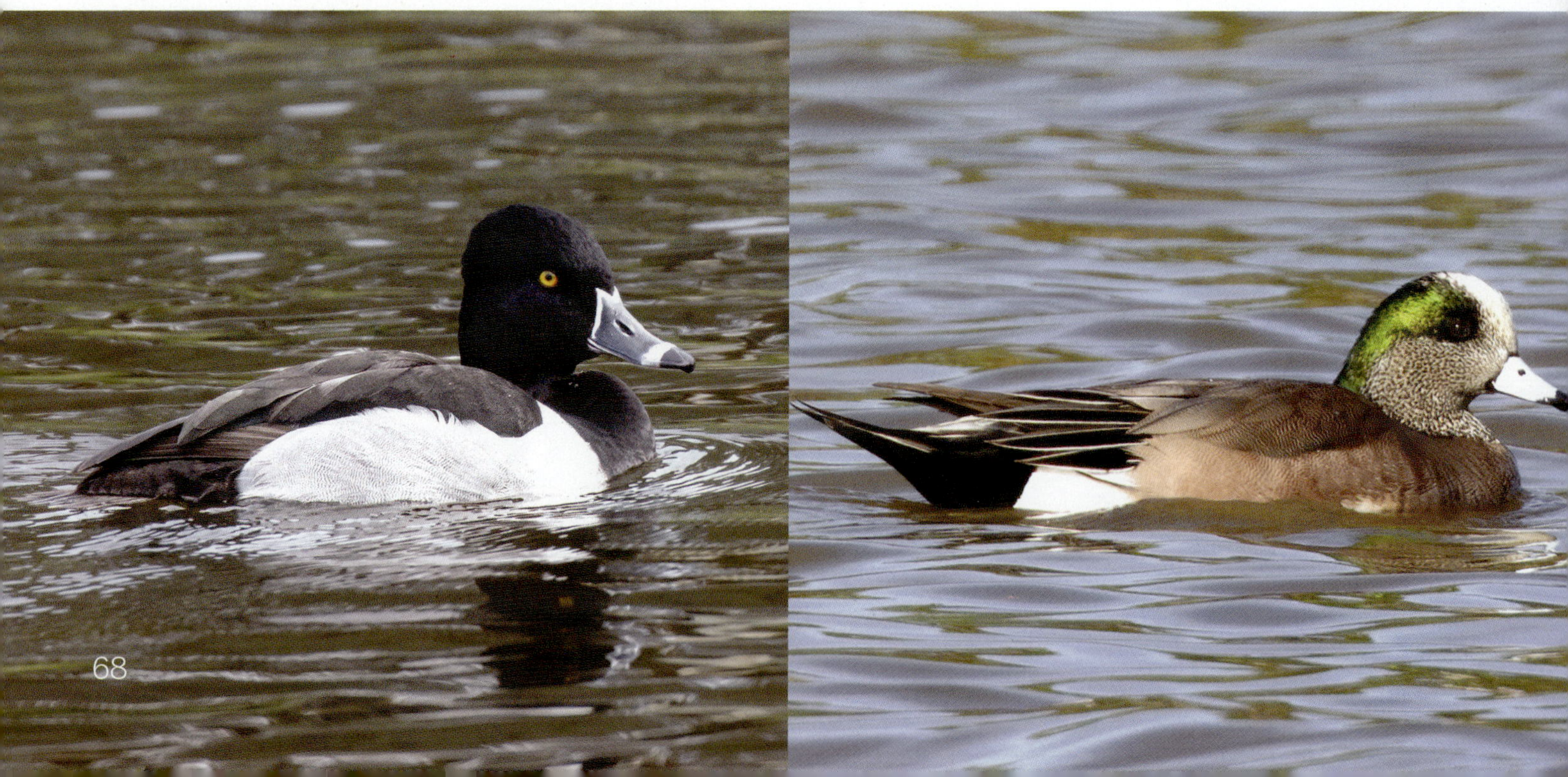

Blue-winged Teal

These small ducks can be found throughout North America. They are migratory with some flying from Canada to South America for the winter, but many large flocks shorten their trip and stop in Florida. Like many ducks, they fly at night and can suddenly appear on a pond in the morning light. They are one of the first ducks to migrate south for the winter and last to head north in the spring.

Blue-winged Teal are small ducks that often hide in the grasses along the edge of a freshwater pond. Be careful not to confuse them with their cousins, the Green-winged Teal. Their blue wing patch is best seen in flight, but, just to make it complicated, they also have some green on their wings. In any plumage, the males have a white crescent on the face that serves as a reliable field mark.

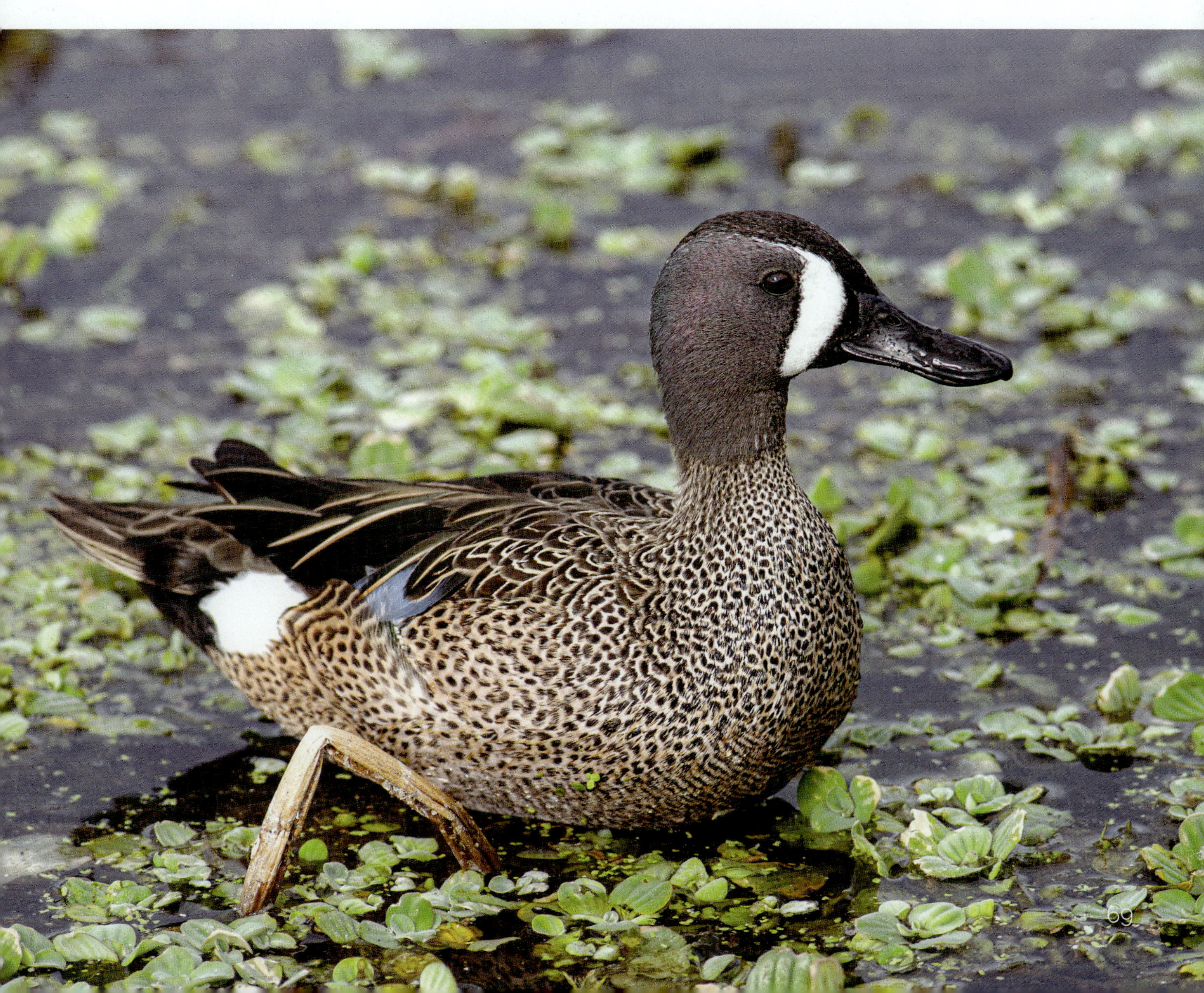

Hooded Merganser

Beautiful little Hooded Mergansers choose to spend the winter in shallow ponds and estuaries along the Gulf Coast despite the fact that they typically breed in the north. In Florida, they usually arrive in late September and depart for the north in April. According to Florida Fish and Wildlife, there are rare instances of them raising young in Florida. Due to their ability to catch and hold fish with their serrated bills, mergansers are also known as sawbills. Thanks to their excellent underwater vision, Mergansers can dive and swim to capture fish, frogs, insects, crayfish, and other aquatic prey.

There are many species of mergansers, but because they are so challenging to photograph, these feisty little "Hoodies" are one of my favorites. This is a dramatic bird with a black face, golden eye, and white crest. They are far more tame in Florida than they are in the north, and occasionally they will allow a photographer close enough for a portrait.

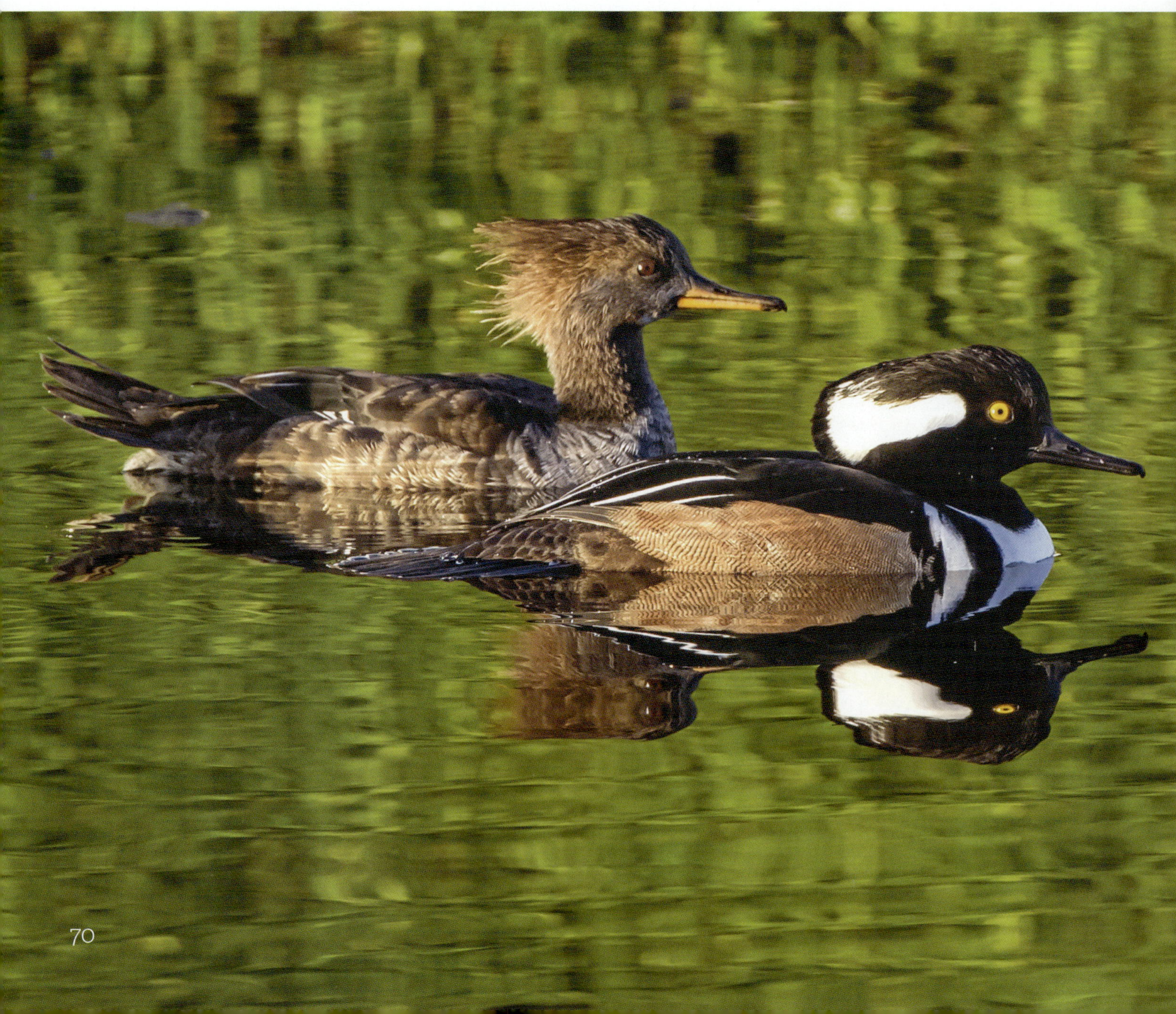

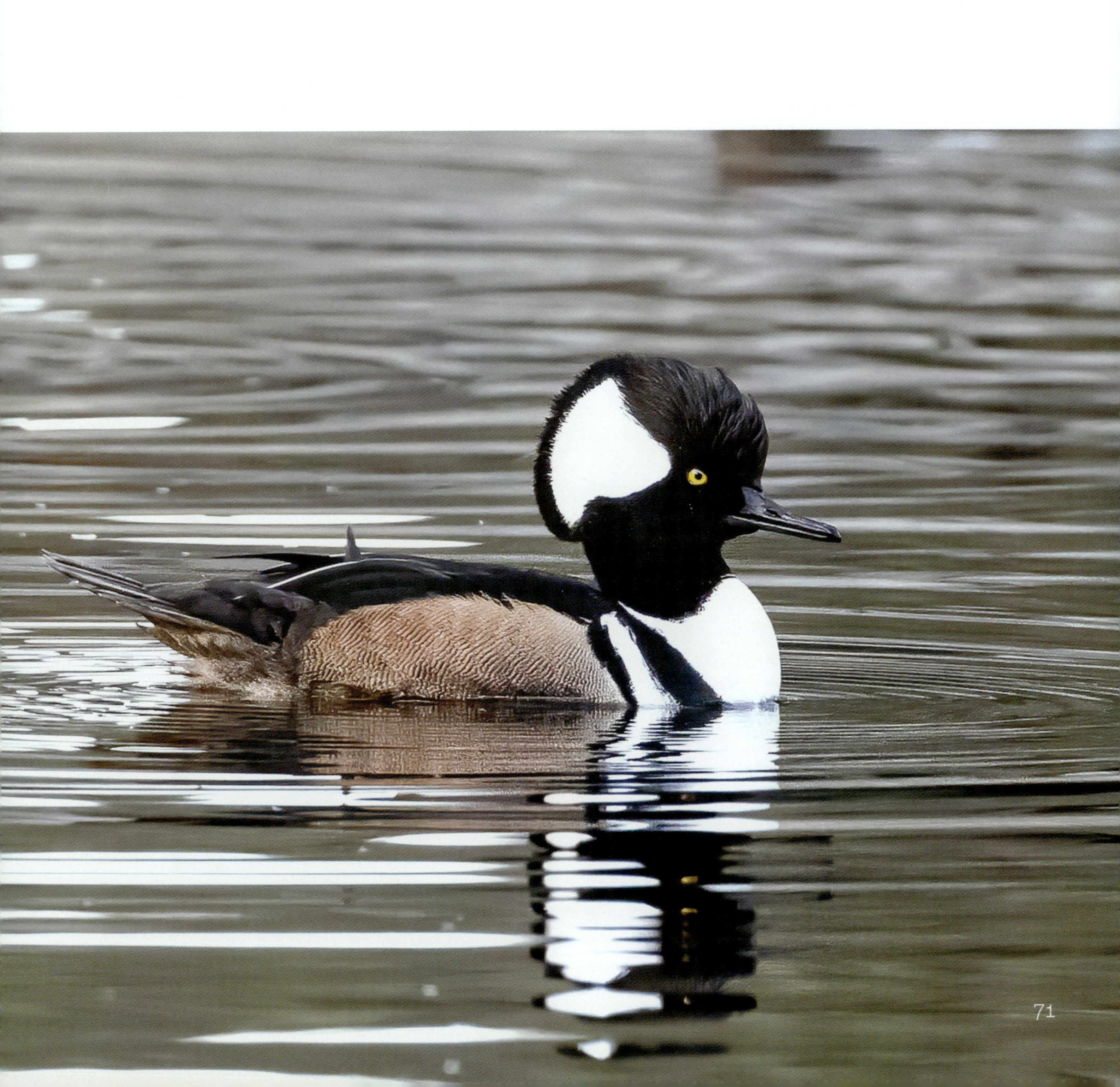

American Coot

Coots are not really ducks although they act like them. Many are migratory but the Florida birds usually nest locally where they build large floating nests. Each hen hatches eight to twelve chicks that start swimming within six hours of hatching. They are gregarious and form large rafts of hundreds of birds in shallow, reed-filled freshwater ponds. Except during migration, coots do not fly much. In order to get airborne, they must get a running start by striding along the water while flapping their wings.

Although these are unattractive plain black birds, often known as Mud Hens, they are aggressive and noisy as the males compete for mates and territory, and it is difficult to ignore them.

Coots are susceptible to brood parasitism where females lay eggs in nests that are not their own. The adult coots are able to recognize parasitic chicks and will reject or even drown them.

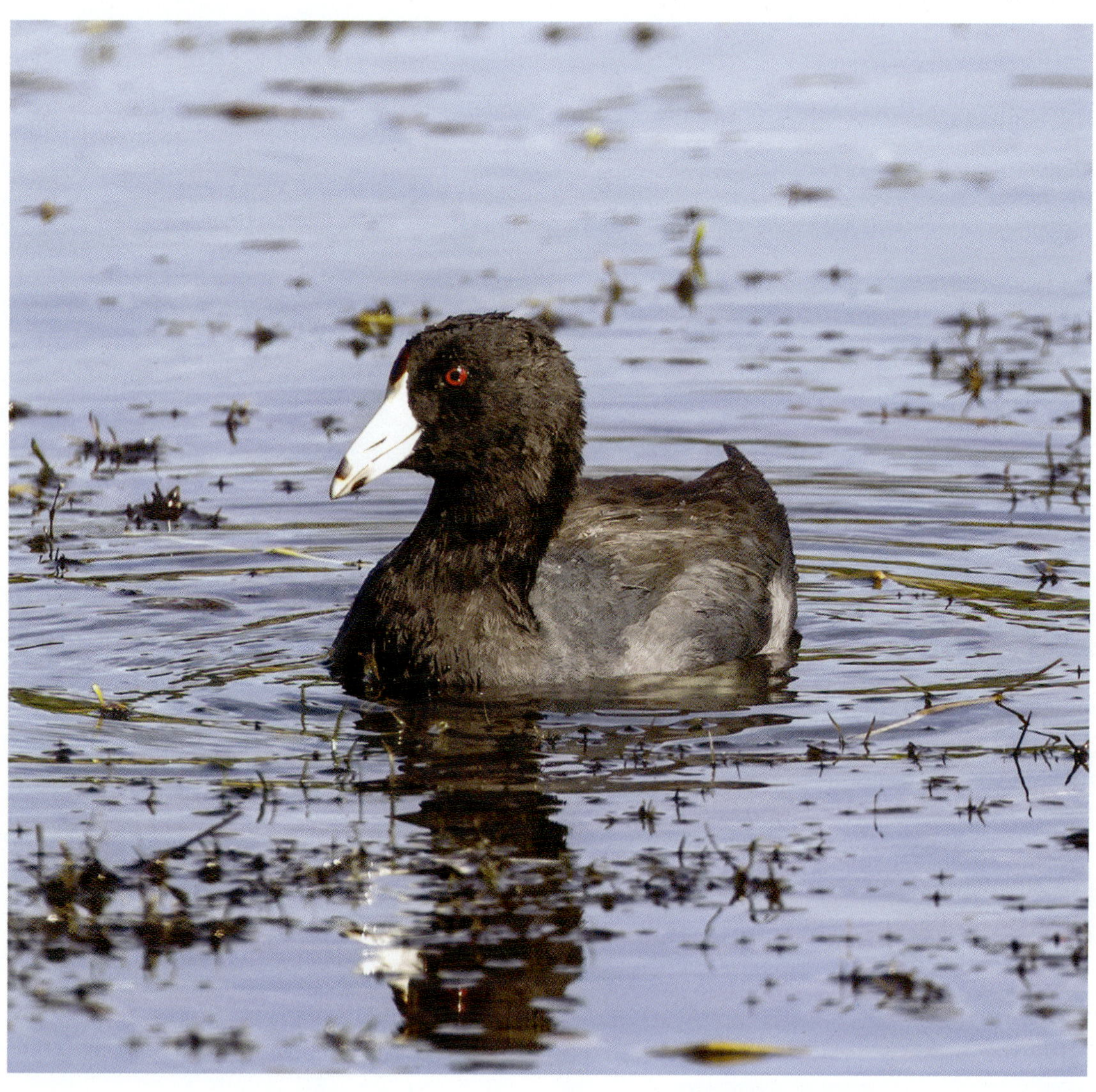

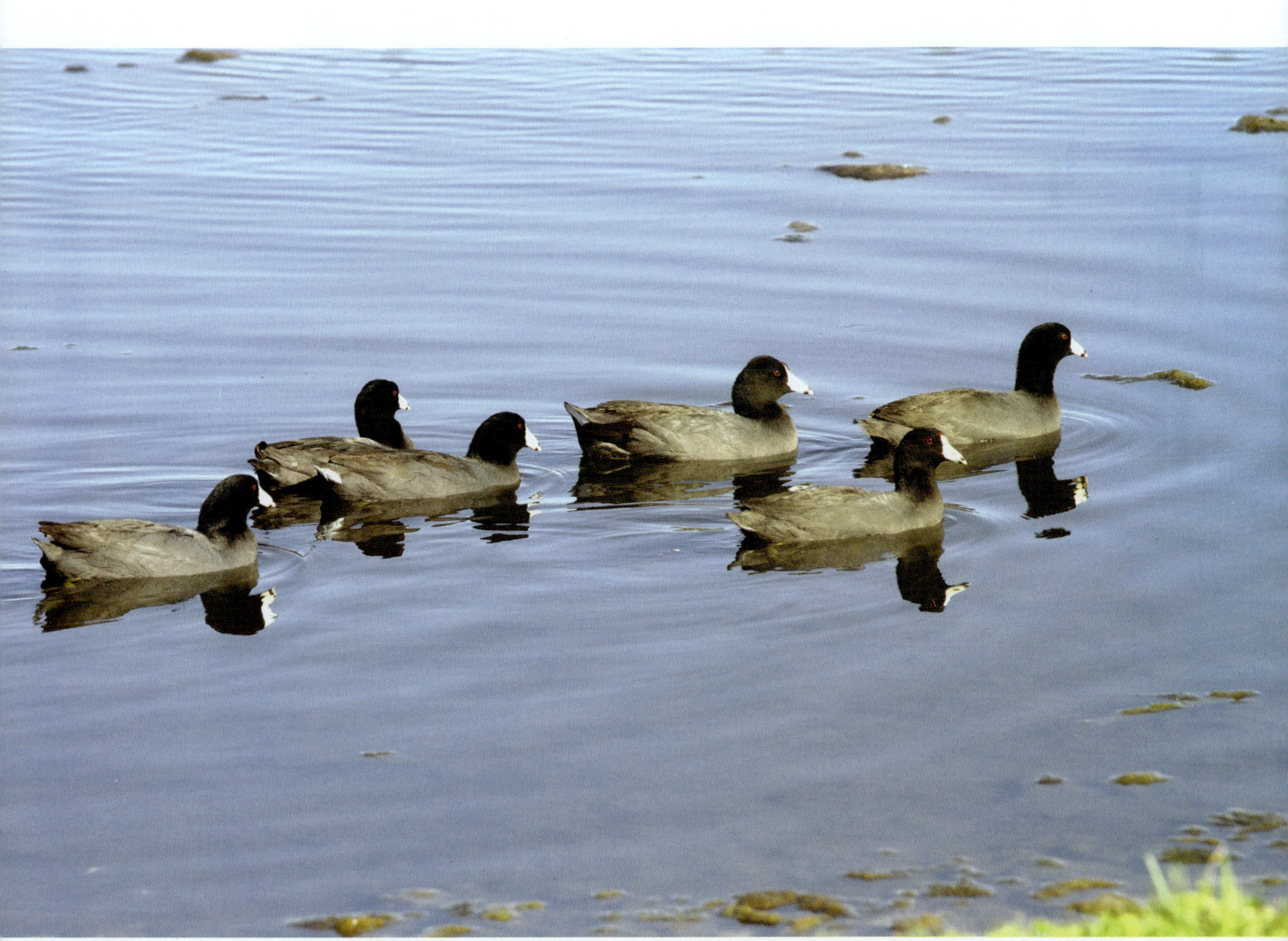

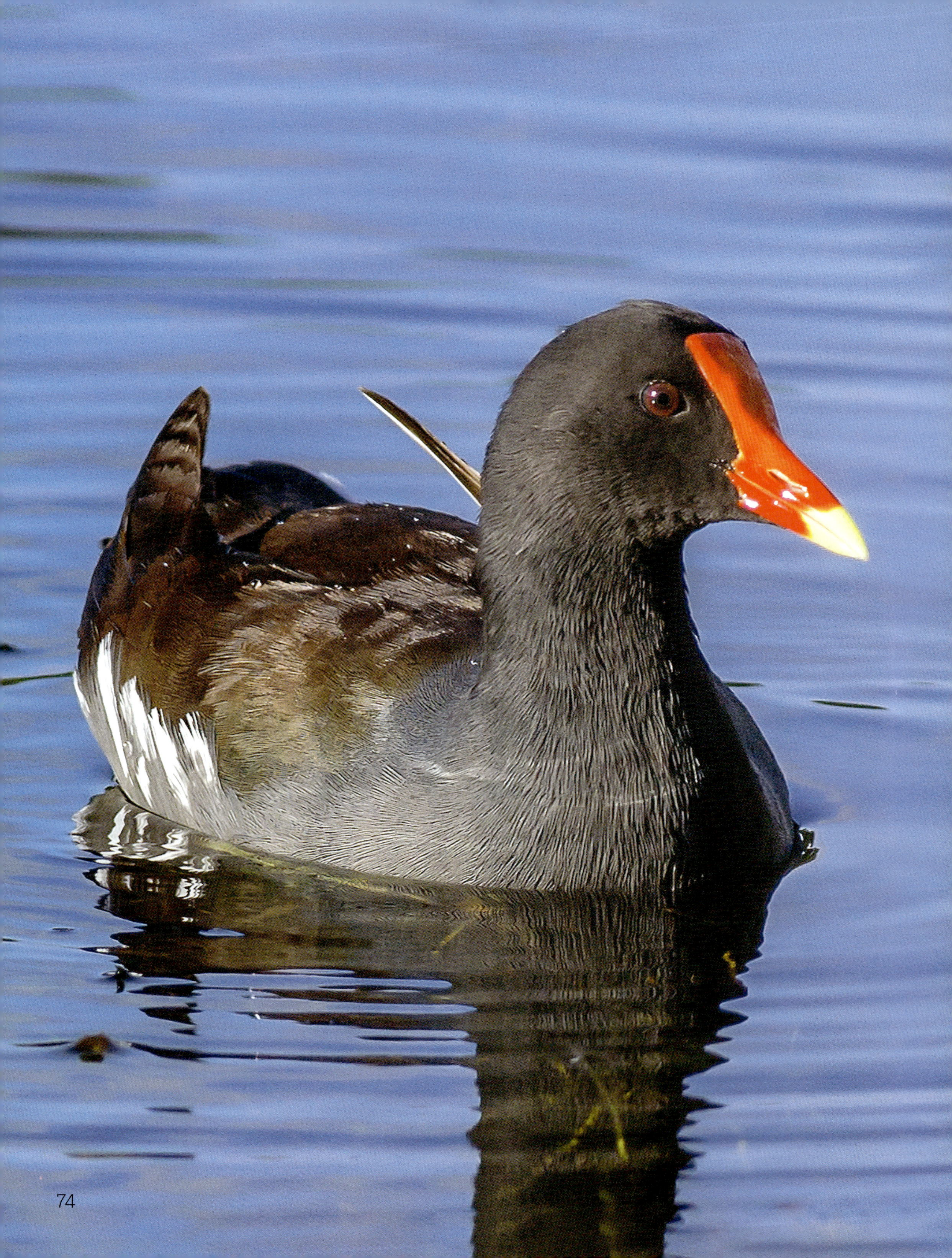

Common Gallinule

Similar to Coots, Gallinules are common and found in shallow water with dense vegetation. They have a distinctive red beak and frontal shield that distinguishes them from coots. Since they rarely fly, their feet have evolved to allow them to walk on aquatic plants. Locally referred to as the Swamp Chicken, they were always called the Common Moorhen until recently. The official name was changed to Common Gallinule in 2011.

Gallinules are prehistoric birds that are descended from ancestors dating back to the Pleistocene era over two million years ago. Fossils of early gallinules have been found in the Ichetucknee River deposits in north-central Florida. Today gallinules are widespread and noisy birds that can be found in any suitable habitat but they are nevertheless vulnerable to the regular challenges posed by pollution, pesticides, and water-management practices.

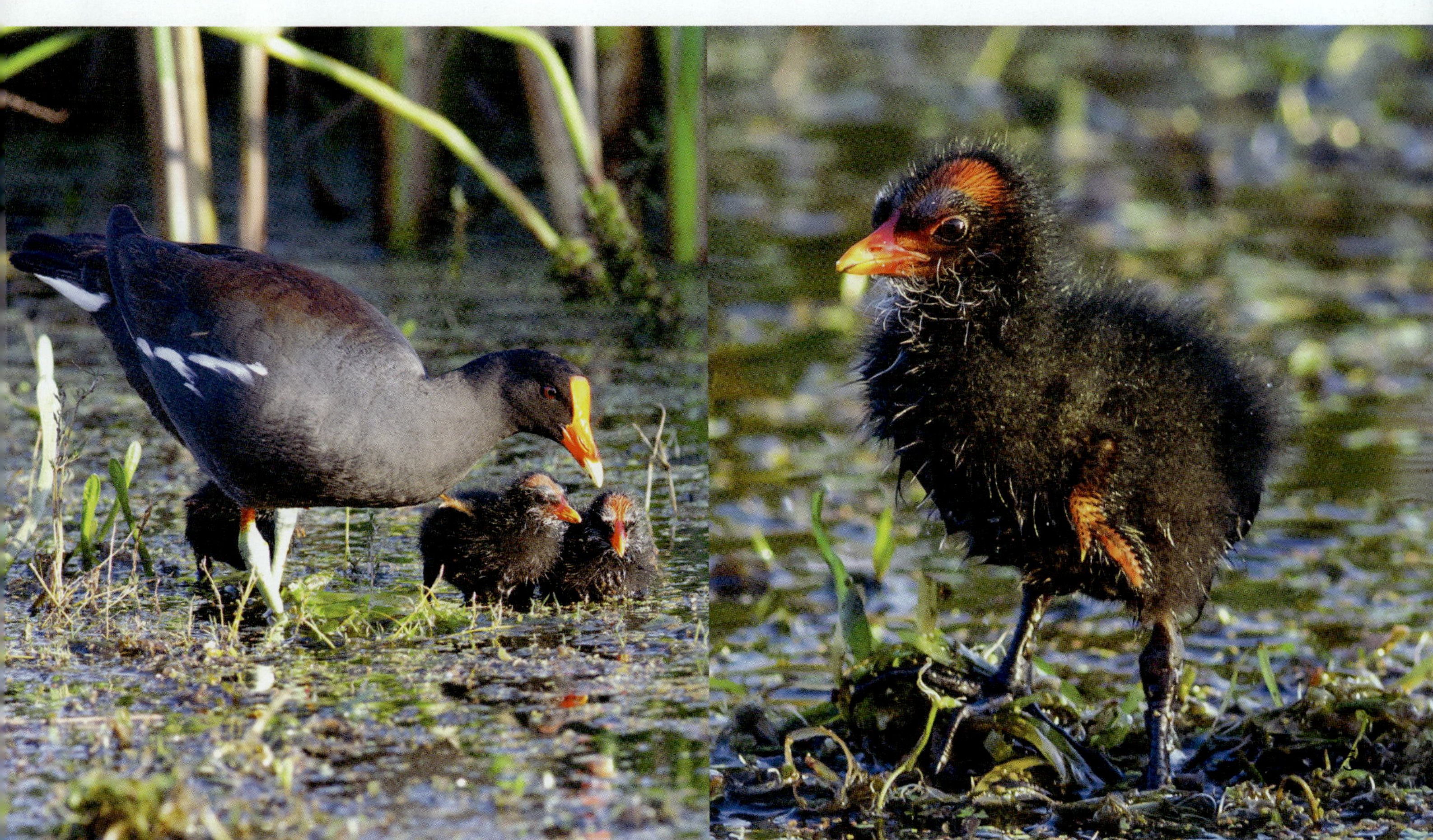

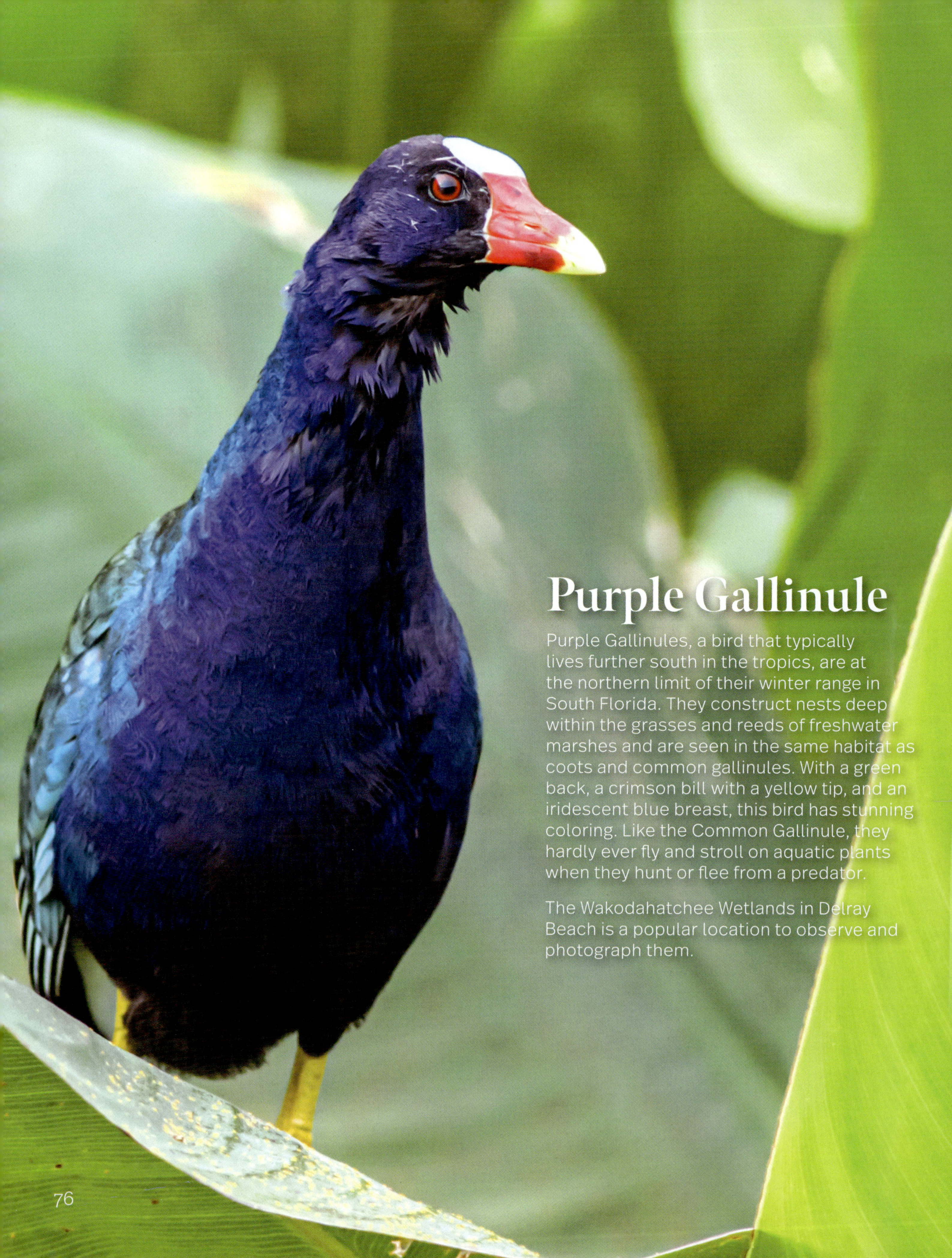

Purple Gallinule

Purple Gallinules, a bird that typically lives further south in the tropics, are at the northern limit of their winter range in South Florida. They construct nests deep within the grasses and reeds of freshwater marshes and are seen in the same habitat as coots and common gallinules. With a green back, a crimson bill with a yellow tip, and an iridescent blue breast, this bird has stunning coloring. Like the Common Gallinule, they hardly ever fly and stroll on aquatic plants when they hunt or flee from a predator.

The Wakodahatchee Wetlands in Delray Beach is a popular location to observe and photograph them.

Gray-headed Swamphen

This is a bird from the Middle East and India that escaped from captivity in South Florida in 1992. They were originally called Purple Swamphens, but the name was changed to Gray-headed Swamphen in 2015. Despite efforts to eradicate them, Gray-headed Swamphens have thrived and are now established in the wild. For birdwatchers working on a Florida life list, Swamphens were added to the American Birding Association checklist in 2013.

They are frequently mistaken for a Purple Gallinule. Look for a larger bird with red legs and all-red bill.

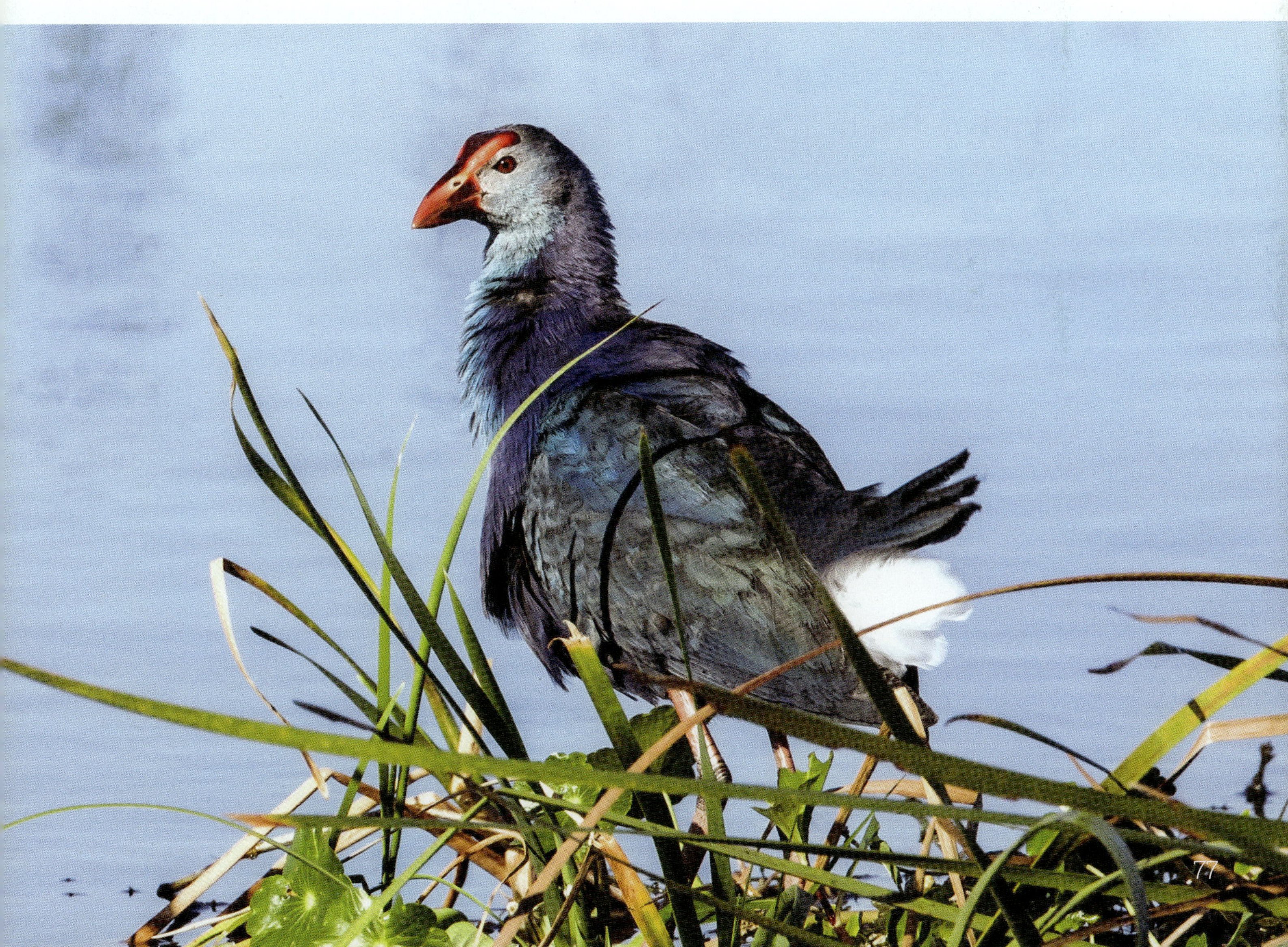

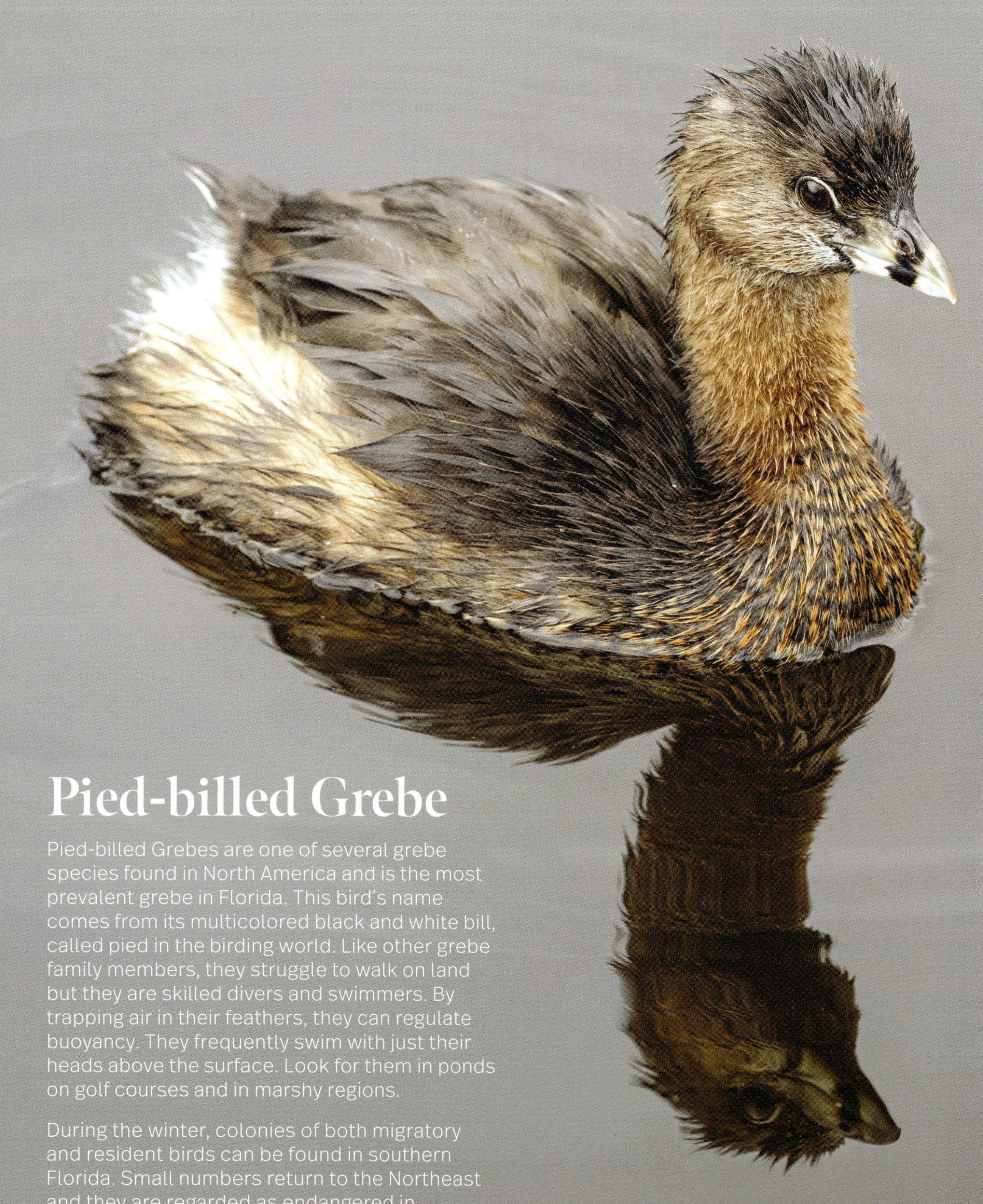

Pied-billed Grebe

Pied-billed Grebes are one of several grebe species found in North America and is the most prevalent grebe in Florida. This bird's name comes from its multicolored black and white bill, called pied in the birding world. Like other grebe family members, they struggle to walk on land but they are skilled divers and swimmers. By trapping air in their feathers, they can regulate buoyancy. They frequently swim with just their heads above the surface. Look for them in ponds on golf courses and in marshy regions.

During the winter, colonies of both migratory and resident birds can be found in southern Florida. Small numbers return to the Northeast and they are regarded as endangered in northern New England states.

Black-bellied Whistling-Duck

The Black-bellied Whistling-Duck is a widespread and common bird in South and Central America. These ducks first appeared in central Florida in 1968, and today they live here all year long. With a chestnut brown and black body and bright pink legs and bill, they are easily identifiable. These friendly, loud birds can completely take over a small pond and usually congregate in large flocks.

They typically live near agricultural areas where rice and corn are grown, browsing on the waste grain. Recently, they have been showing up in Florida's suburbs, particularly in areas where people have placed food out for ducks and geese.

There is a closely related species called the Fulvous Whistling-Duck that has established itself in South Florida. I have seen them but have not been lucky enough to get an adequate photograph.

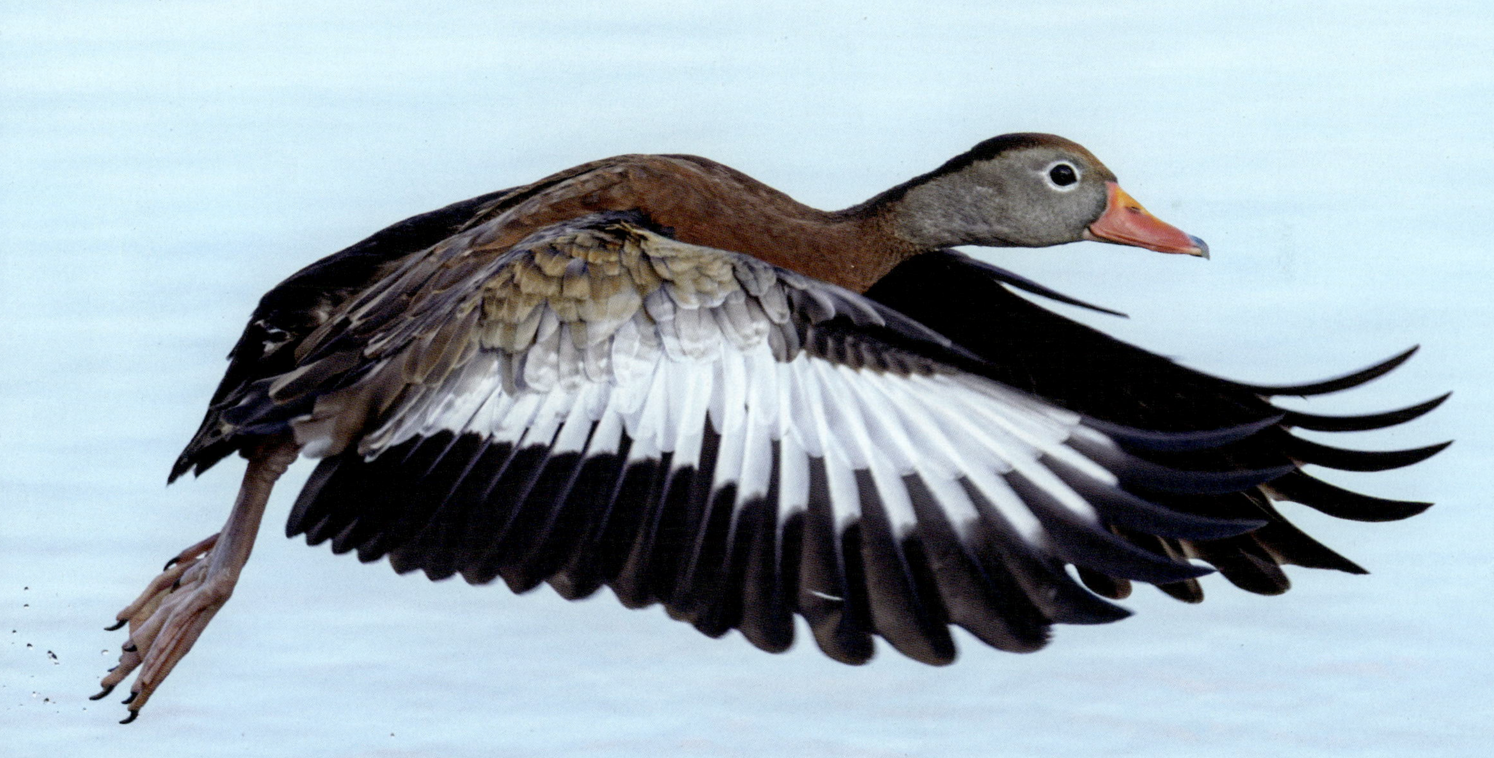

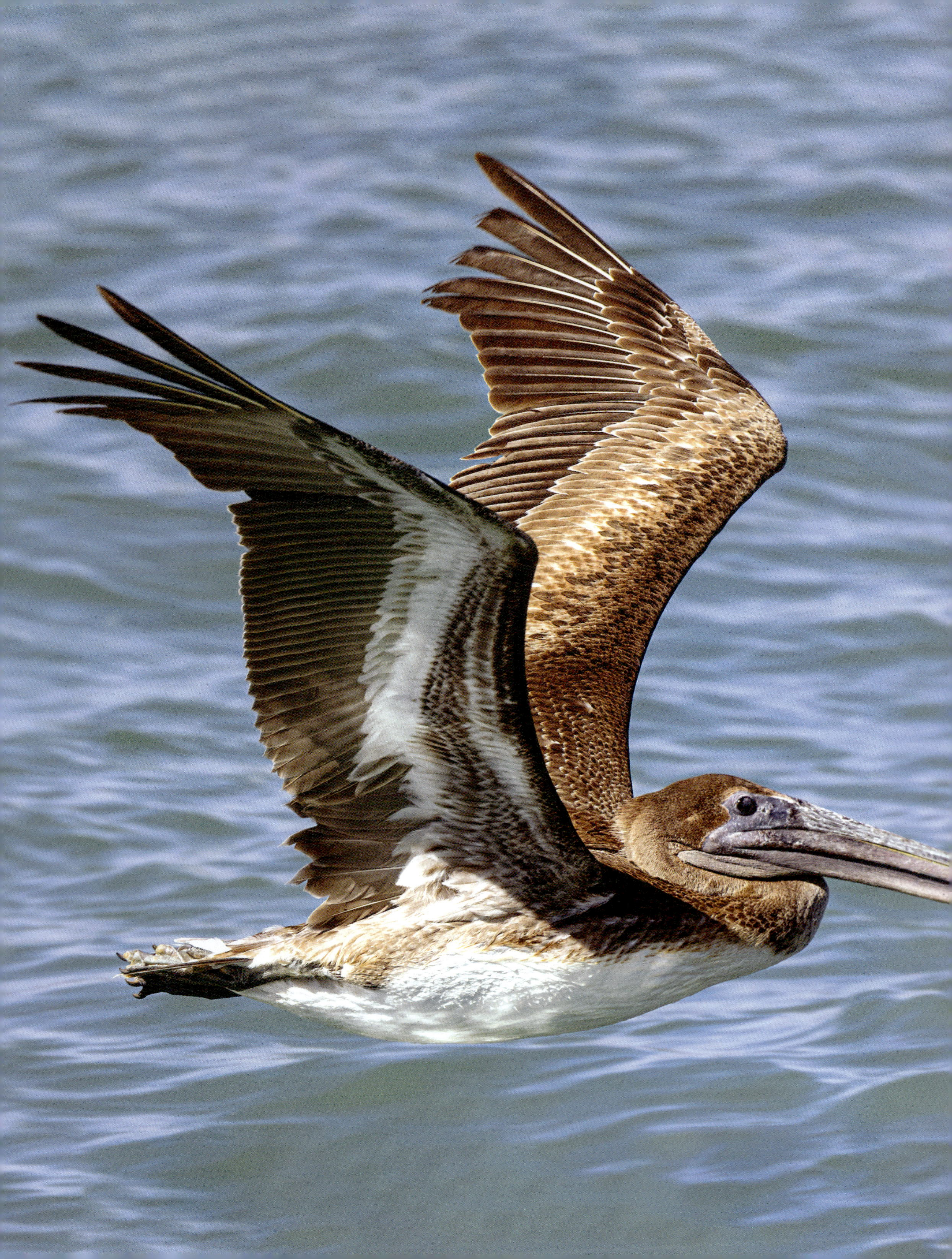

Pelicans

Pelicans live in all temperate areas of the world and are recognizable by their long beaks and throat pouches. Despite being coastal birds, they nest in large inland colonies. Brown Pelicans stay in Florida year-round, whereas White Pelicans migrate north to spend the summer in the central plains. Pelicans are known for their large gular pouch, which is used to scoop up fish. By using special throat muscles, they can contract the pouch, expel excess water, and swallow their catch. Fossilized remains of birds with elongated fishscooping bills from around 30 million years ago that are very similar to present-day pelicans, show that this adaptation has been successful for a vast expanse of time.

Pelicans need predator-free islands for roosting and nesting. In 1903, President Theodore Roosevelt created the first national wildlife refuge at Pelican Island in Sebastian, Florida, in order to protect pelicans from market hunters. Birdwatchers visiting Pelican Island NWR can hike miles of trails and see dozens of Florida bird species, including the famous pelicans.

American White Pelican

White Pelicans are dramatic twenty-pound birds with a nine-foot wingspan. In flight they display their black wing tips that are not visible while swimming. The population of American White Pelicans has increased from a low point in the 1950s when spraying and pollution of wetlands was common. Today there are thousands of pelicans wintering in Florida and along the Gulf Coast. They typically congregate in protected lagoons, ponds, or harbors but never on the open ocean like the Brown Pelicans. Every year we are entertained by a flock of hundreds of white pelicans who swoop into Grand Harbor Golf and Yacht Club.

They are fascinating to watch as they work in groups to corral fish into a shallow corner of a pond. When the breeding season begins in March, their beaks develop a large bump indicating sexual maturity. By the end of the month, they will have flown hundreds of miles back to their breeding grounds in the Great Plains and mountain lakes of the American West.

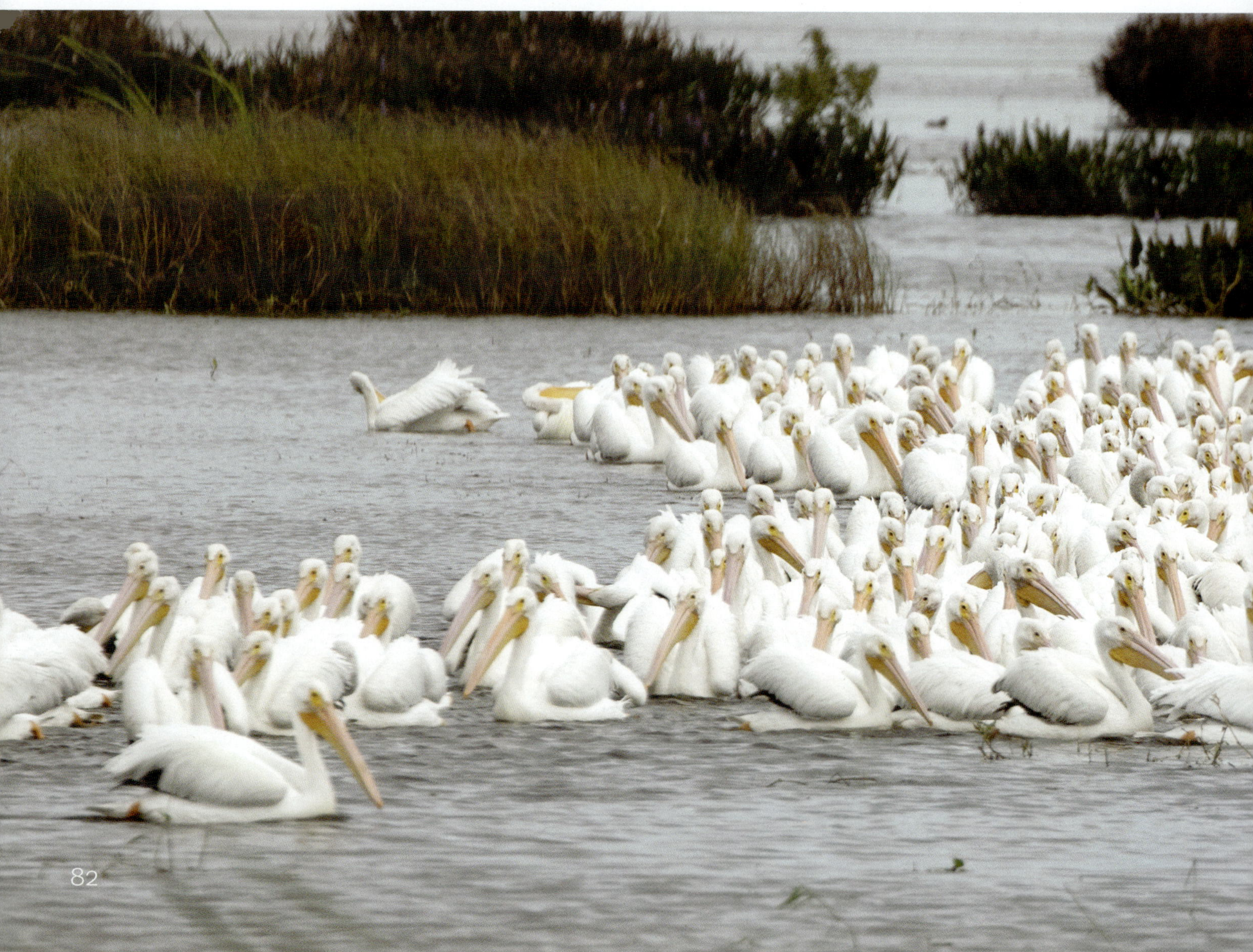

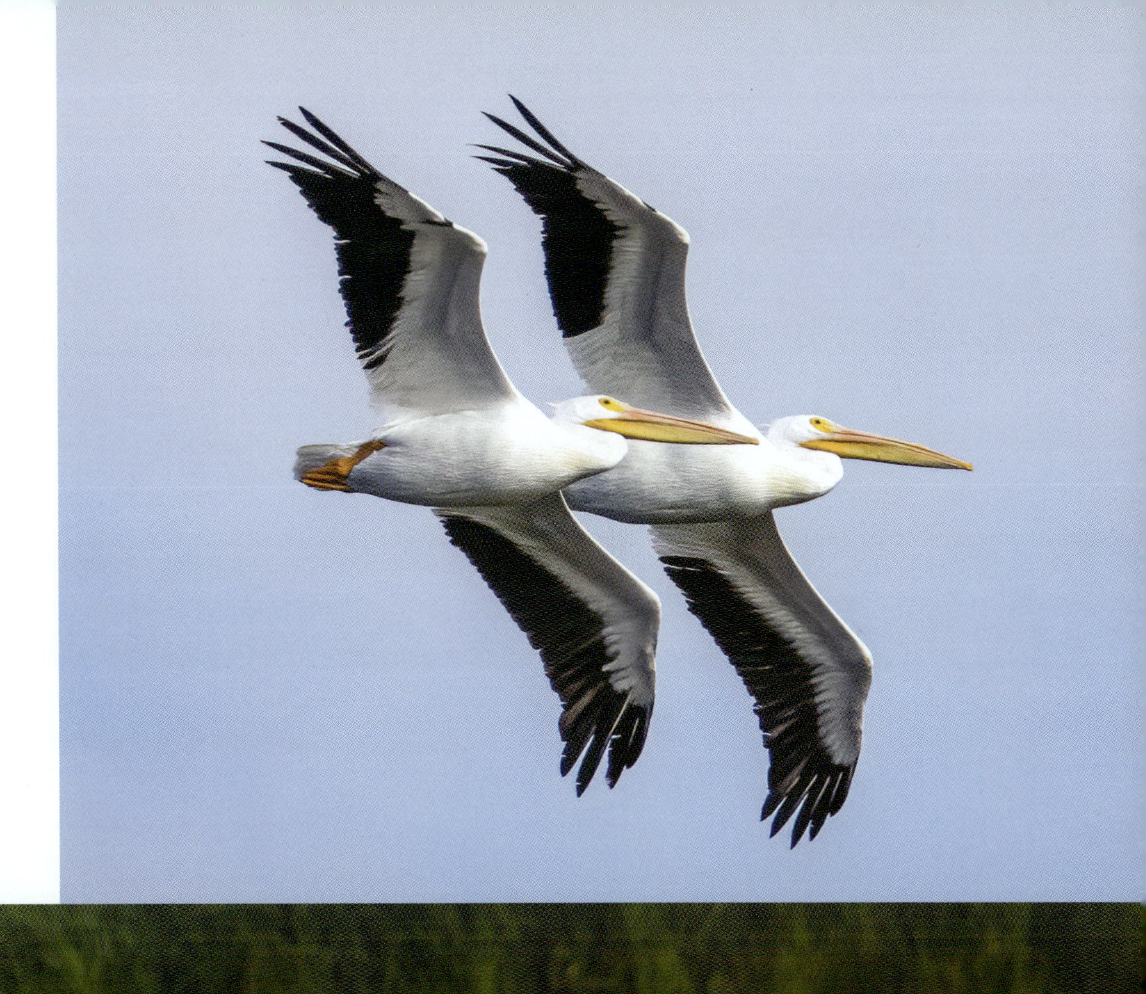

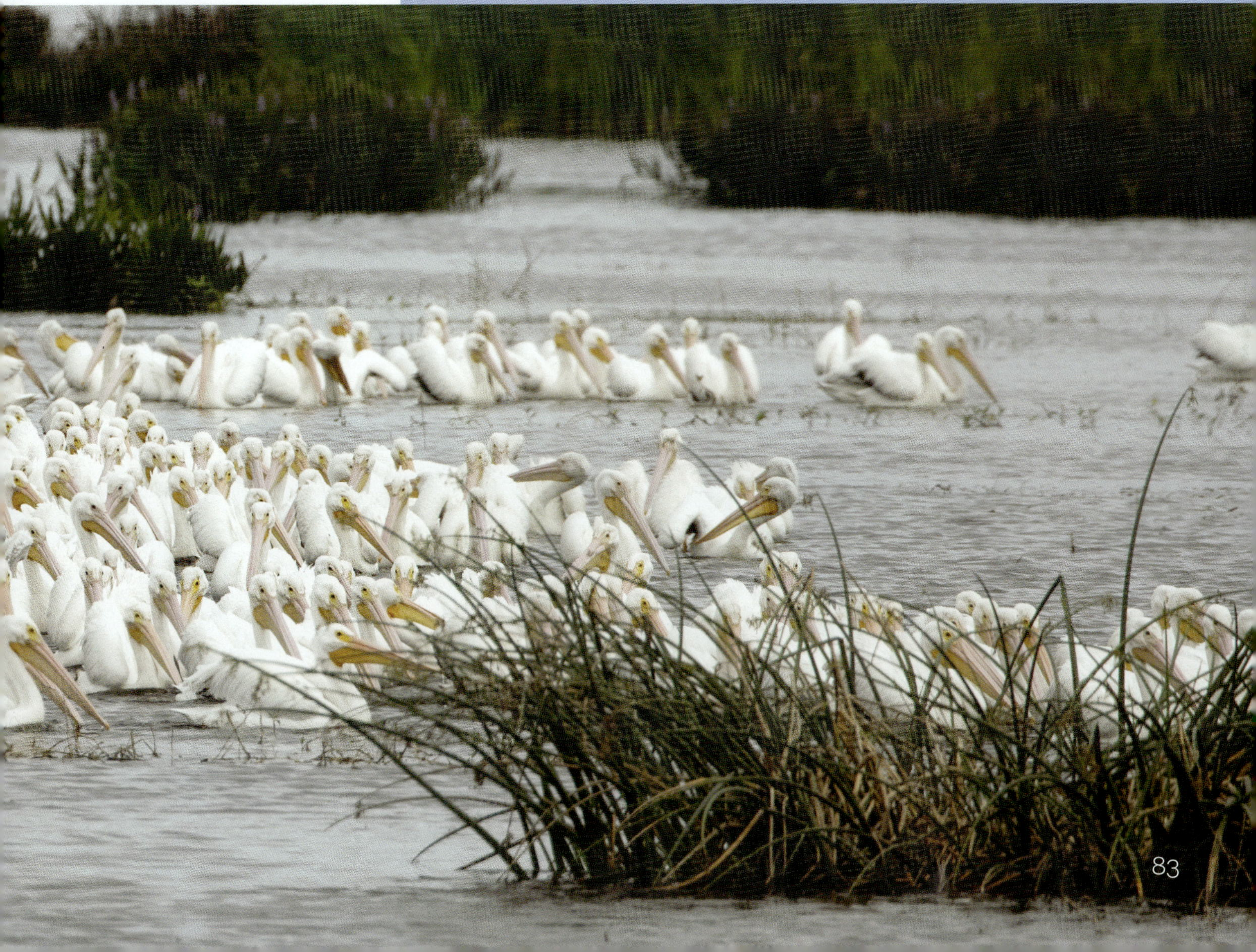

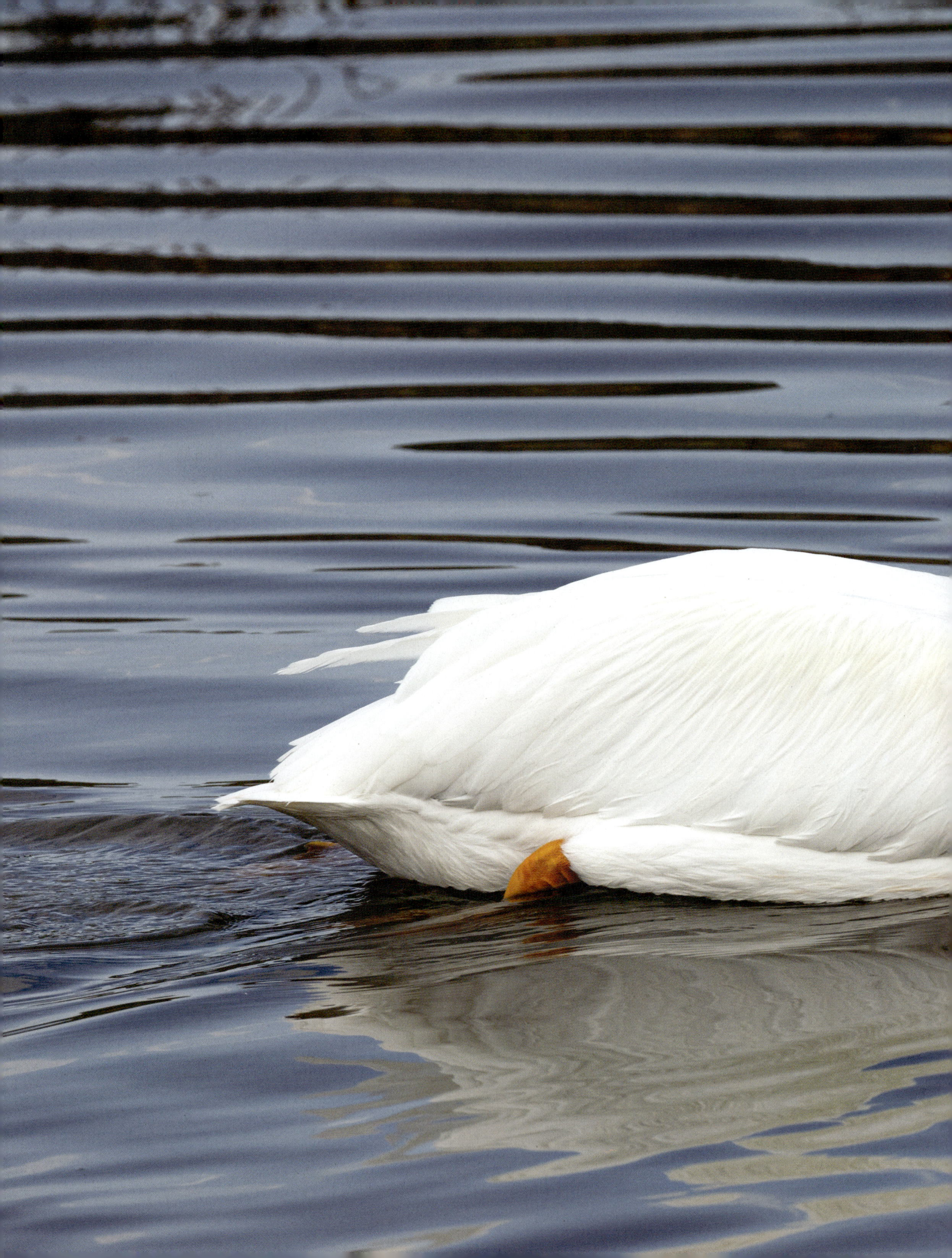

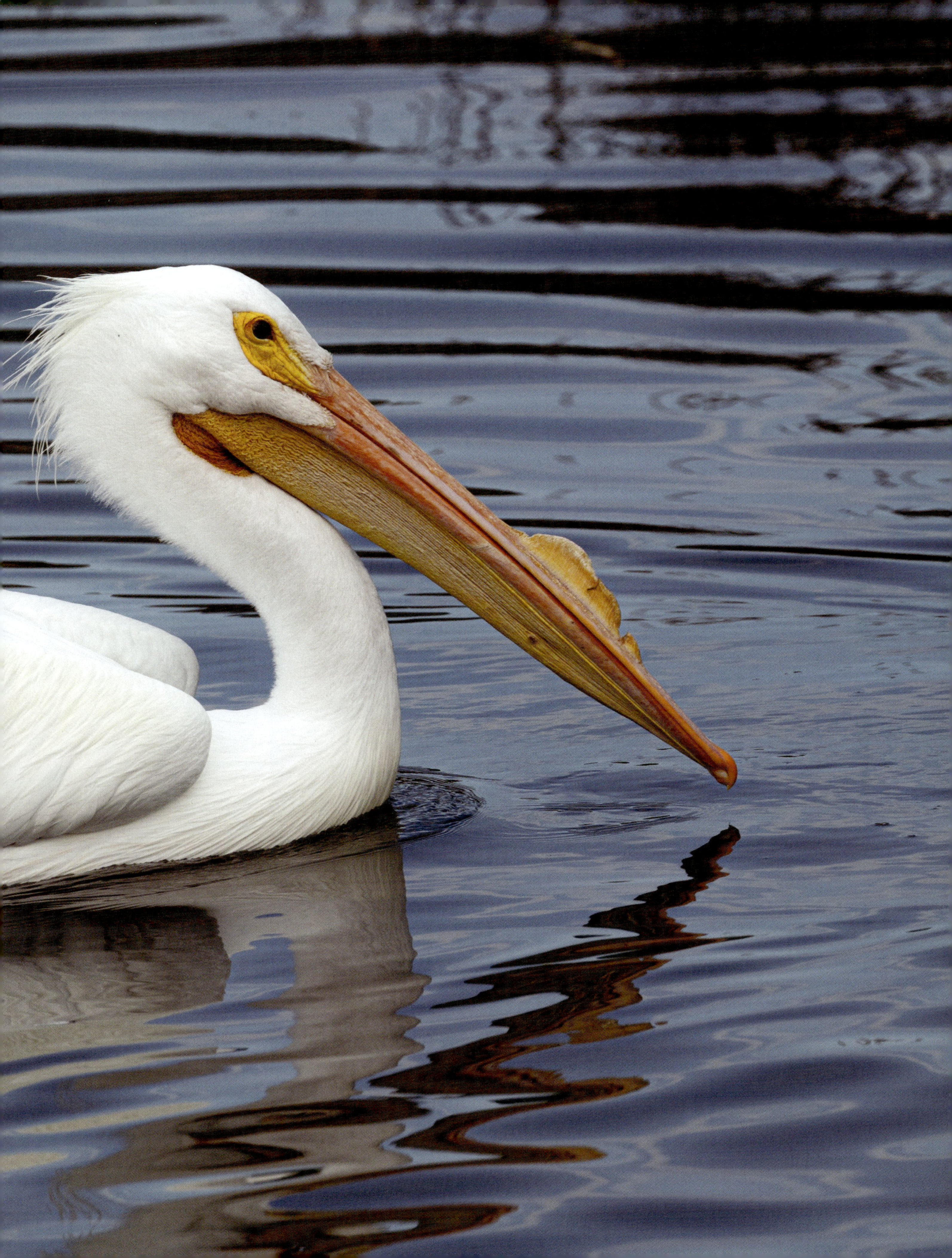

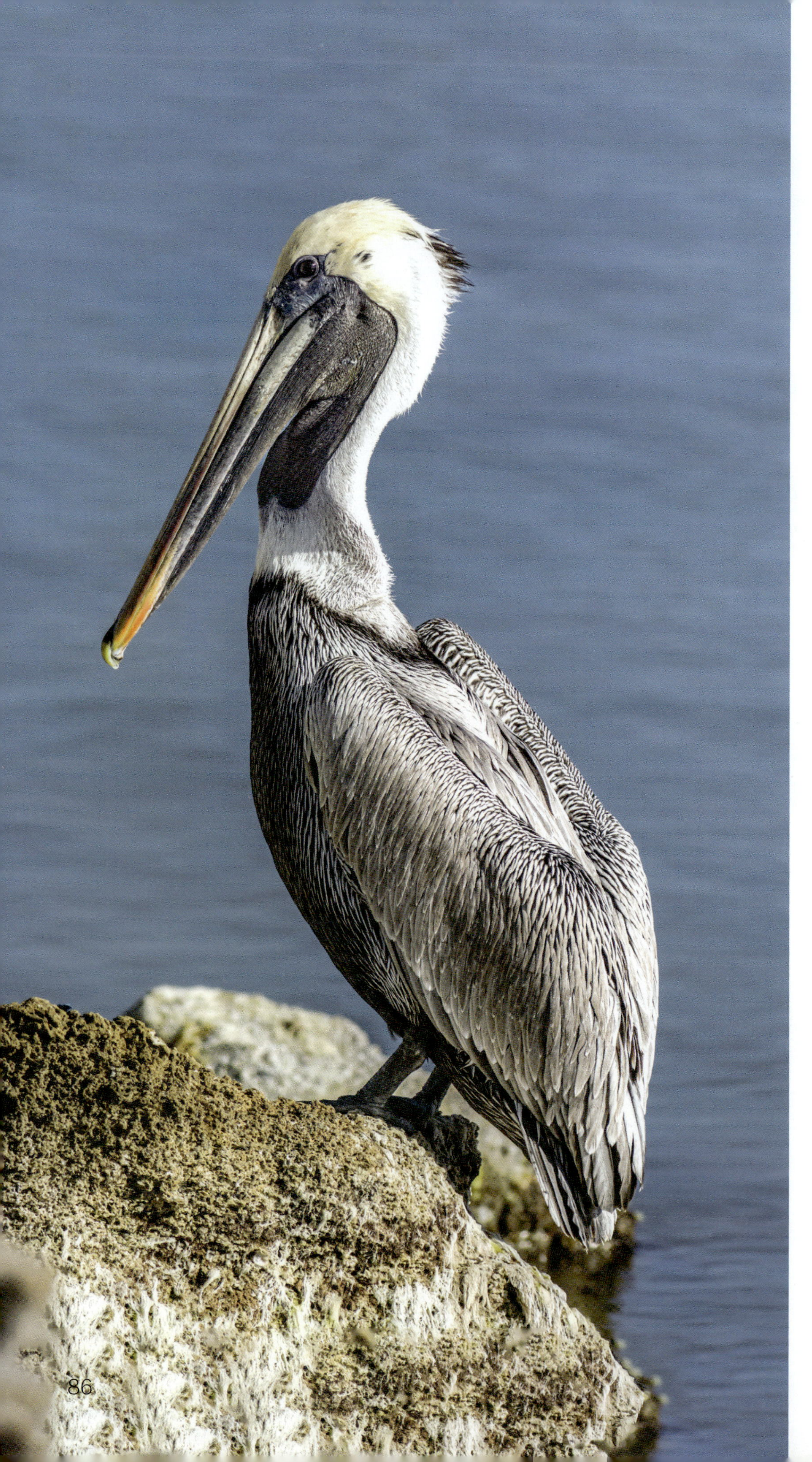

Brown Pelican

Brown Pelicans, unlike American White Pelicans, are year-round residents of South Florida and can be found plunge-diving for fish in any inlet or harbor. With amazing eyesight, they can spot a fish from seventy feet in the air, fold their wings, and dive headfirst at speeds up to forty miles per hour. They can be quite tame and sometimes get caught picking up fish that have already been hooked by an angler.

While ugly and awkward on land, they are accomplished fliers and are often seen in formation, flying just above the waves as they return to their roost. Newspapers advertised shotgun shoots on the beach for tourists in the early 1900s, but fortunately that pastime is long gone. DDT had a devastating effect on Brown Pelican populations in the 1960s. The Brown Pelican was designated as endangered following the signing of the Endangered Species Act in 1973. With this protection, populations in Florida have recovered.

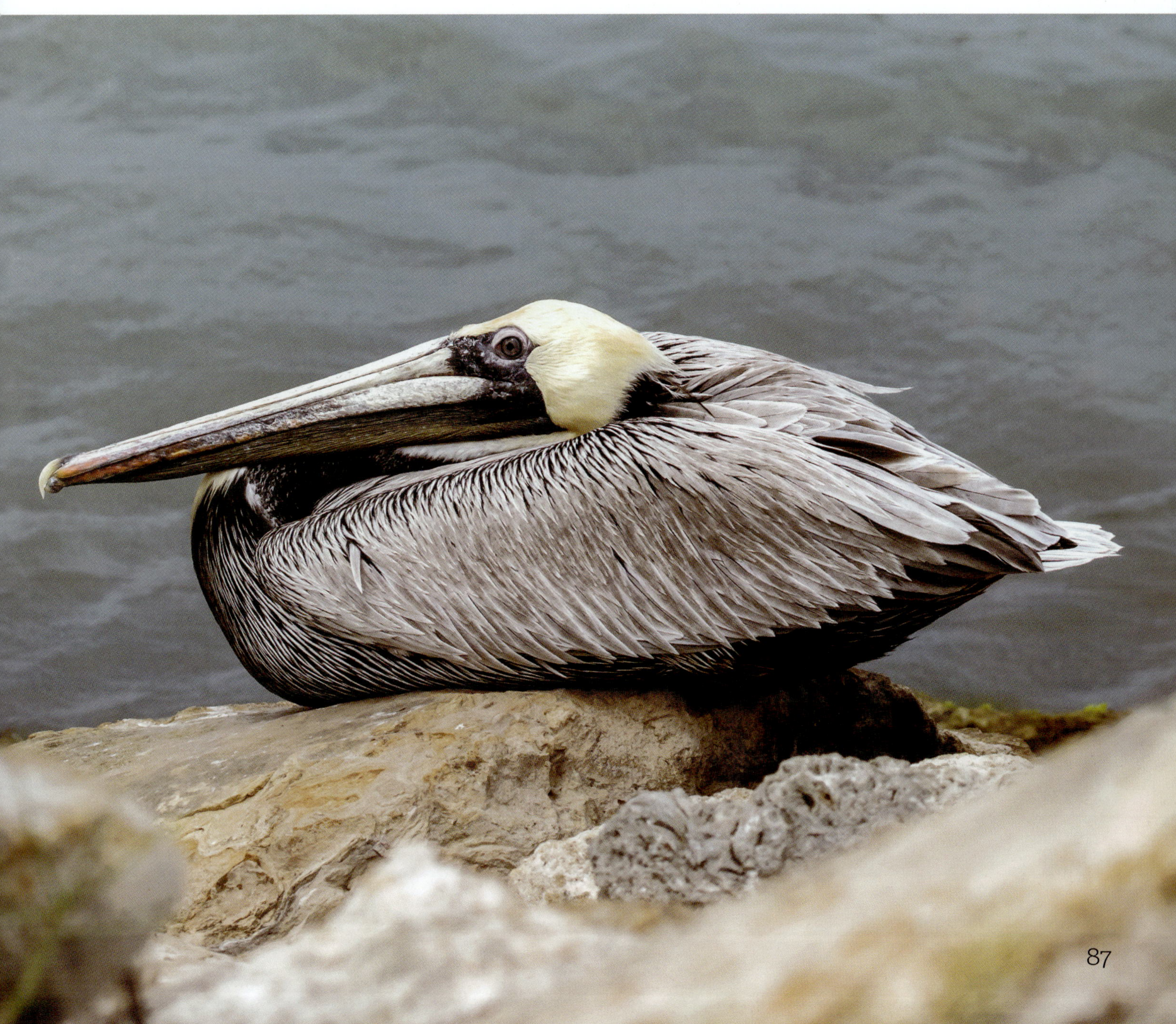

Double-crested Cormorant

Double-crested Cormorants dive, swim underwater, and are experts at catching fish. These are large birds, gray-black, with long necks and tails and an orange face with a long orange bill. Cormorants are often considered pests by anglers because they can decimate ponds and fish farms. If you look closely, you can see this one is about to snare a fish that's already been hooked.

Cormorants have a waterproof inner layer of feathers that allows them to swim underwater easily, but these feathers must be dried before flying. They are frequently seen perched with their wings spread, drying out before taking flight.

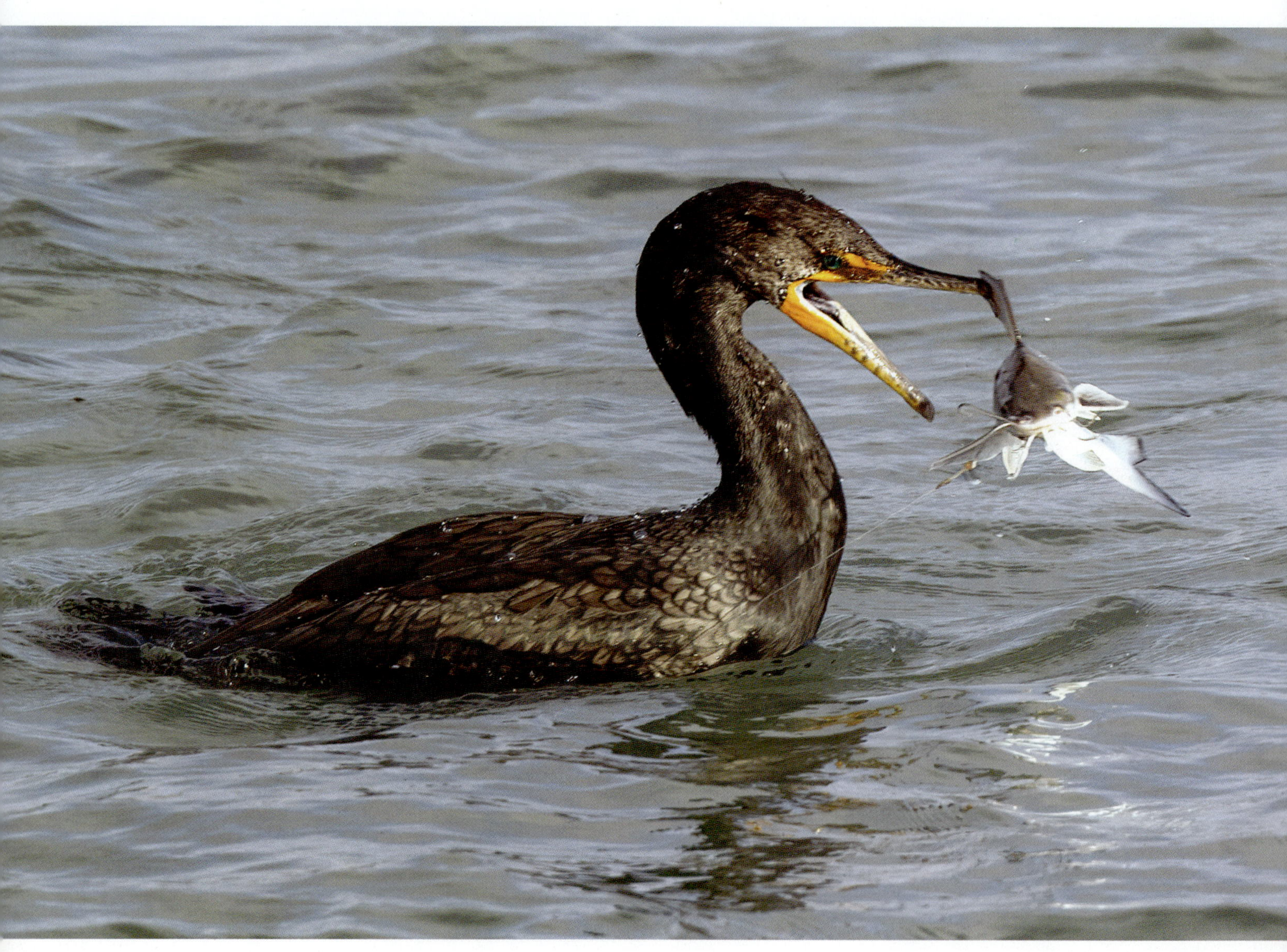

Anhinga

This bird is commonly referred to as the Snakebird because it swims with only its long, thin neck and head out of the water. It is similar in size and color to a Double-crested Cormorant and shares many of the same habits, but they lack the orange bill and are not related.

Anhingas catch prey with a long daggerlike bill. After spearing a fish underwater, they will surface and toss it in the air, catching it headfirst before swallowing it. Although considered a waterbird, they are often seen soaring high, enjoying the afternoon thermals with vultures.

While cormorants migrate north for the summer, Anhingas are strictly birds of warm climates, rarely straying north of the Gulf Coast.

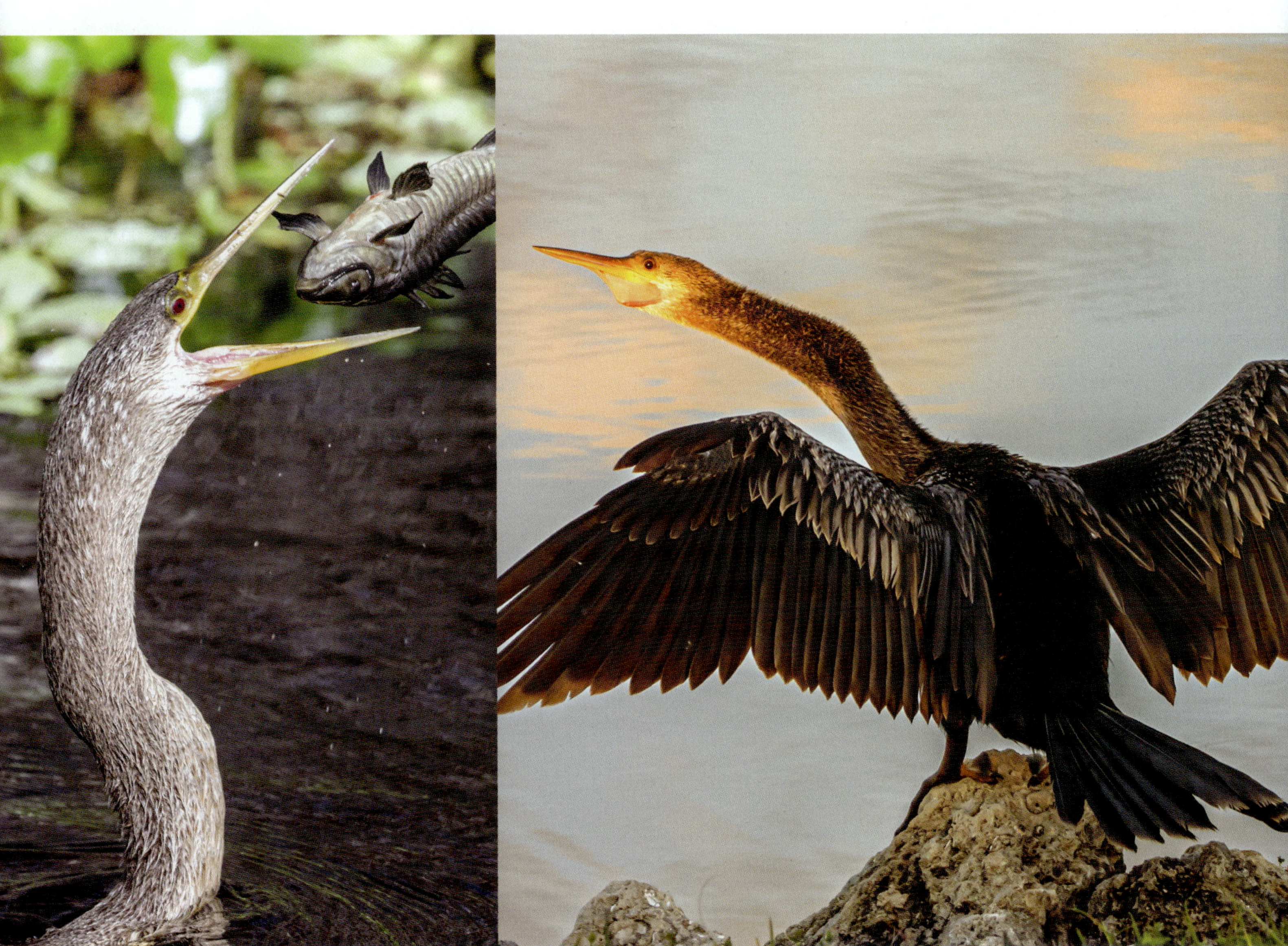

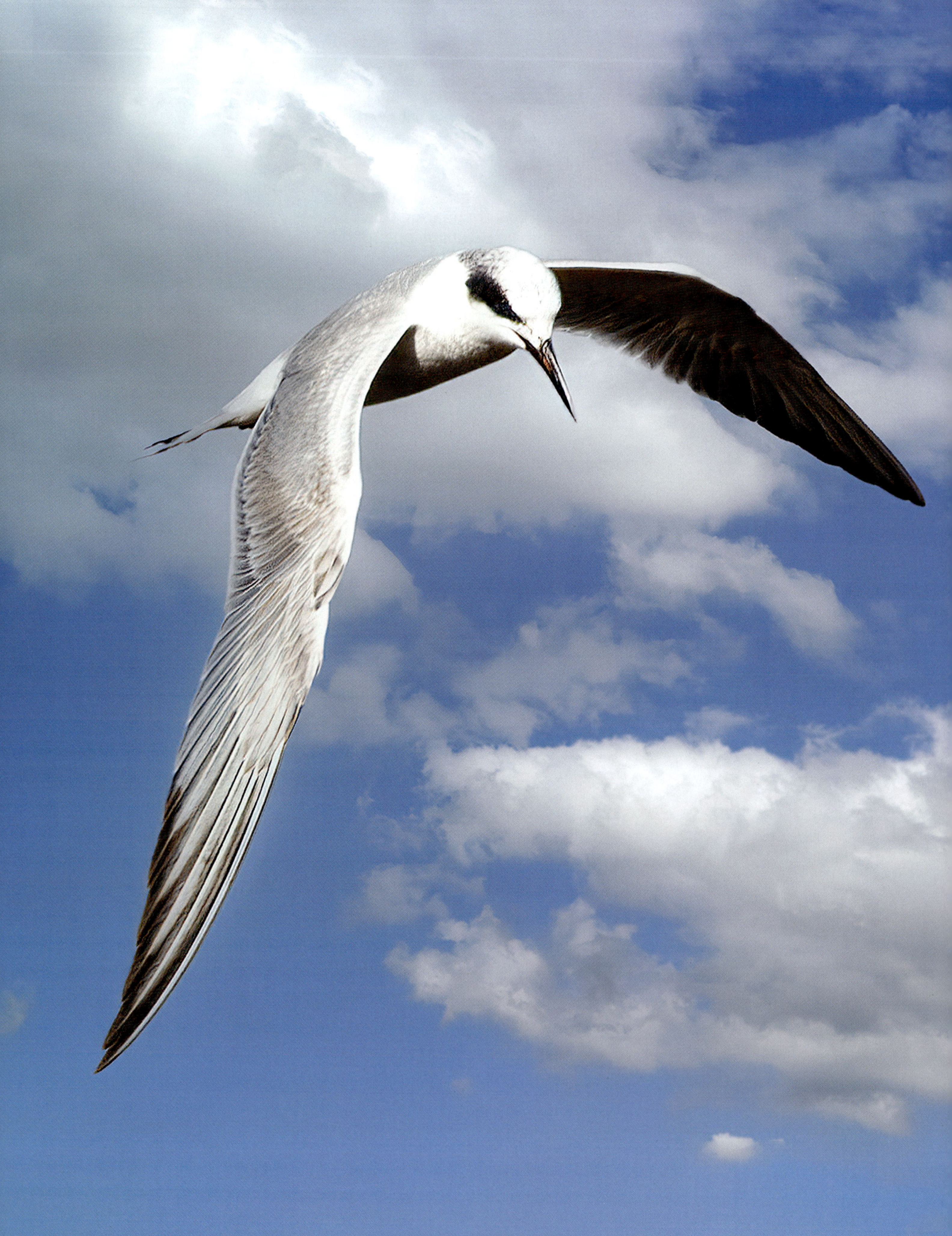

Gulls & Terns

There is no such bird as a "seagull," but Florida is home to a variety of gulls and terns. Gulls prefer coastal areas, specifically parking lots, beaches, fishing piers, and seawalls, as well as any other place they can pick up a quick meal. The more agile terns dive head-first into the water to snatch fish and shrimp. Unlike gulls, they are rarely found inland, except in breeding colonies.

Tern identification is difficult, because their winter plumage differs significantly from summer breeding plumage. Gulls complicate matters even further, because adult patterns take three to four years to develop, depending on the species.

Royal Tern

Still common along the Vero Beach coastline, Royal Tern numbers are decreasing these days primarily because of their preferred habitat: the beach. These birds rarely travel inland. They feed in offshore waters and they nest in colonies on the beach, where they are sensitive to disturbances from people, dogs, and predators. They, like all terns, dive for small fish, crabs, and shrimp. The usual technique is to hover in place, then plunge-dive for prey just below the surface. Sometimes they will fly along the water, picking food off the surface with their bright orange bill. Their crests turn completely black during breeding season, but during the rest of the year it recedes to the sides leaving the top white, creating a bald look.

These are large birds, capable of stealing fish from Brown Pelicans. Unfortunately, they can become entangled in fishing gear if they dive for a baited hook or get caught in carelessly discarded line.

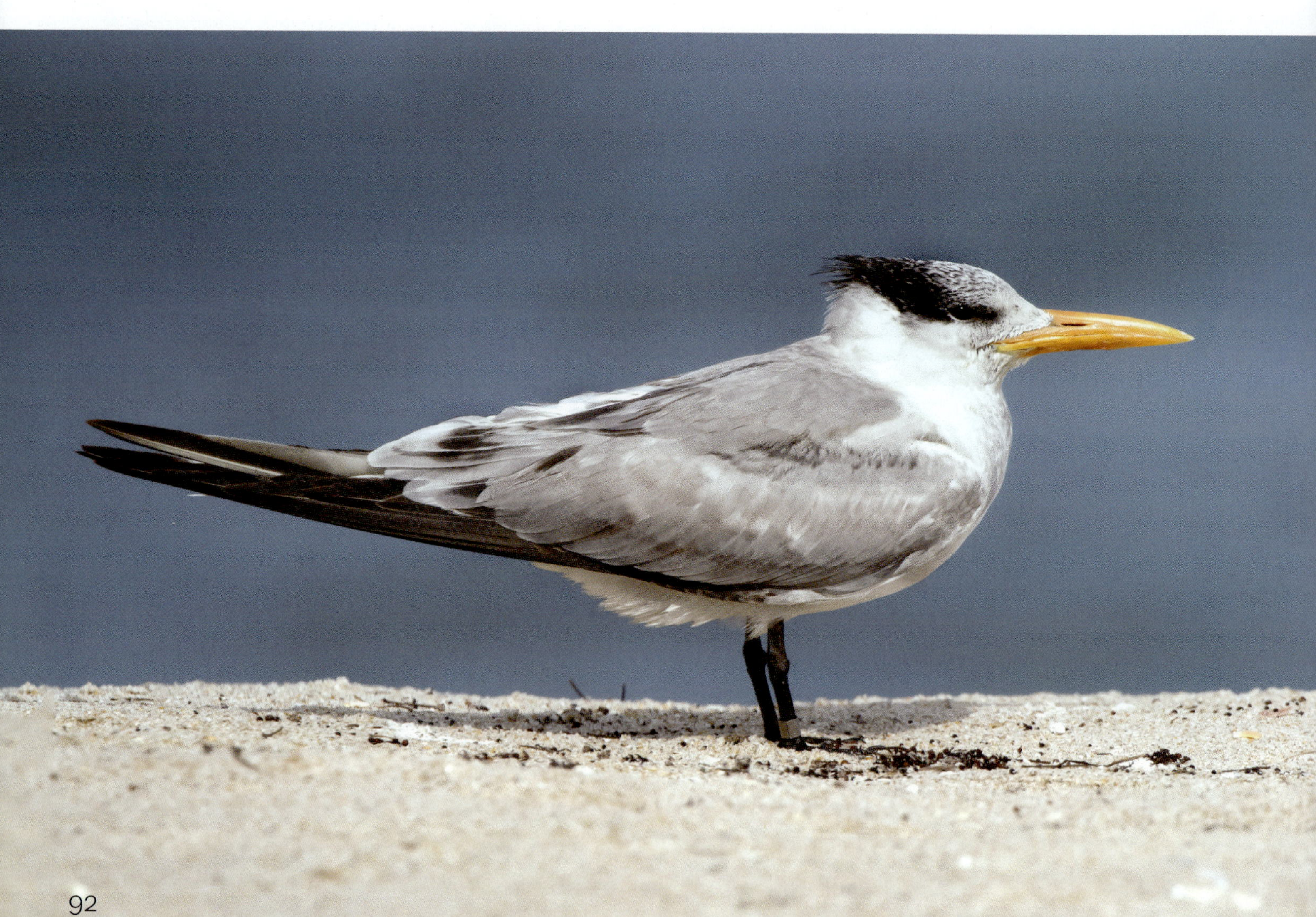

Caspian Tern

Caspian Terns are the largest of the terns and easily identified by their striking bloodred bill. They can be found on both coasts of North America as well as around large inland lakes such as Lake Okeechobee. They spend the winter along the Gulf Coast before returning to large lakes in the north to nest and raise their young. Although most Caspian Terns in Florida are migratory, there is a small breeding colony on an artificial island in Tampa Bay. Juvenile birds remain dependent on adults for up to eight months after leaving the nest.

I usually notice them as individual birds rather than in flocks, patrolling the wastewater treatment facility or a nearby freshwater pond.

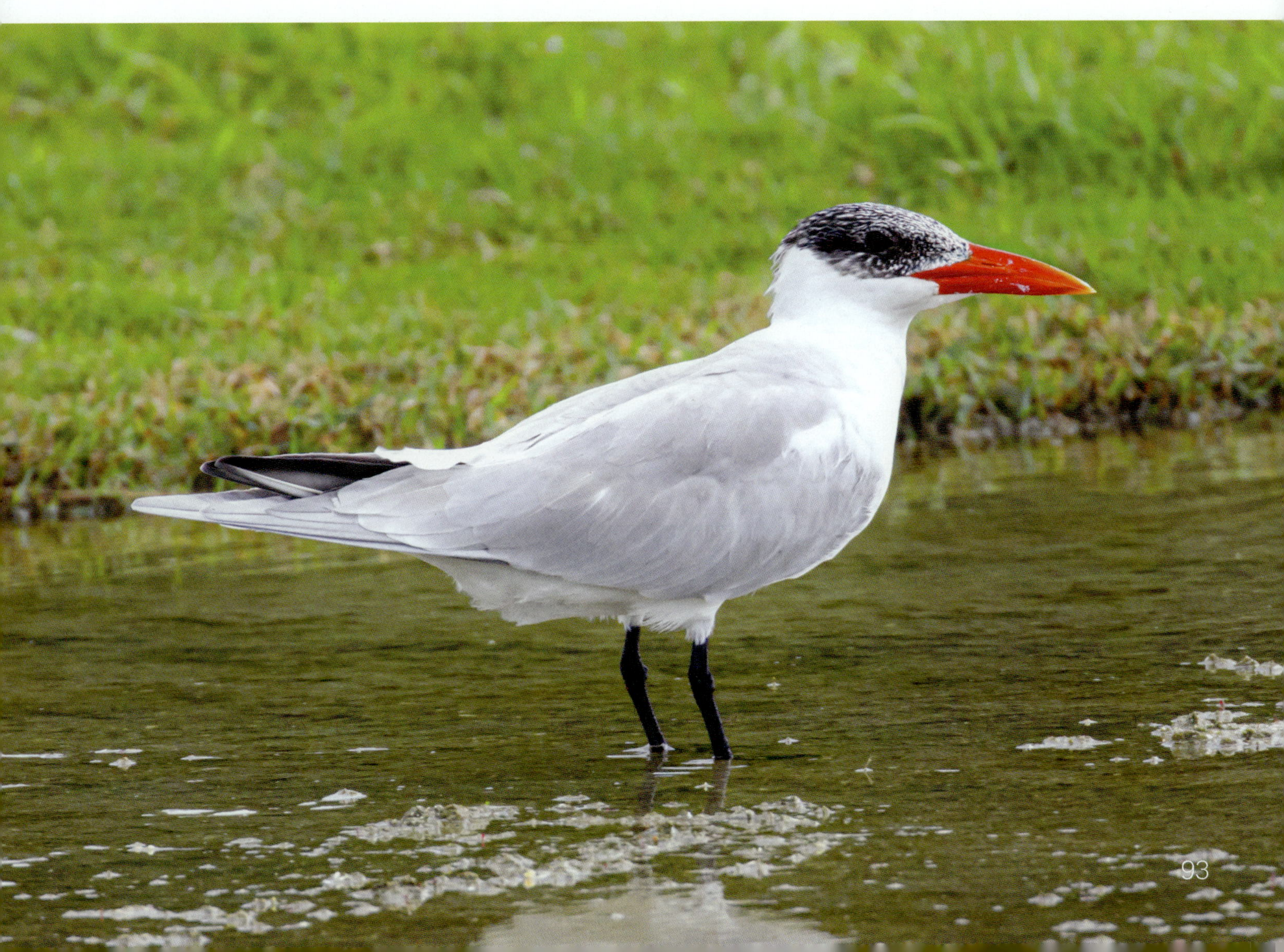

Sandwich Tern

If you look carefully at any group of roosting Royal Terns, there is likely a Sandwich Tern among them. They are slightly smaller than Royals, and their black bill with a yellow tip makes them easy to identify. Northern birds migrate to southern beaches, including the Caribbean Islands, before returning north in the spring, occasionally reaching Cape Cod. There is a year-round population in Florida south of Daytona Beach and along the Gulf Coast. Sandwich Terns were quite common in the early nineteenth century, but they almost disappeared and have only recently begun to make a comeback. Breeding birds have a shaggy crested black cap that recedes in the winter. This bird is an example of the white forehead seen in the winter plumage.

They are named after the English town of Sandwich in the county of Kent, where they were first discovered in 1787. Recent DNA studies have shown that although they look alike, the terns of the New World may be a different species, and a new name of Cabot's Tern has been proposed.

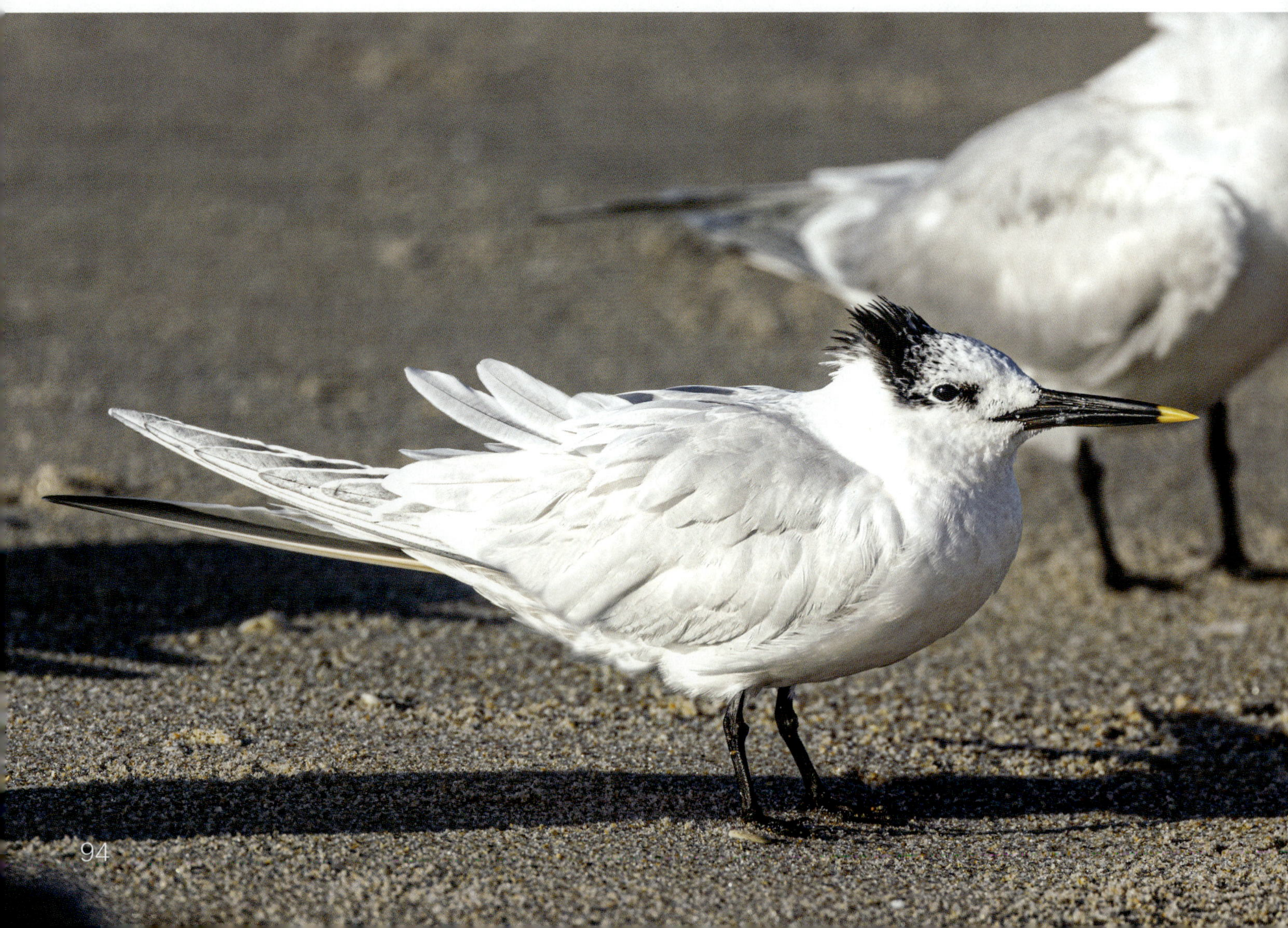

Forster's Tern

Forster's Tern is a small graceful tern named after Johann Forster, an eighteenth-century German naturalist who accompanied Captain Cook on his second voyage around the world in 1772–1775. They are similar to the Common Tern that we see in Maine, but they would be unusual that far north. Early ornithologists mistakenly classified them as a subspecies of the Common Tern, but that error has been corrected. This tern spends the winter near salt water and is abundant along the Florida coast, but it prefers to breed in large freshwater marshes. It is the only tern species that is found exclusively in North America.

They lose their black caps in the winter, but can be identified by their prominent black eye patch.

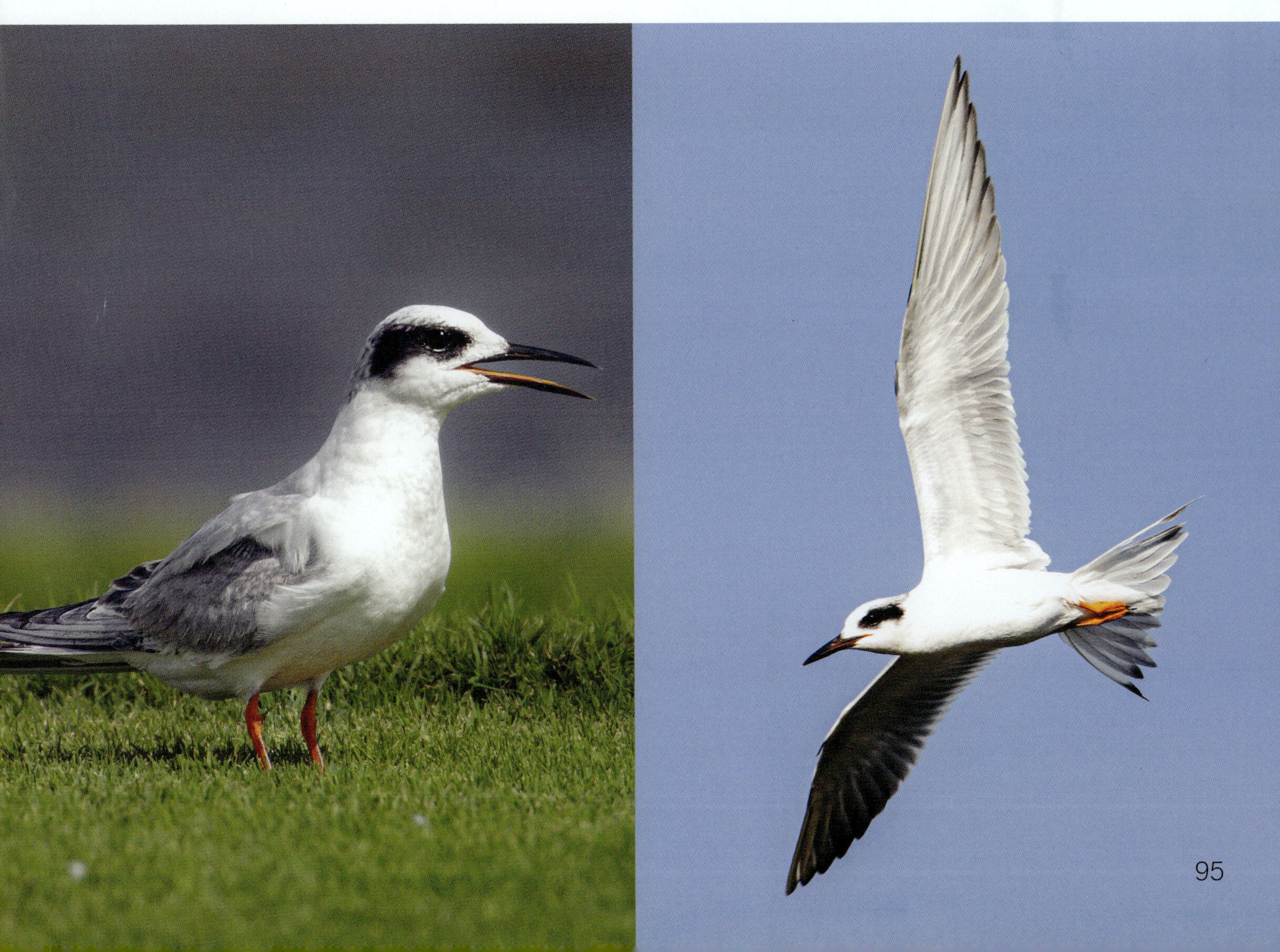

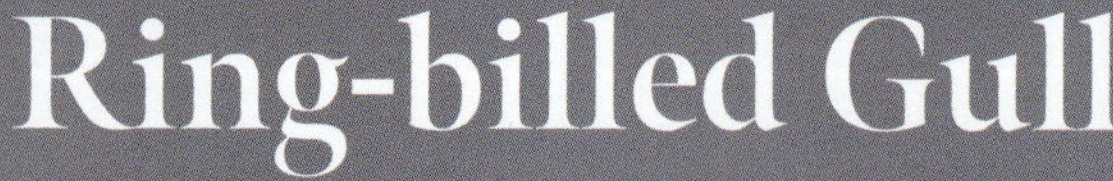

Ring-billed Gull

The Ring-billed Gull, the most common gull in North America, migrates to the Gulf Coast and Florida for the winter. These are the gulls you see on beaches, in parking lots, and at marinas, often stealing picnic lunches. Maybe their fondness for french fries is why some birders call them the "fast-food gull." They are more likely than other gulls to be seen at freshwater lakes. Look for the distinctive black ring near the tip of the bill and bright yellow legs.

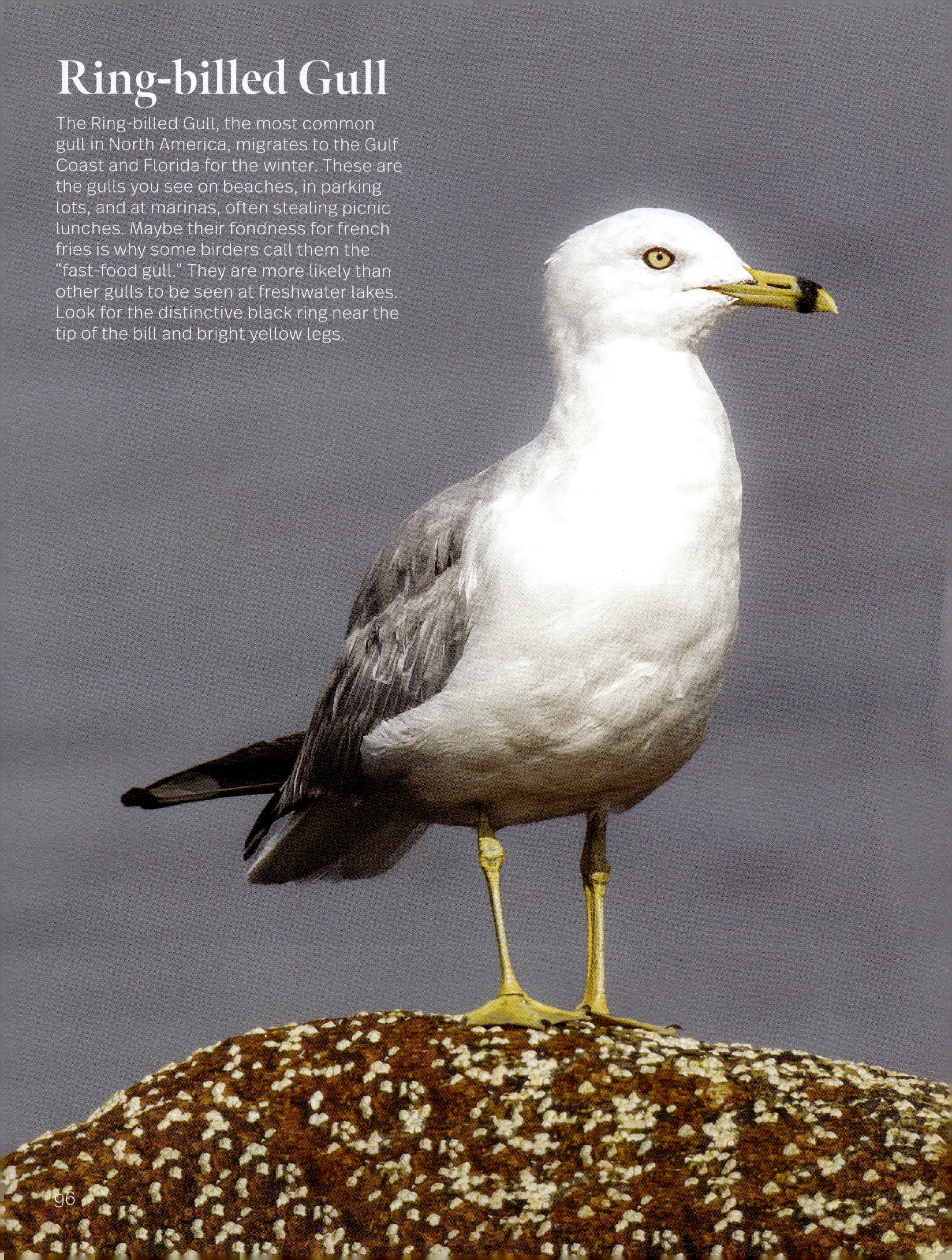

Laughing Gull

Recognizable by its laugh-like call, this is a warm-weather gull. Laughing Gulls are nonmigratory in Florida, but northern birds move south and join locals for the winter. They molt into nonbreeding winter plumage shortly after arriving on southern beaches. Summer birds have a distinct black hood, white arcs around the eyes, and a bright red bill.

Because of their omnivorous diet, which includes, insects, fish, crabs, and any available human food, Laughing Gulls are extremely successful. They are common on any beach, often mingling with other gulls and terns.

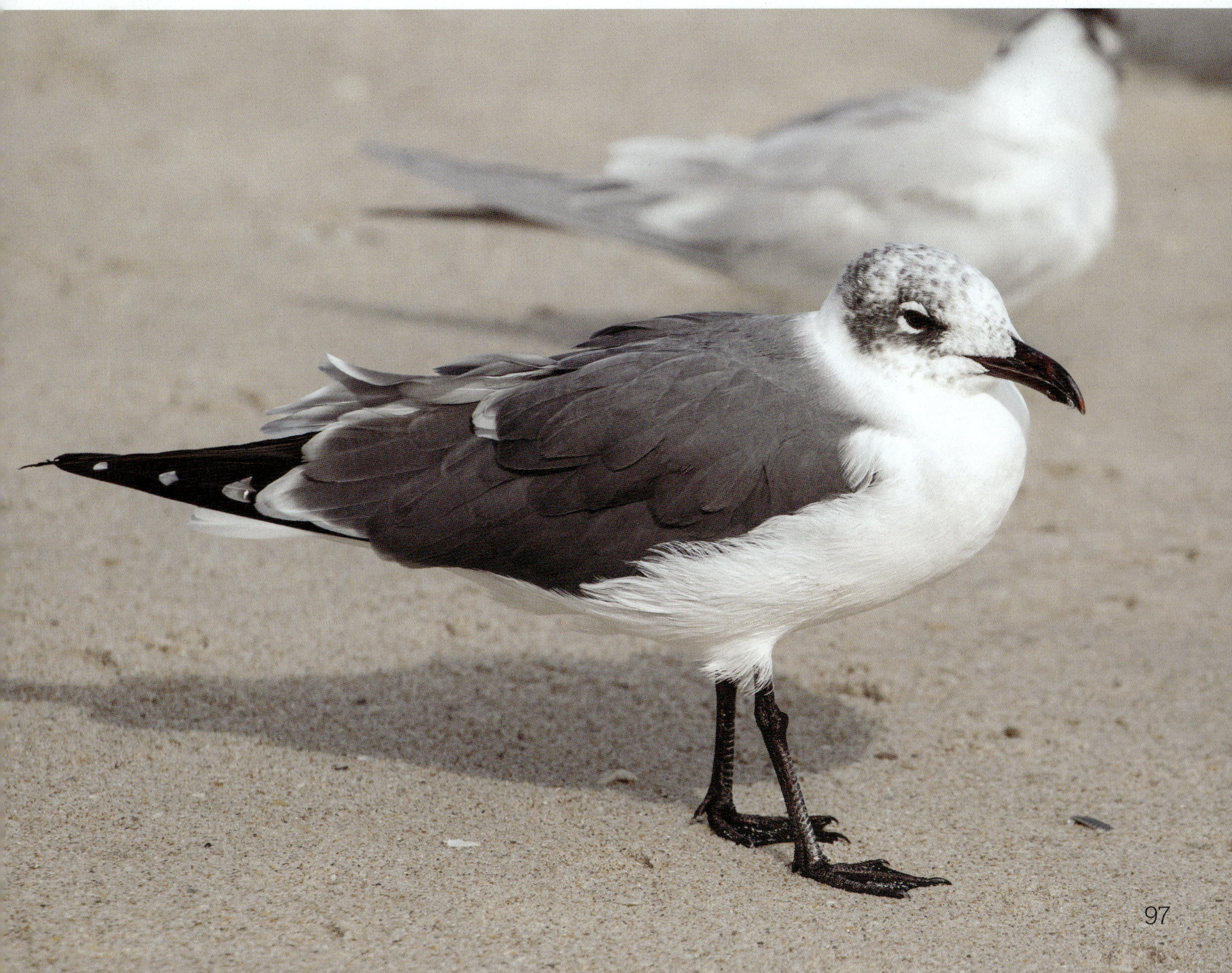

Lesser Black-backed Gull

This is a large gull found on the Atlantic coast of the British Isles that migrates to West Africa for the winter. A few appear at Sebastian Inlet every year, and it appears that there are more with each passing year. There have been no reports of them nesting in North America. The birds found here during the winter are thought to be migrants from the breeding colony in Iceland.

Their darker, gray-black plumage distinguishes them from other gulls, and their bright yellow legs make them stand out in a crowd.

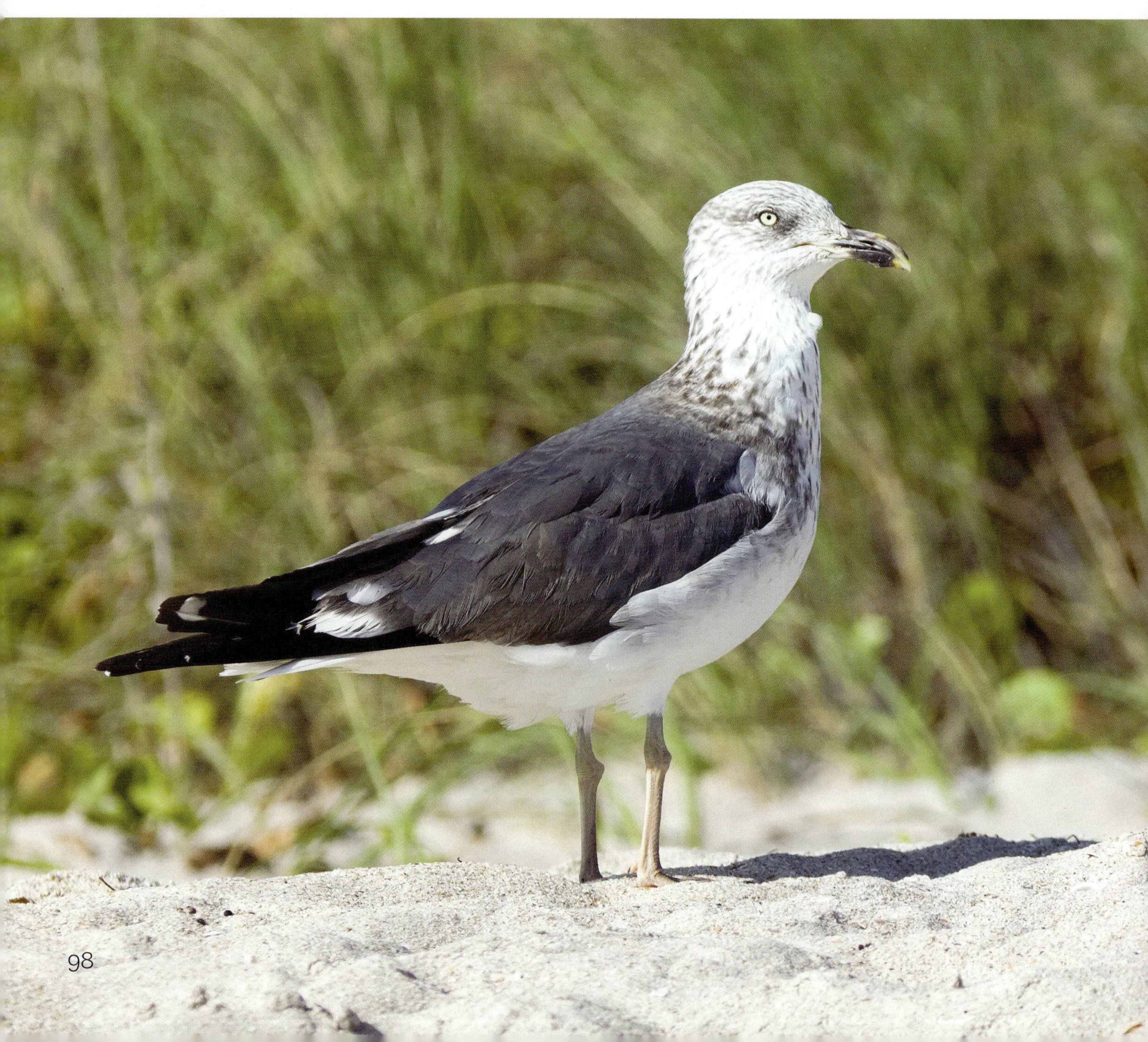

Bonaparte's Gull

This small gull, named after Napoleon's nephew Charles Lucien Bonaparte, breeds in northern forests, then migrates south along both the East Coast and the West Coast in the winter. In the fall, we see them along the coast in Maine as they travel south to the Gulf Coast. Like all black-headed gulls, its winter plumage turns white with a prominent black ear spot.

They fly more gracefully than most gulls and have the appearance of a tern. The bright white feathers on the leading edge of the wing help me identify them at a distance.

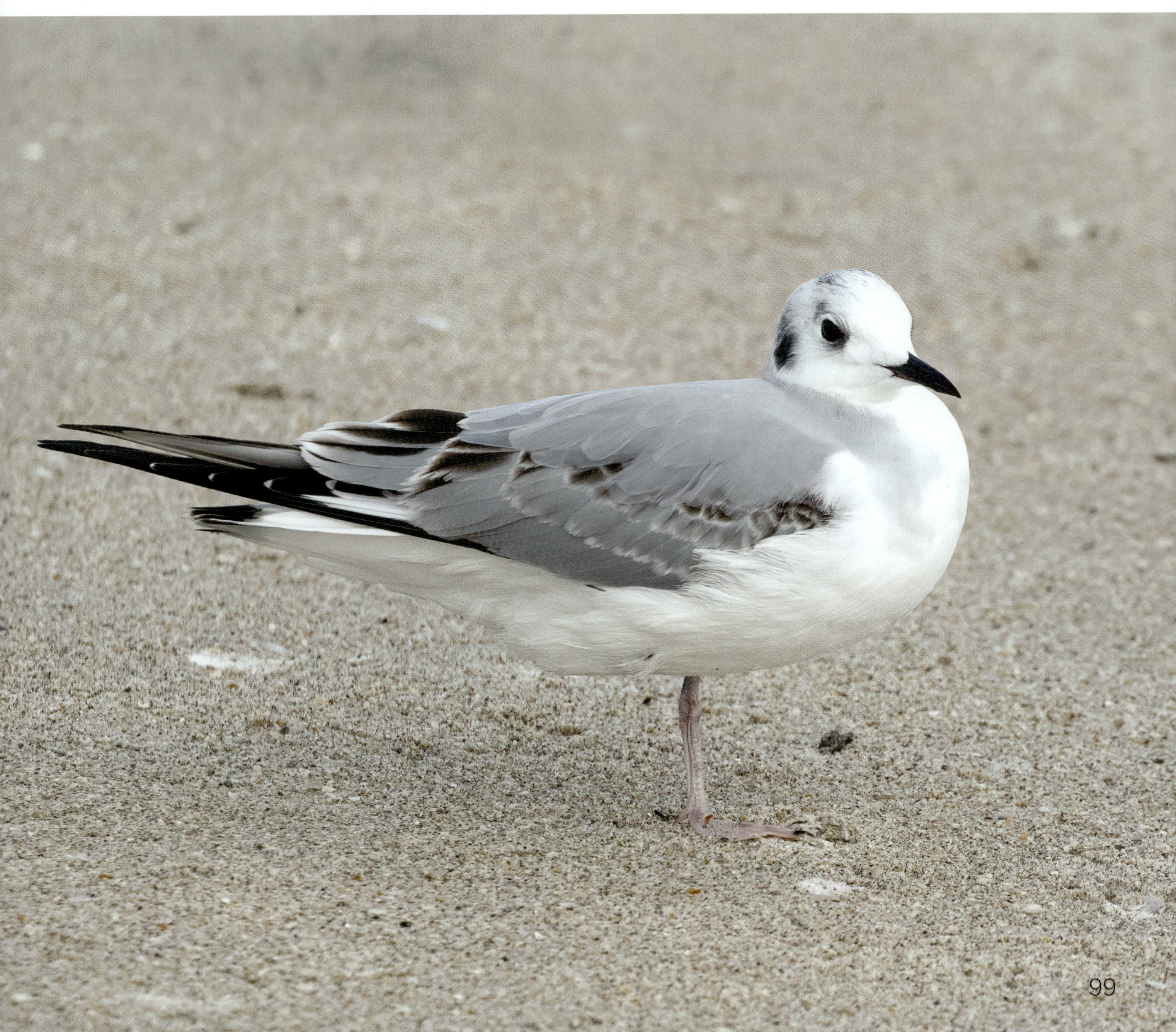

Magnificent Frigatebird

During the winter, this striking bird can be found all over the Caribbean and as far north as Florida. They are often seen soaring along the beach, riding the afternoon wind and occasionally stealing food from another bird while in midair. These are huge birds, four feet long with a V-shaped tail and a seven-foot wingspan. The best place to see them is at Fort Jefferson in the Dry Tortugas National Park off Key West. The only breeding colony in the United States is at nearby Long Key.

To attract females, the male displays its bright orange throat sac. Females have an entirely different plumage, with white heads and chests. Their eggs take almost three months to hatch, and the parents continue to feed their young for a year.

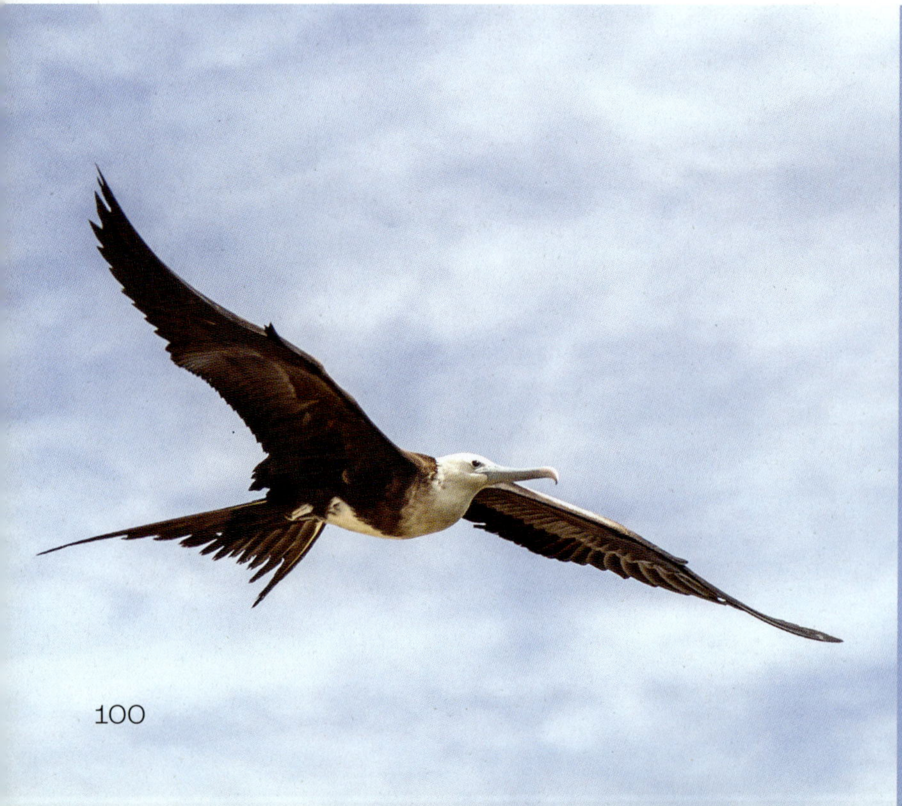

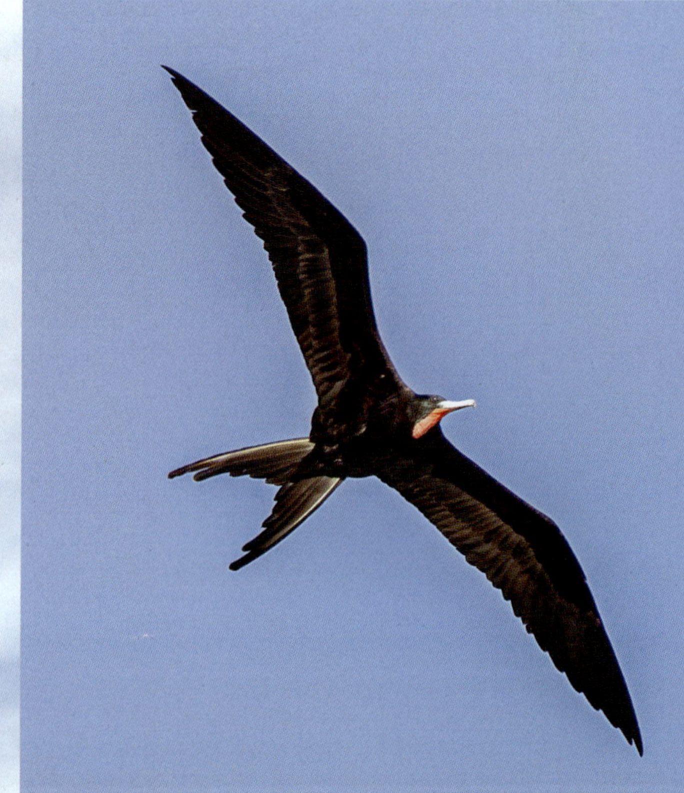

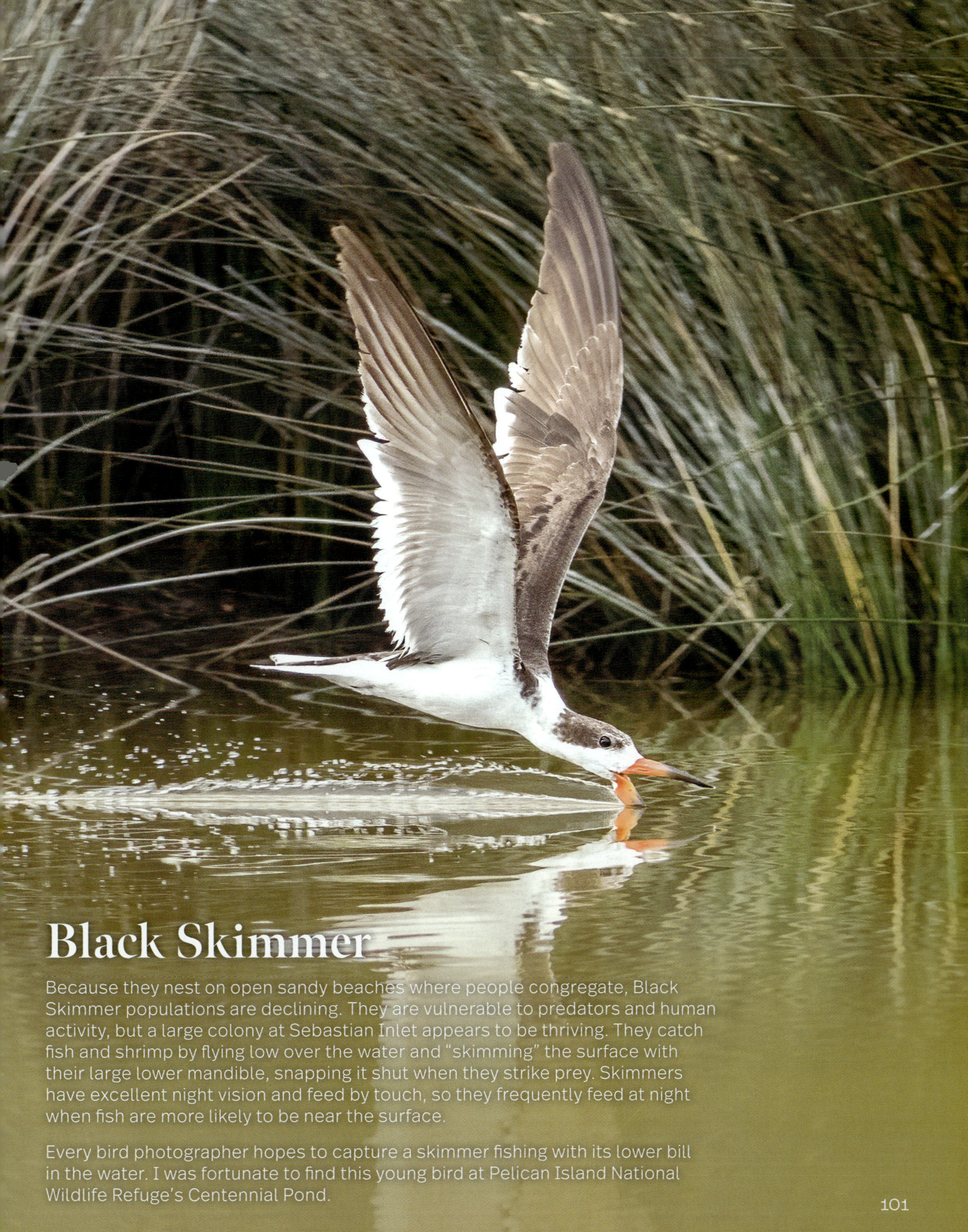

Black Skimmer

Because they nest on open sandy beaches where people congregate, Black Skimmer populations are declining. They are vulnerable to predators and human activity, but a large colony at Sebastian Inlet appears to be thriving. They catch fish and shrimp by flying low over the water and "skimming" the surface with their large lower mandible, snapping it shut when they strike prey. Skimmers have excellent night vision and feed by touch, so they frequently feed at night when fish are more likely to be near the surface.

Every bird photographer hopes to capture a skimmer fishing with its lower bill in the water. I was fortunate to find this young bird at Pelican Island National Wildlife Refuge's Centennial Pond.

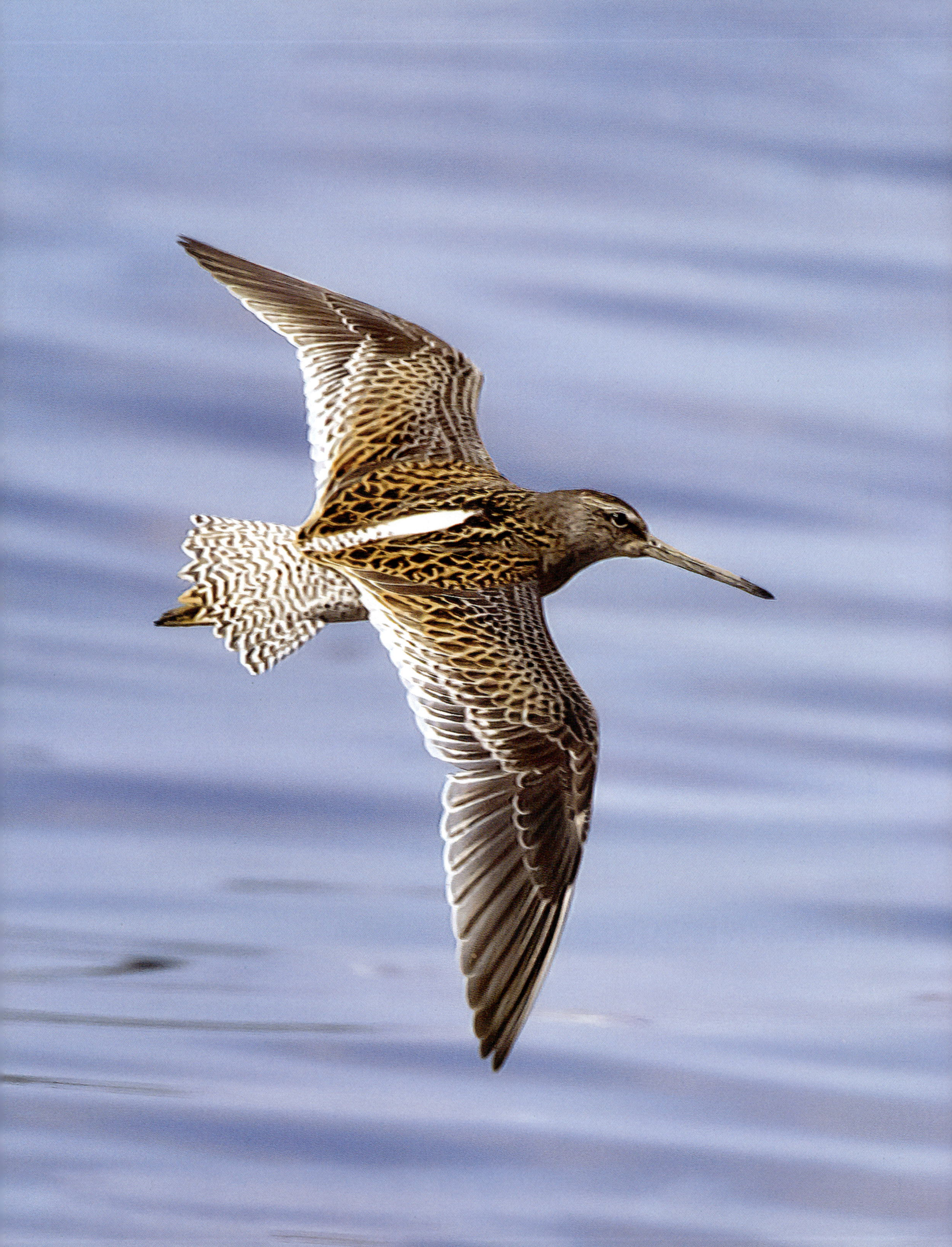

Shorebirds

Shorebirds include sandpipers, plovers and curlews, birds that comb beaches looking for insects, small fish, and crustaceans. After breeding in the high Arctic, the majority of these birds move south across North America in late summer and early fall on their way to Central and South America. These amazing bits of fluff, some only an ounce or two in weight, fly alone or in flocks of hundreds. They can be found flying just over the waves or at heights of a mile or more. Their annual spring migration begins in April, so we see them on Florida beaches before they head back north. Some species, such as Willets and Ruddy Turnstones, remain in Florida for the winter.

Willet

Willets are large, long-legged shorebirds with a large, straight bill that is black at the tip. Willets were nearly hunted to extinction in the late 1800s. Audubon described them as "fat and juicy." They have made a comeback with the passage of new hunting laws and are now common. The Eastern race, which breeds along the Atlantic coast, migrates to South America every winter, while the inland Western race does not migrate as far south and can be found on Gulf Coast and Florida beaches in the winter. Western birds are larger with a darker dull gray plumage. Like all Willets, they display distinctive black-and-white wing markings and a white patch at the base of the tail during flight.

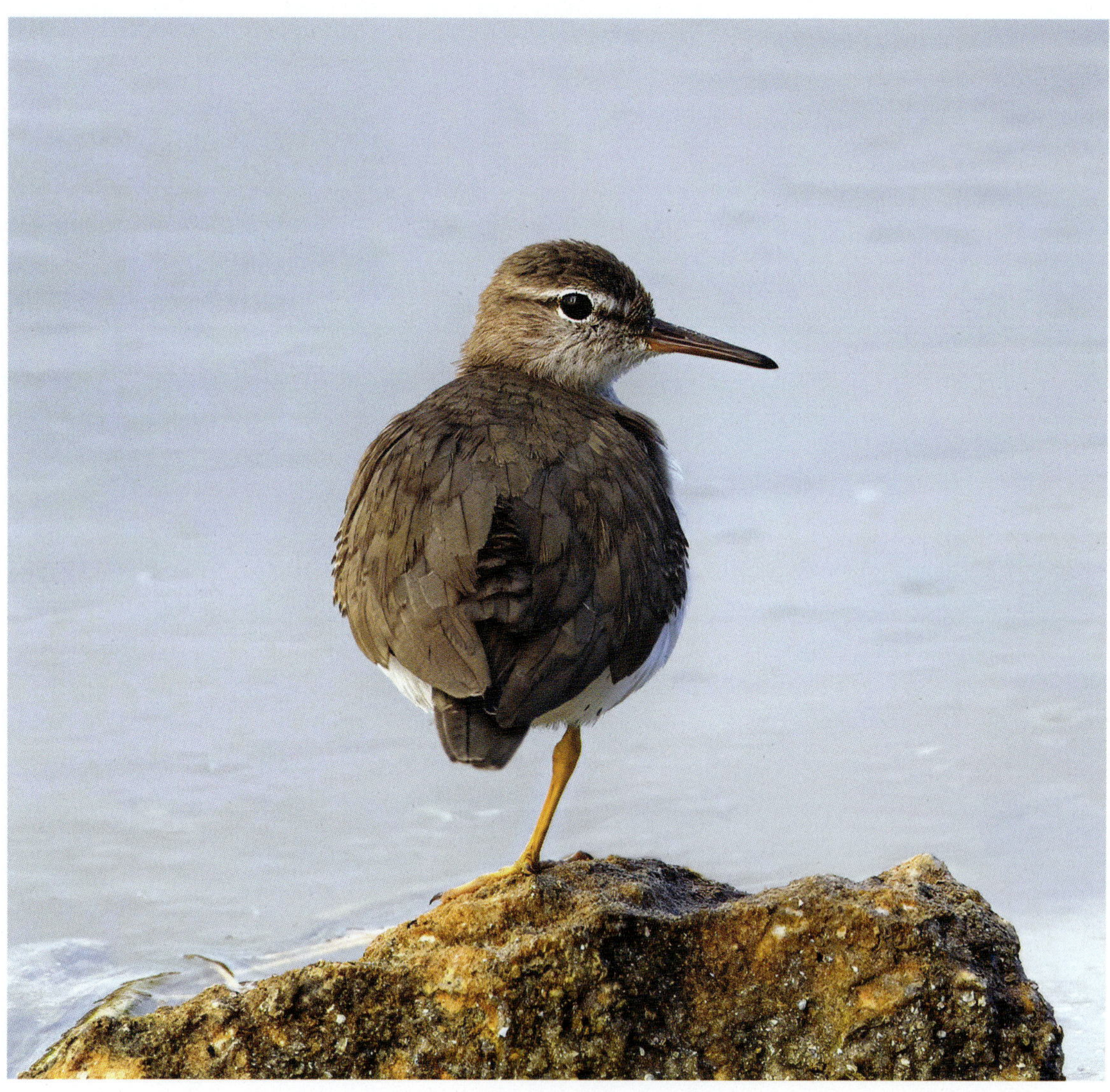

Ruddy Turnstone

Ruddy Turnstones are small, stocky shorebirds with a black-and-white pattern on their heads and beautiful chestnut brown colors on their backs. They also have prominent orange legs. They are unique among shorebirds because of the presence of special spines on their toes that aid in keeping a grip on slippery wet rocks as they scavenge for food. They insert their bills under stones and shells, literally turning them over to find food underneath. They are long-distance migrants who leave their Arctic breeding grounds to spend the winter on warm beaches. Many fly all the way to South America, but others can be found along the Florida coast.

Dunlin

This small, sandpiper-like shorebird can be found all over the world, with three distinct subspecies in North America. The subspecies are difficult to distinguish in the field, but their long, downcurved bill is recognizable anywhere. They display bright red and black plumage during breeding season, but we only see the dull brown color in winter, hence the name, a shortened version of Dunling. Dunlin spend the winter along the south coast of the United States, rarely venturing to South America.

During the migration season, Dunlin roost in coastal habitats such as mudflats, so they are very susceptible to disturbance by wetland development projects. They also have the unusual ability to forage at night, giving them an advantage over other shorebird species. Unfortunately, populations have decreased over 30 percent in the last thirty years, possibly due to loss of winter habitat.

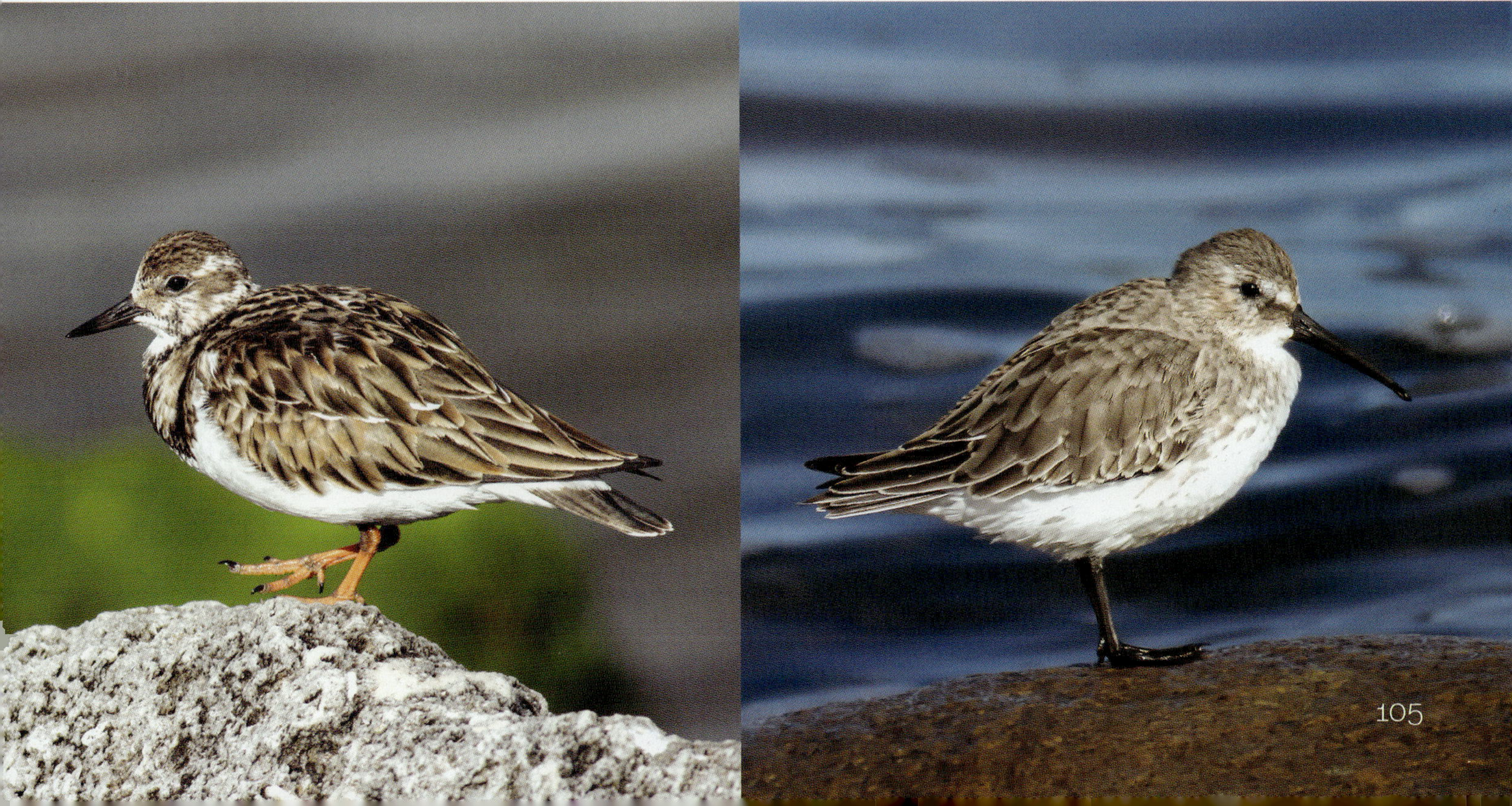

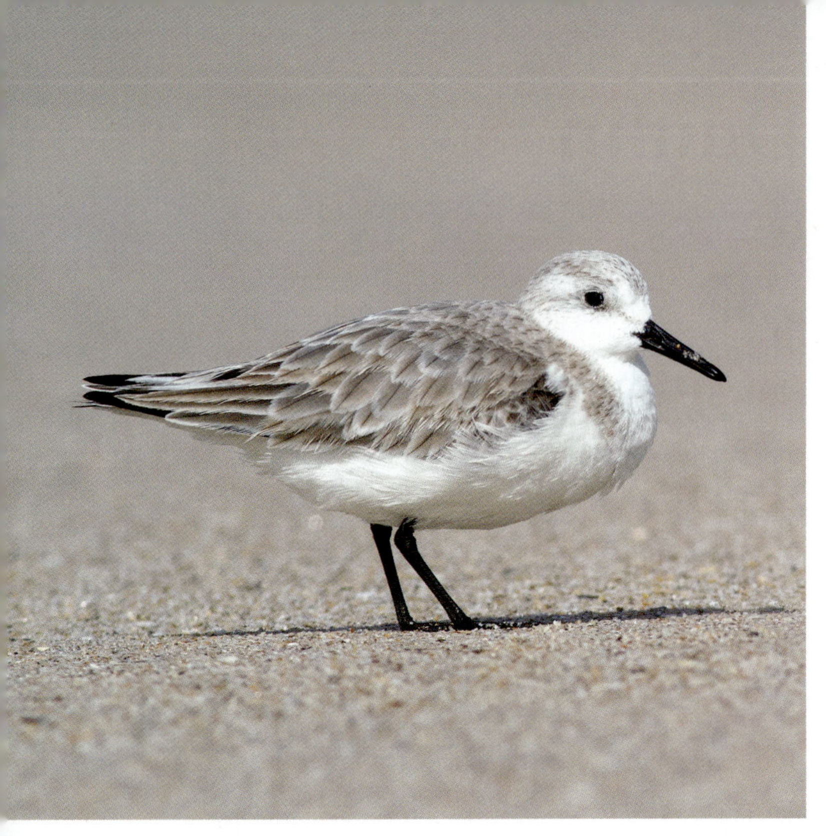

Sanderling

When you hear the word "sandpiper," this is the bird that comes to mind. Sanderlings are the sandpipers that gather in small flocks on the beach, running just ahead of the the incoming waves as they probe for food. In the winter, they are pale gray above and white below, but by the time they reach their Arctic breeding grounds in the spring, they have black-and-white speckled plumage with bright reddish-brown highlights.

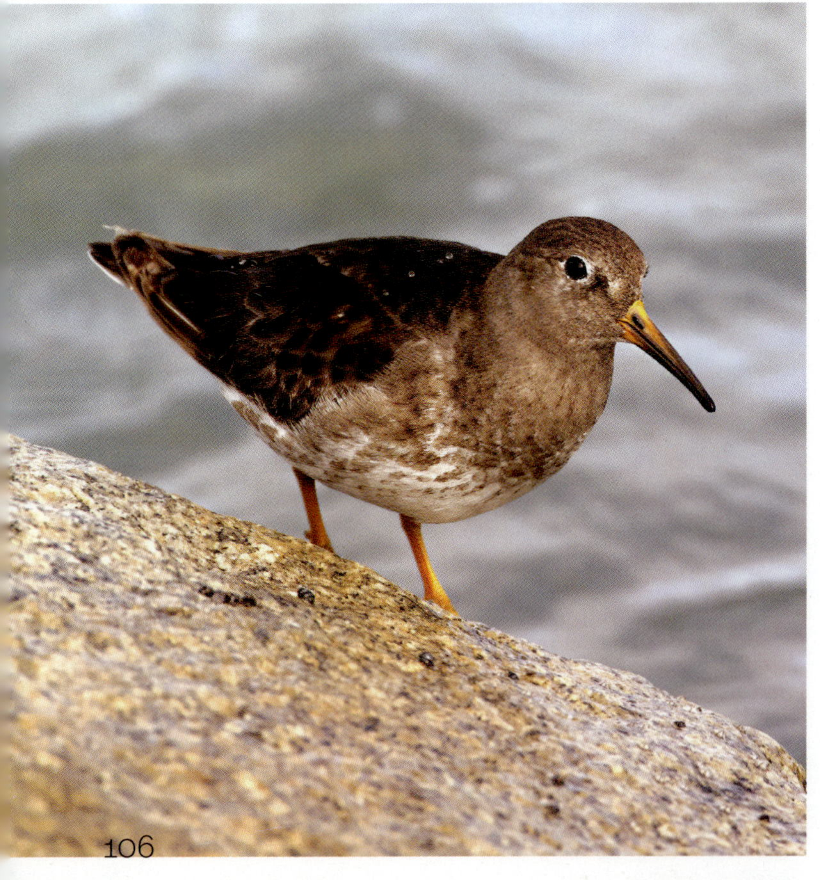

Purple Sandpiper

Purple Sandpipers nest on the Arctic tundra and spend the winter farther north than any other sandpiper. They are common winter visitors along Maine's rocky coast, usually in flocks of ten to twenty birds. This solitary Purple Sandpiper somehow found its way to Sebastian Inlet in 2021, much to the delight of southern birdwatchers.

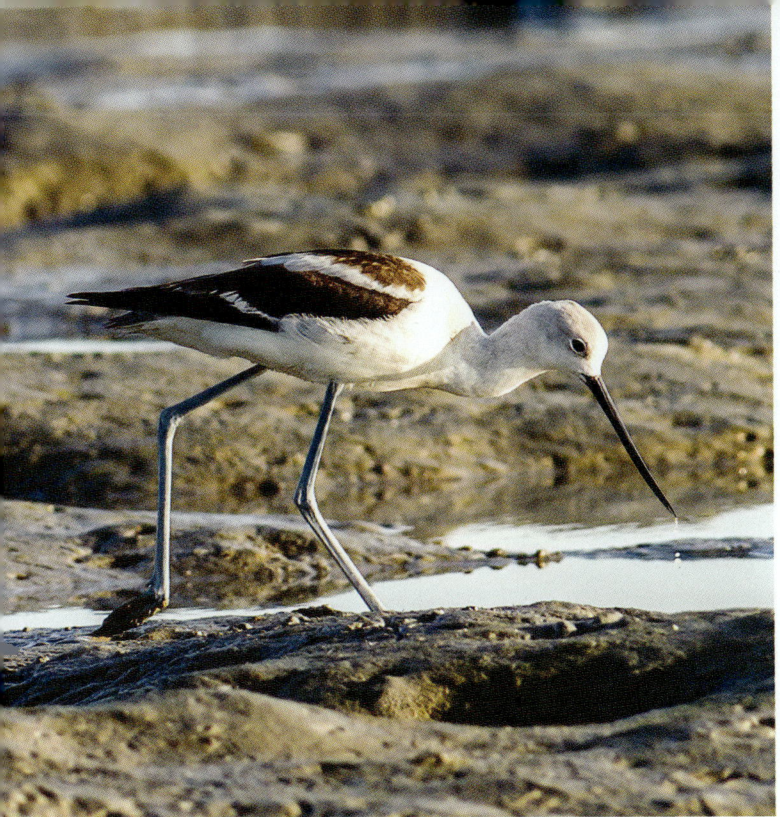

American Avocet

Avocets are more common out west, but a few find their way to Florida every year. They congregate in flocks on mudflats and in shallow water where they spend the day searching for tiny crustaceans and insects with their dainty, upturned bills.

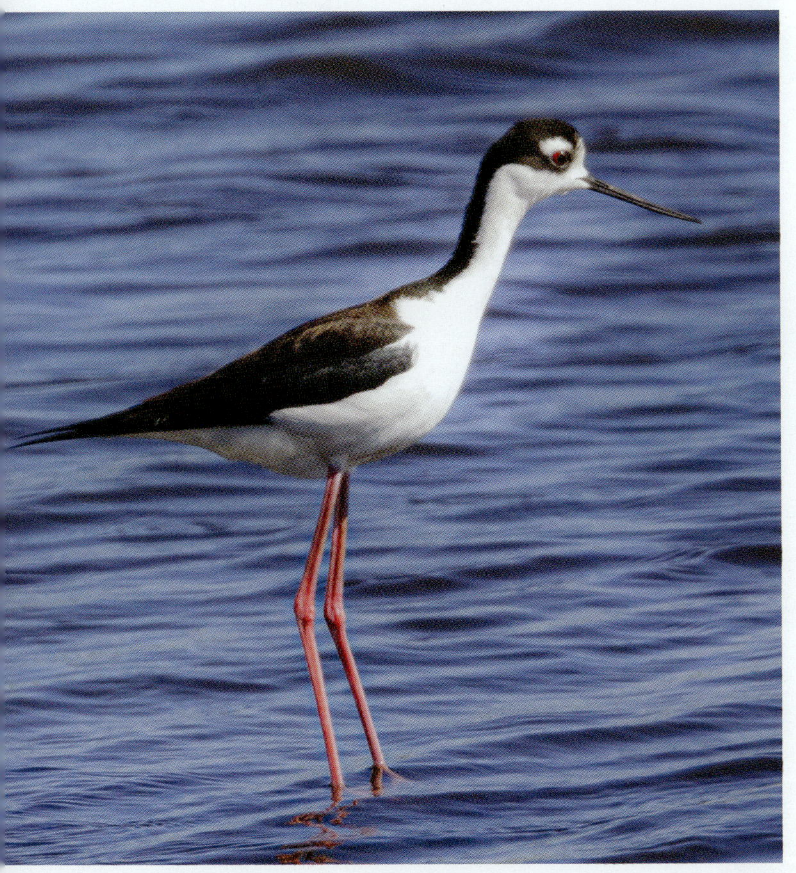

Black-necked Stilt

This long-necked shorebird is more common on the West Coast, but it can be found in Florida salt marshes and mudflats on occasion. They frequently associate with avocets. Their striking black-and-white plumage with long needlelike black bill is distinctive, but the comical long pink legs always make me laugh.

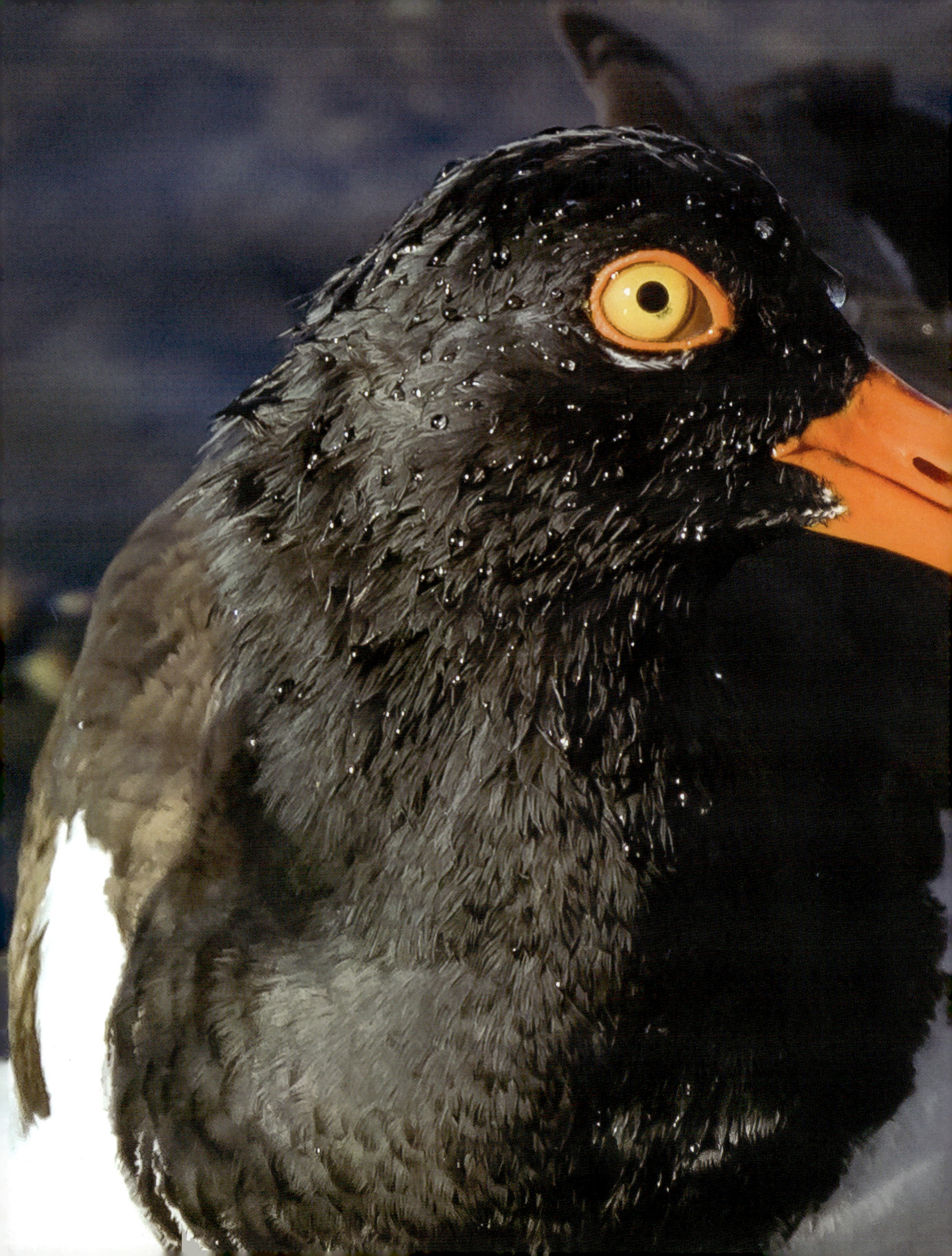

American Oystercatcher

Oystercatchers visit barrier beaches along the Florida coast during the winter. They are large and easy to identify because of their orange eye and large orange bill. As the name suggests, they open oysters, clams, and mussels with their powerful bills. They are susceptible to human traffic, because they wait out the high tide in dunes along the beach before venturing out to search for clams at low tide. They are doing well because they readily colonize man-made dredge islands in places like Indian River Lagoon.

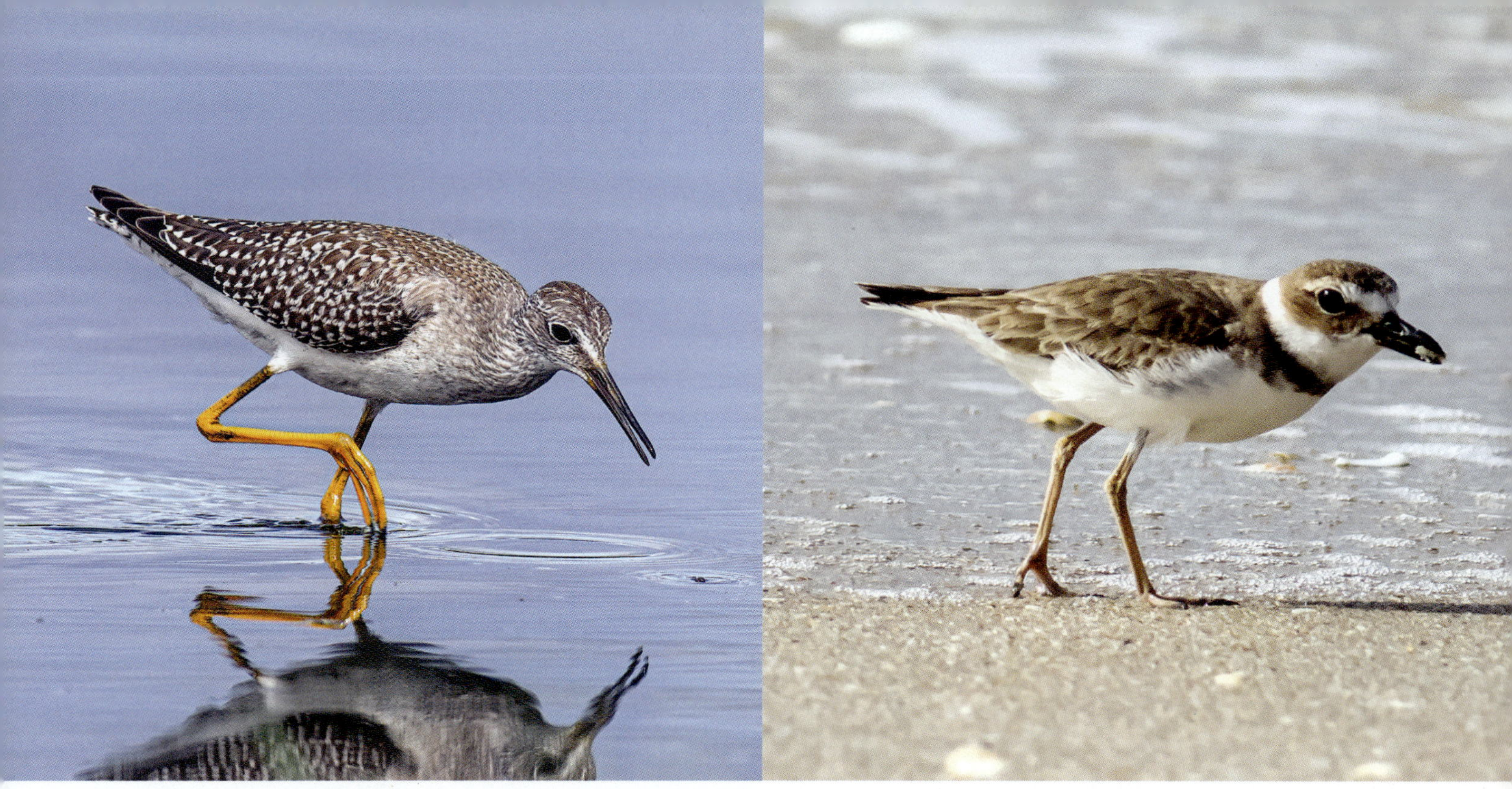

Lesser Yellowlegs

Long, bright yellow legs help identify this graceful midsized wader, but like the dowitchers, there are two varieties that are very similar. When the two species are standing together, the differences become more apparent. A Lesser Yellowlegs is smaller and more dainty, while a Greater Yellowlegs is slightly larger and has a longer, more upturned bill. They breed in Alaska and northwestern Canada before migrating south for the winter.

Wilson's Plover

Wilson's Plovers are not common in Florida. They specialize in hunting fiddler crabs and, as a result, are vulnerable to beach disturbances and human activity. They are now on the endangered watch list for species with a limited range.

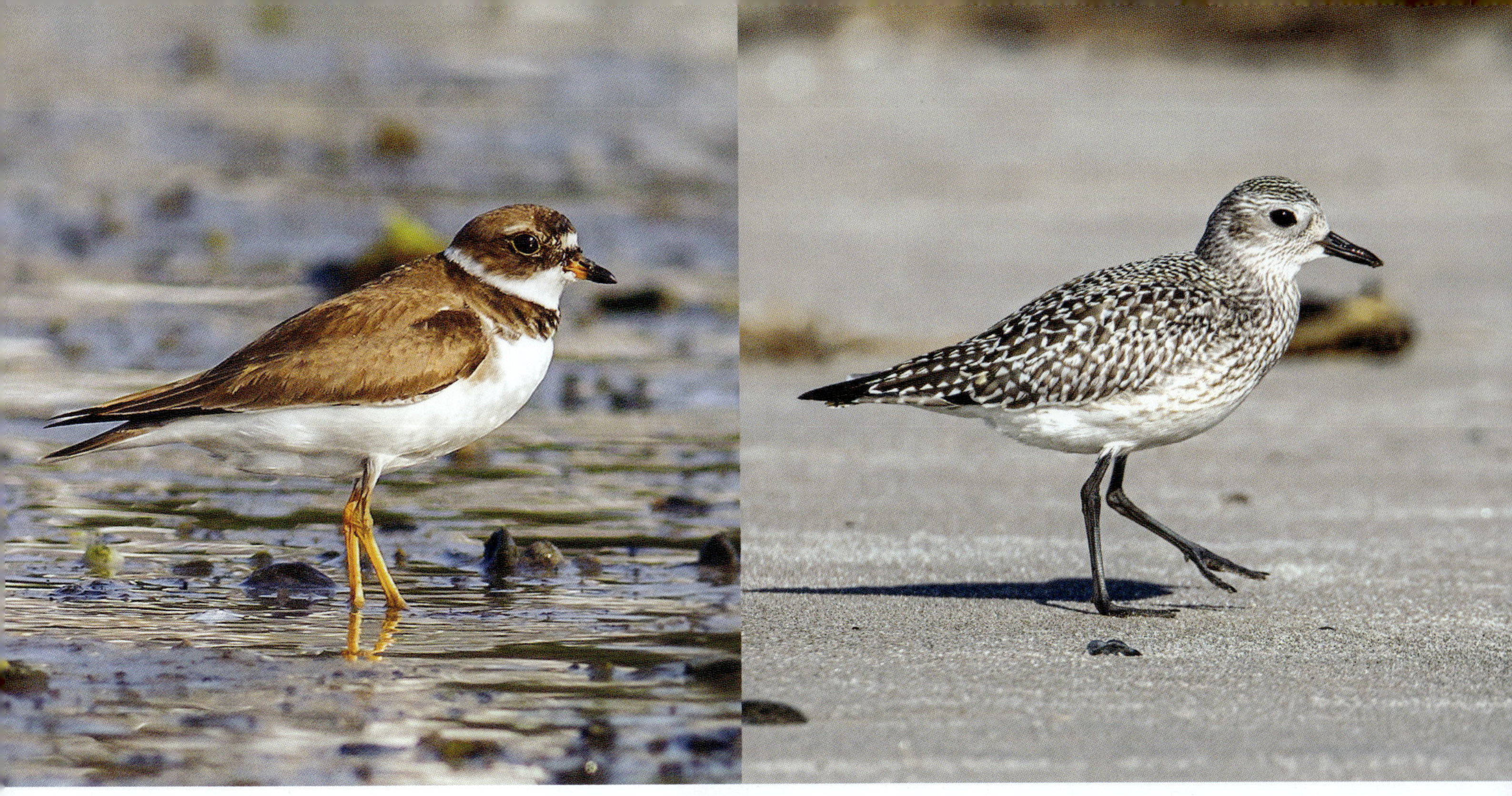

Semipalmated Plover

There are numerous plover species in the world, with the Semipalmated being the most common and widespread in North America. Adults are brown above and white below, with one black band on the breast. The term "semipalmated" refers to the partial webbing of their toes. They gravitate to shallow and muddy water, even inland locations like farmland and golf courses. They often forage alongside other species, but stand out with their distinct stop-and-go feeding style.

Black-bellied Plover

The Black-bellied Plover is one of the many shorebirds named after their distinctive breeding plumage. During the winter, we see only plain, gray-checked birds on Florida beaches. They begin to develop their characteristic black bellies before returning to the Arctic later in the spring. Like all plovers, their short stocky bills are perfect for picking small insects and crustaceans from the sand.

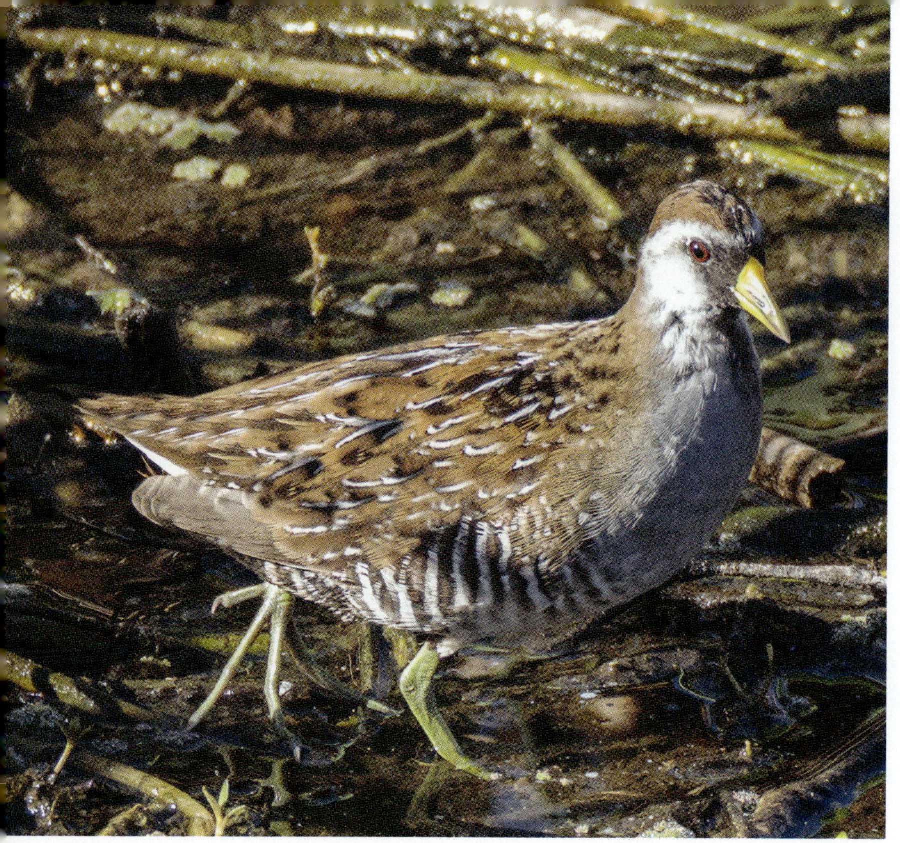

Sora

Soras are small, secretive birds that build their nests in dense vegetation. Although they are rarely seen, they are one of the most common members of the rail family. Occasionally, they come out in the open long enough for a photograph. The best time to find them is early morning or late afternoon. If you hear their distinctive whinny call, just wait patiently and one may appear.

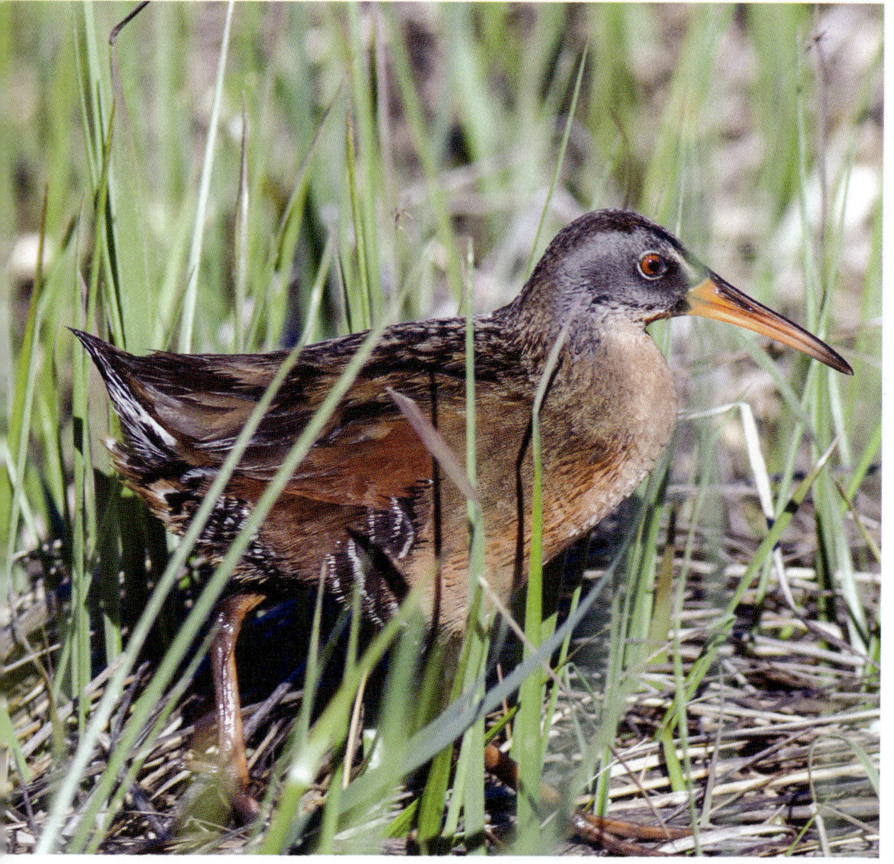

Virginia Rail

These birds favor the same habitat as Soras but they eat insects rather than vegetation. And, like Soras, they are rarely seen because, when threatened, they run through thick grass, rather than fly. Interestingly, rails can compress their bodies laterally so the grass does not move as they run. Although birders like to think the expression "thin as a rail" owes its origin to the bird, it really refers to the rail of a fence.

Wilson's Snipe

This is another elusive freshwater bird that leaves the marsh at dawn and dusk to feed. They look and behave like their relatives, the American Woodcock. They are legally hunted in Florida, but their fast erratic flight makes them difficult targets. When flushed, they burst out of their cover and fly in a zigzag pattern at speeds of up to sixty miles per hour.

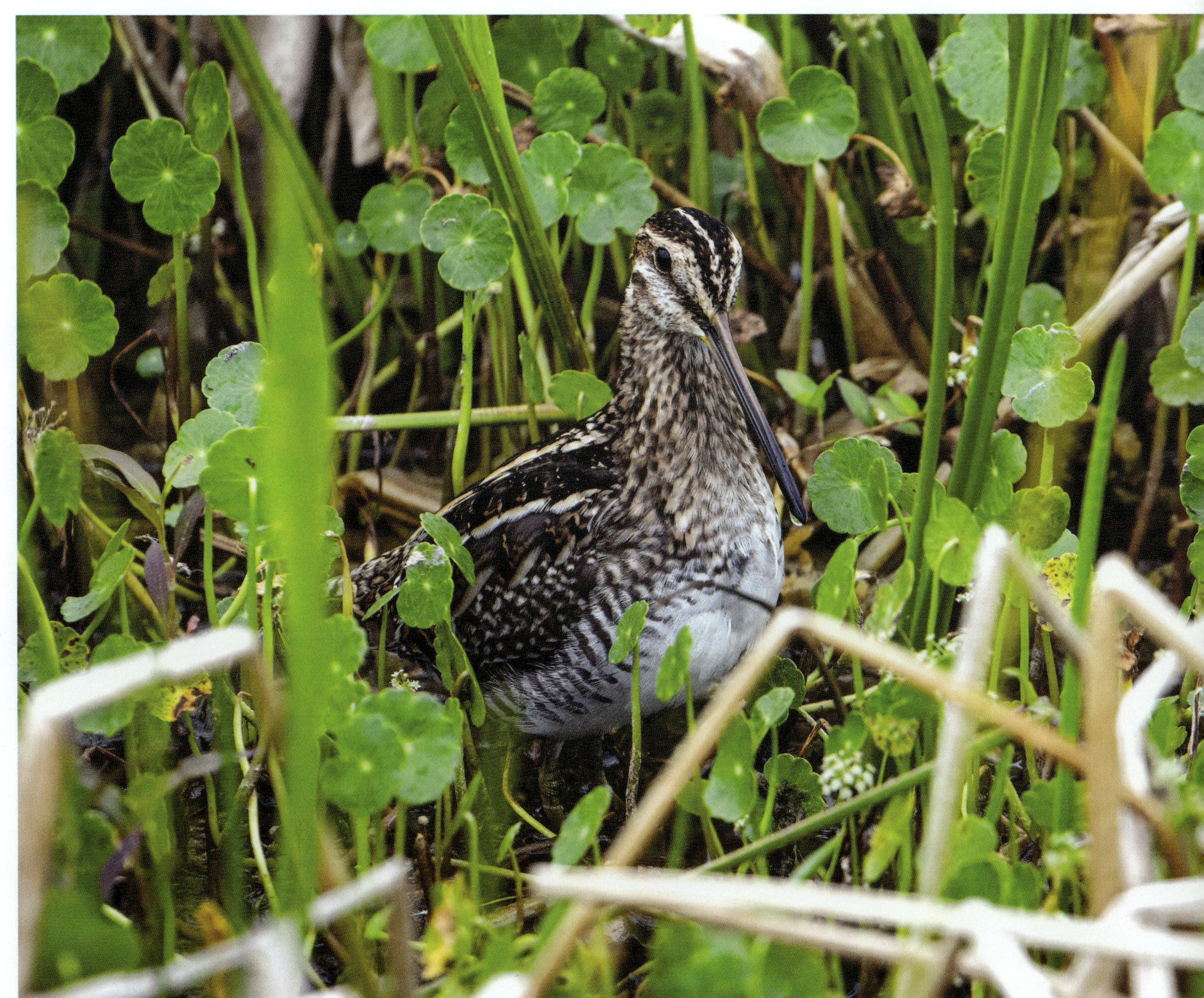

Short-billed Dowitcher

Dowitchers have beautiful reddish coloration on their heads and necks in breeding plumage, with prominent black-and-white barring on their backs and flanks. During the winter months, their feathers are mostly dull gray. Their cousins, the Long-billed Dowitchers, are almost identical but have a slightly different call. It's nearly impossible to tell them apart. Since this dowitcher was found in brackish water, its preferred habitat, I'm going with Short-billed Dowitcher.

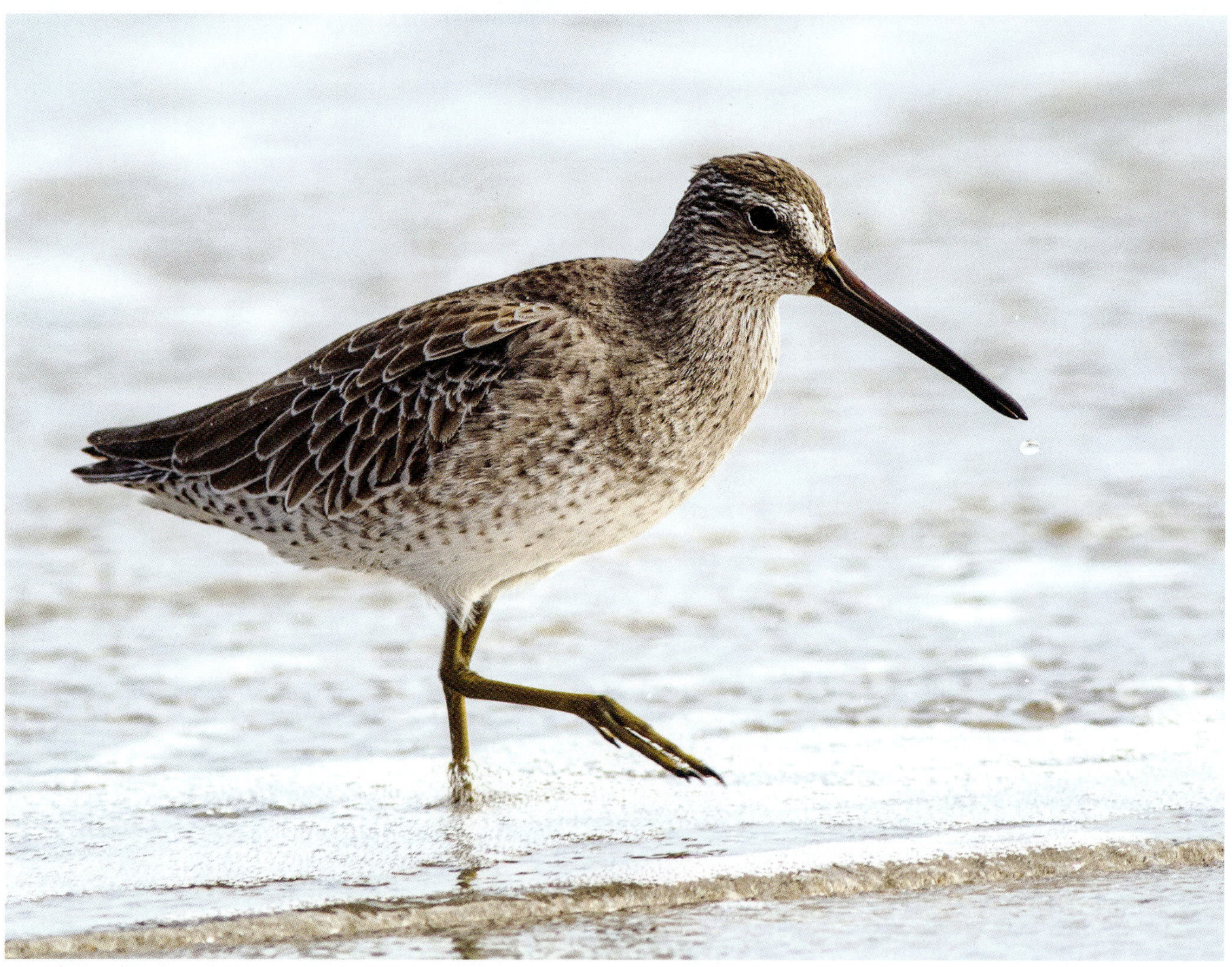

Whimbrel

Favoring nesting grounds across the northern tundra, the Whimbrel spends winters along the coasts of North and South America. These are large, brown speckled shorebirds that have a long curved bill they use to probe for food in mudflats and shallow lagoons. Their diet is primarily crabs, shrimp, marine worms, and mollusks. They can form large flocks at times, making them susceptible to market hunting on some Caribbean islands.

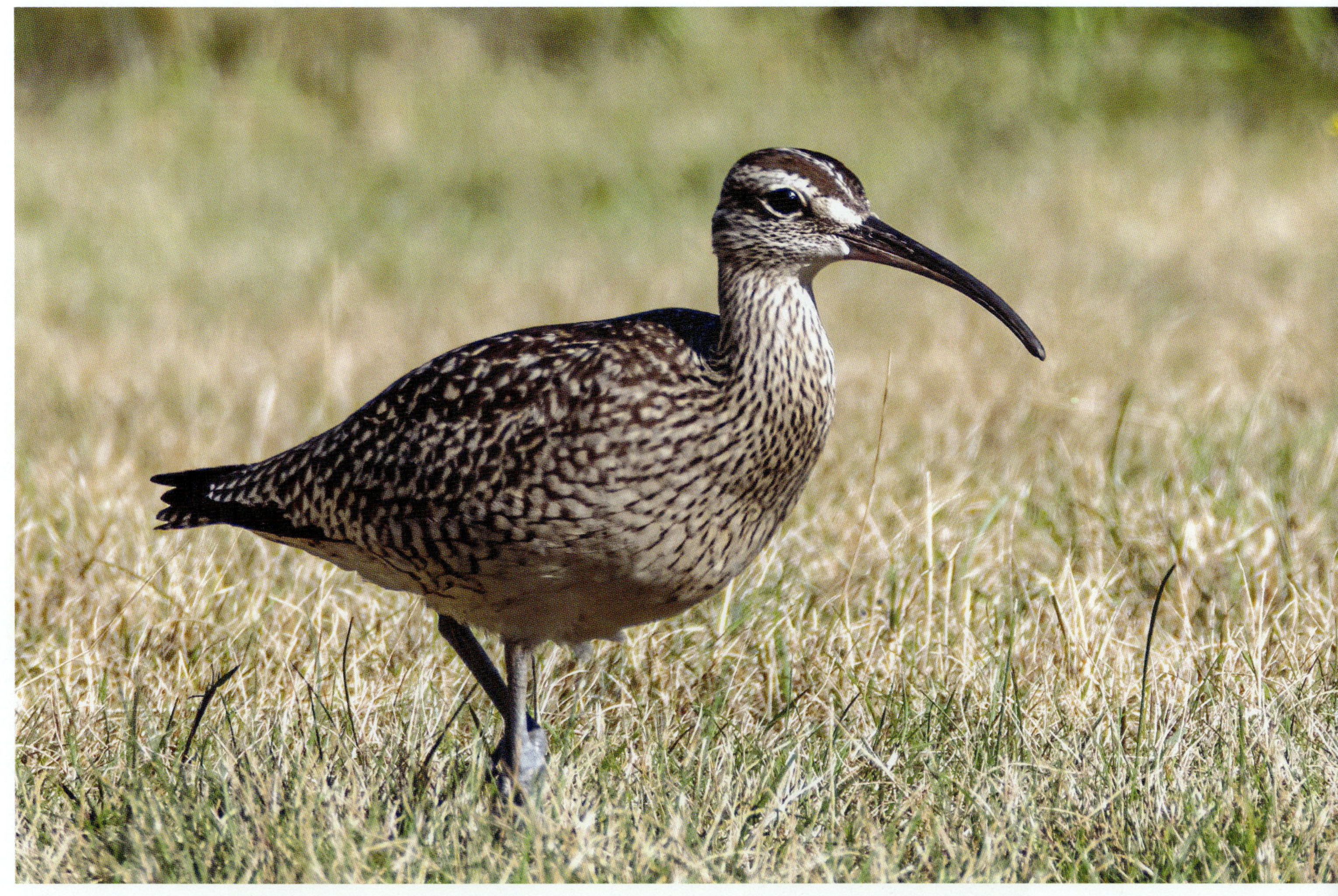

Red-winged Blackbird

No Florida wetland is complete without the raucous calls of blackbirds competing for territory and mates. Red-winged Blackbird males have bright red and yellow epaulets that they flash as they chase rivals out of their area. Males can have from ten to fifteen females in their breeding territory, so they have a full-time job, sometimes going after larger animals or people, just to keep things in order. Nesting season is March through mid-July. The drab, brown-streaked female builds a nest of grasses and leaves a few feet off the ground in shrubs or reeds in a wetland.

The majority of Red-winged Blackbirds in Florida are not migratory, but many birds do travel north and will be in Maine by March 1st, just as the ice begins to melt.

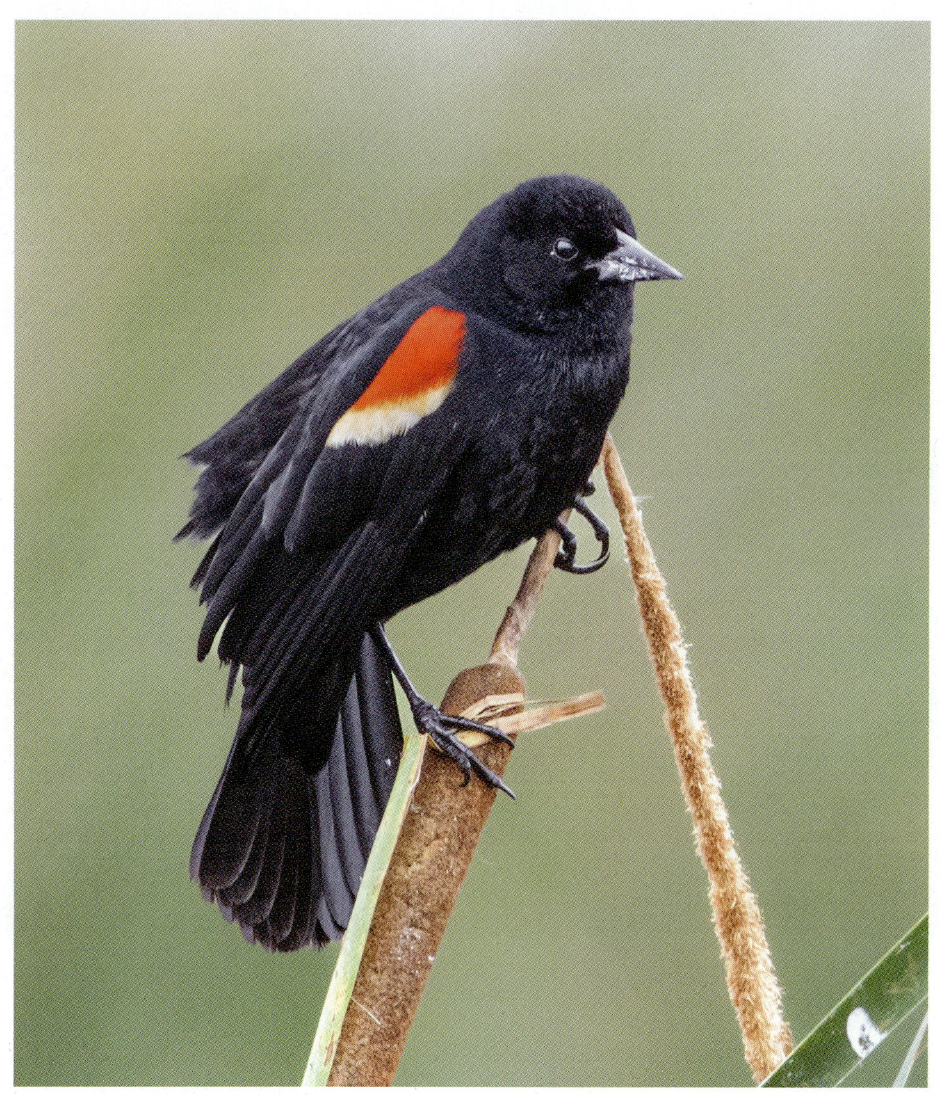

Boat-tailed Grackle

There are two species of grackles in Florida, the Common Grackle and the impressive Boat-tailed Grackle. All Grackles appear to be ugly and aggressive black birds until you look closely at their feathers, which have an amazing purple and bronze iridescence. Boat-tailed Grackles get their name from the long, keel-shaped tail. They are usually found only in coastal areas, however, in Florida, they are permanent, nonmigratory residents of ponds and marshes throughout the peninsula, often far from the coast. Individuals on the Gulf Coast have dark brown eyes while on the Atlantic coast their eyes are bright yellow.

As a novice birder, I assumed these were invasive species like European Starlings, but grackles are native to North America. Grackles are ubiquitous, forming large flocks of hundreds of birds. It's worth looking closely, because you might pick up a rare vagrant like a Great-tailed Grackle from Louisiana.

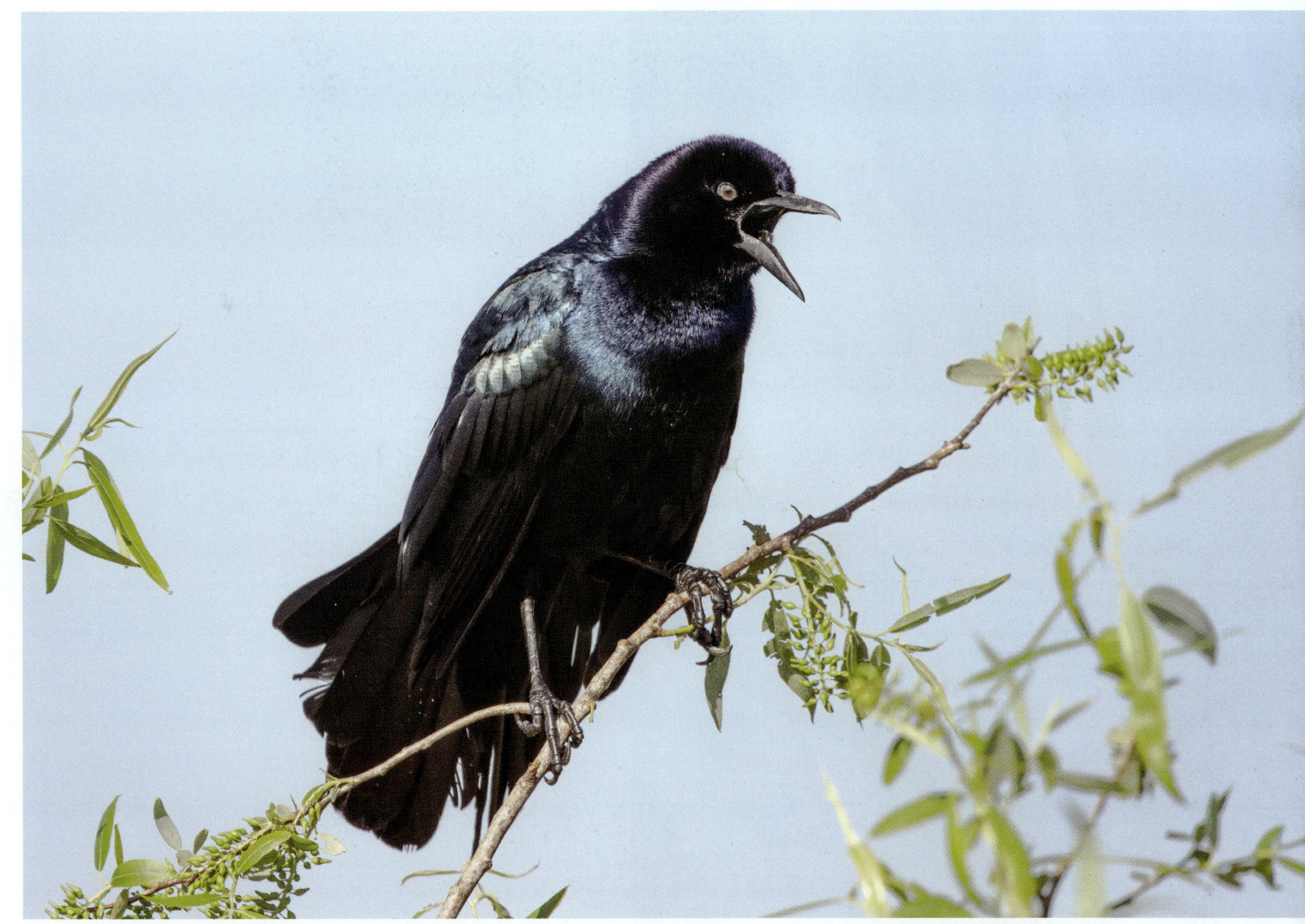

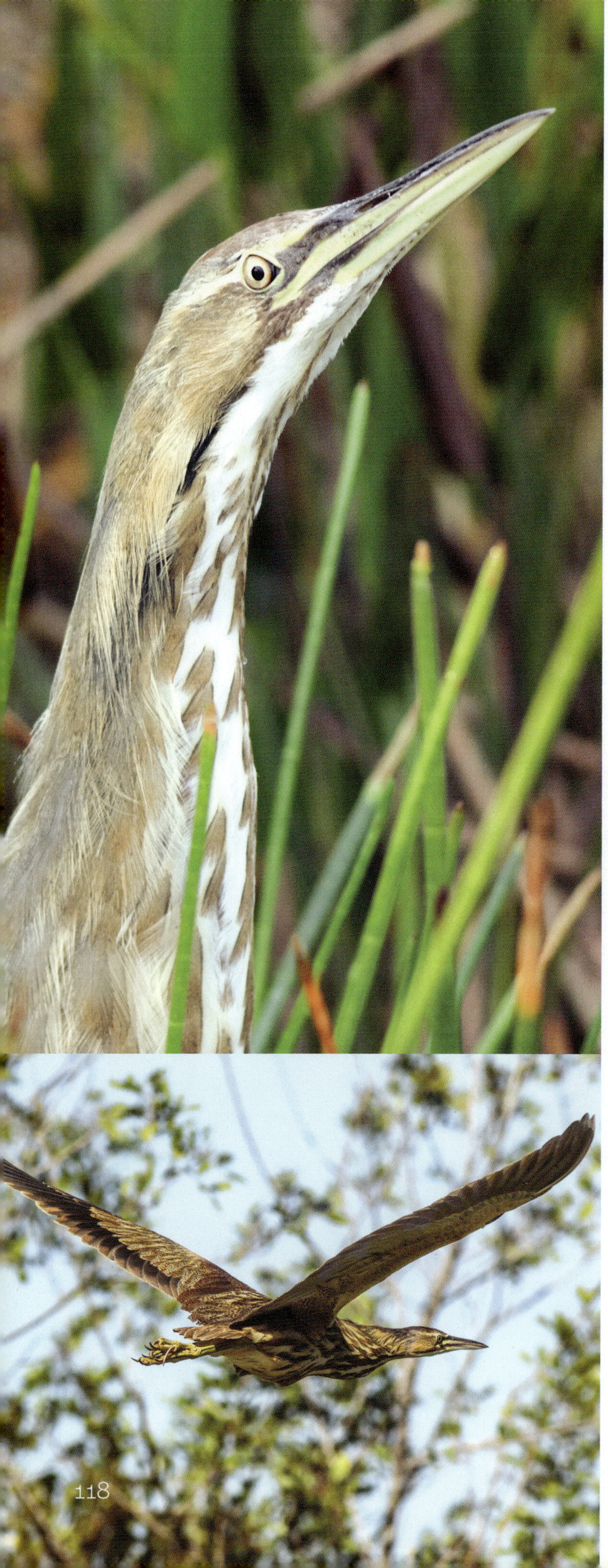

American Bittern

The Bittern is a large bird with excellent camouflage that is usually seen flying away after being flushed from its hiding place in thick vegetation. Male bitterns have a loud booming call that is used to alert others to their presence. In an effort to conceal themselves among the reeds, they are noted for "freezing" in place with their bills extended in a vertical position.

Bitterns can found in wetlands all across North America and during the winter many northern birds migrate south to spend the season in the Everglades. They are not considered to be endangered because of their extensive distribution, but their numbers are dwindling due to development and pollution of wetland areas.

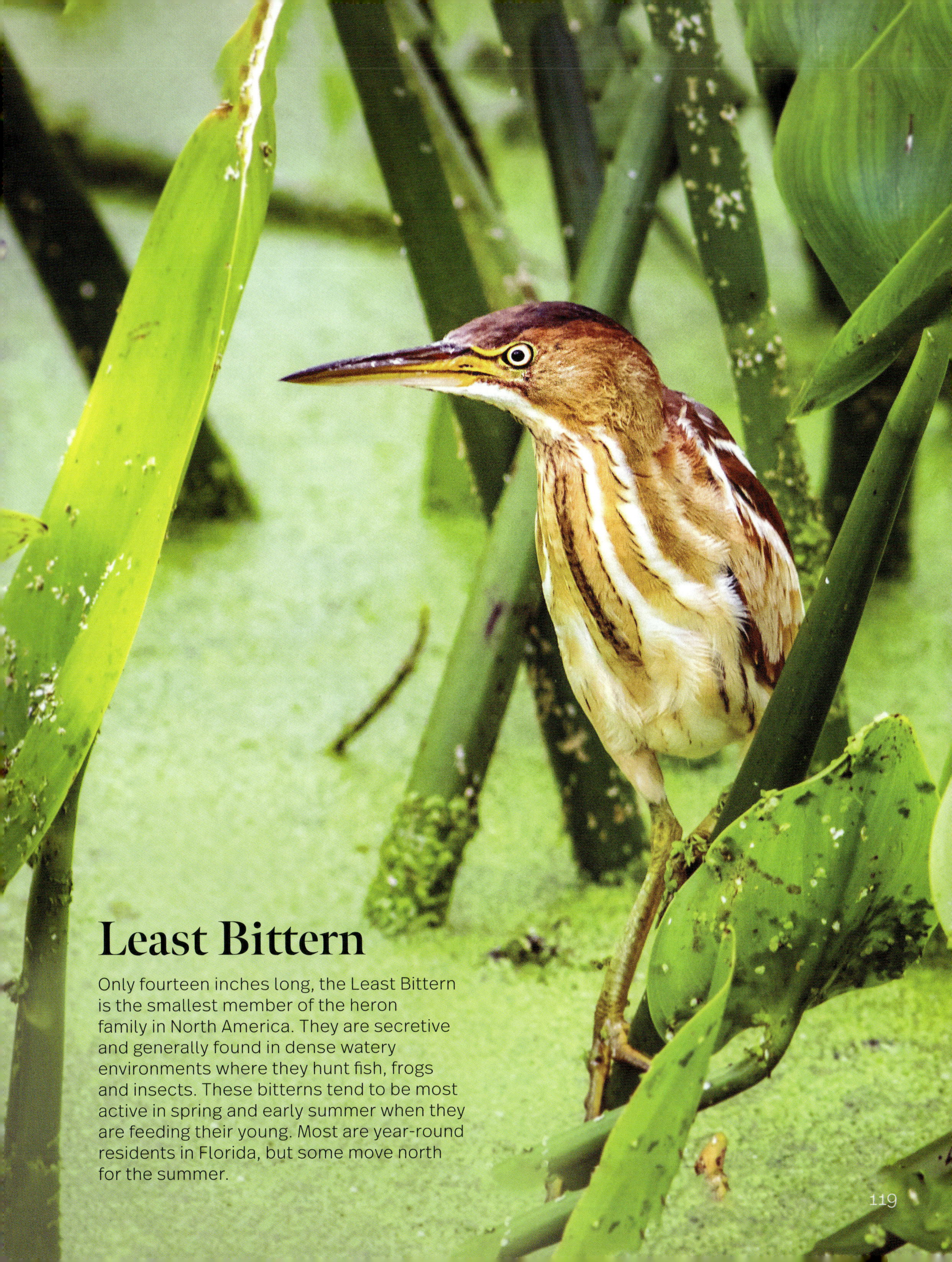

Least Bittern

Only fourteen inches long, the Least Bittern is the smallest member of the heron family in North America. They are secretive and generally found in dense watery environments where they hunt fish, frogs and insects. These bitterns tend to be most active in spring and early summer when they are feeding their young. Most are year-round residents in Florida, but some move north for the summer.

Belted Kingfisher

Kingfishers are found all over the world from the Amazon to Australia. The North American species is called the Belted Kingfisher because of the broad, blue band across a white breast. This is one of the few bird species where the female has a more elegant plumage as she sports a rusty orange band across the belly as well. Kingfishers spend a lot of time perched over the water then diving to spear a fish. They can also hover in midair before making a plunge on a target. These birds make a noisy chattering call as they move around a pond going from perch to perch. Since they live almost exclusively on fish, they are rarely found far from water.

Kingfishers can be very skittish and for me have been notoriously difficult to photograph. They never seem to sit still and they're gone long before a decent photo op. Imagine my surprise when we came upon this male perched on a stick out in the sun. He was very tame and allowed us to get fairly close for many excellent shots, even showing off his shaggy crest in the wind.

This photo illustrates many of the features we look for in a classic "bird-on-a-stick" image. The light is optimal, so the exposure allows a good depth of field, blurring the background, but sharp focus bringing out detail in both the white and dark feathers. There is even a "catchlight," the reflection of the sun in the bird's eye.

One of the best things about bird photography is that you never forget when you get those great photos of a nemesis bird or a lifer. Whenever I see this photo, even years from now, I'll remember the day and this very cooperative, handsome young male.

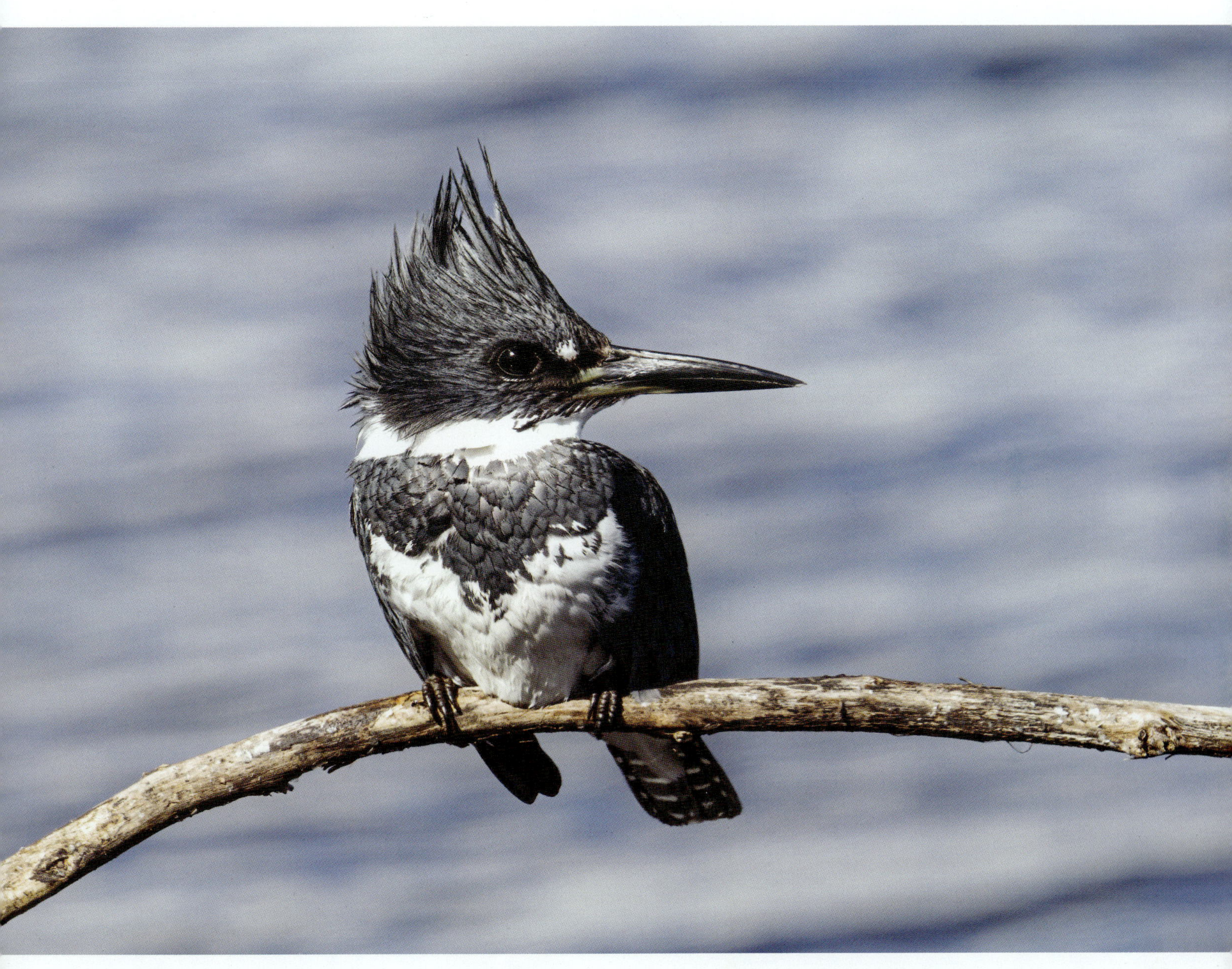

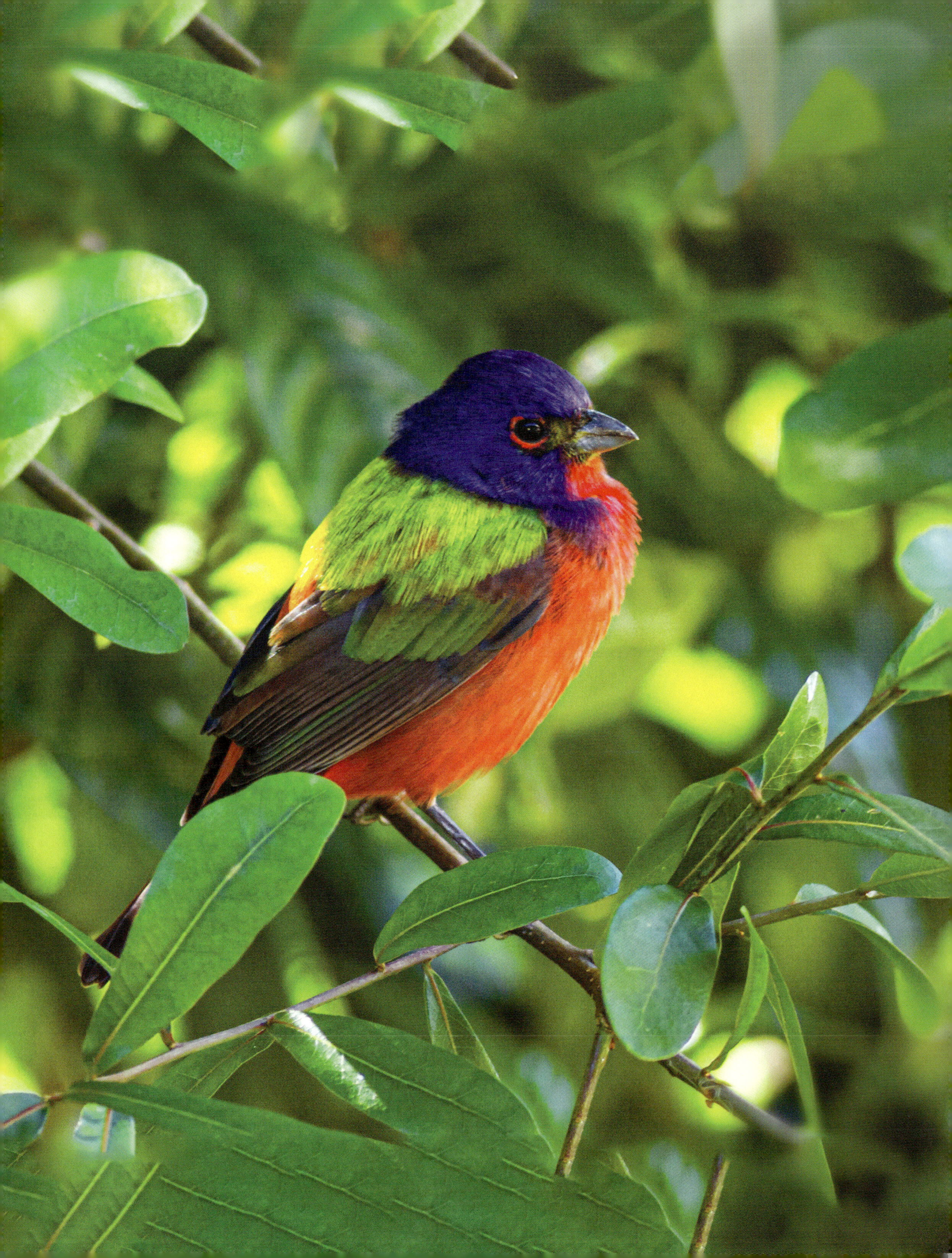

Songbirds

Songbirds are also known as passerines or perching birds. Unlike ducks, gulls, or waterbirds, their feet are uniquely designed to automatically "grip and lock," allowing them to hold on to a perch using a combination of muscles and tendons. It is this feature that allows them to roost in trees and sleep without falling to the ground.

Just to make things confusing, ornithologists exclude woodpeckers, kingfishers, pigeons, and doves from this group, but songbirds make up at least half the birds in the world and most of the ones we see in fields, woods, and our own backyards.

Painted Bunting

The French call Painted Buntings "nonpareil" (without equal), and the males certainly are unique in the bird world with their gleaming purple, blue, green, and red feathers. Females and young males display beautiful soft green and yellow plumage.

They will come to feeders but usually hide in dense shrubs, creating a distinct challenge for photographers. Perhaps their evasiveness is justified, as they are still trapped for the illegal caged bird trade. According to Florida Fish and Wildlife, the eastern population of Painted Buntings that breeds along the northeast coast of Florida has been declining 4.6 per cent a year since 1966.

No one is certain about the cause for the decline, but the restricted range makes them vulnerable to habitat loss and nest parasites like Brown-headed Cowbirds may play a role.

These little jewels are a special treat for birders from the North, and I always enjoy visiting my neighbor's feeders trying to get an adequate photo for my collection.

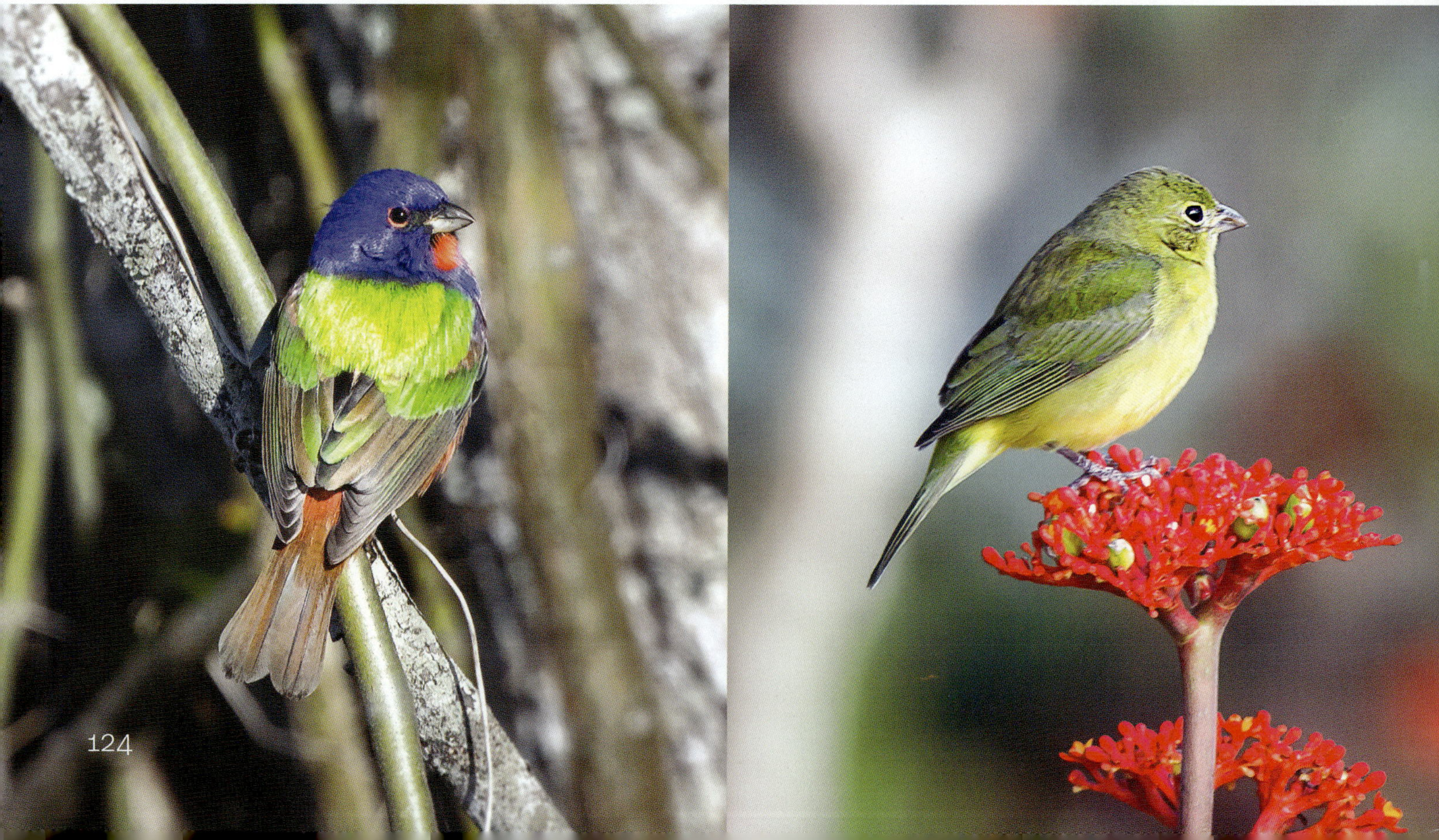

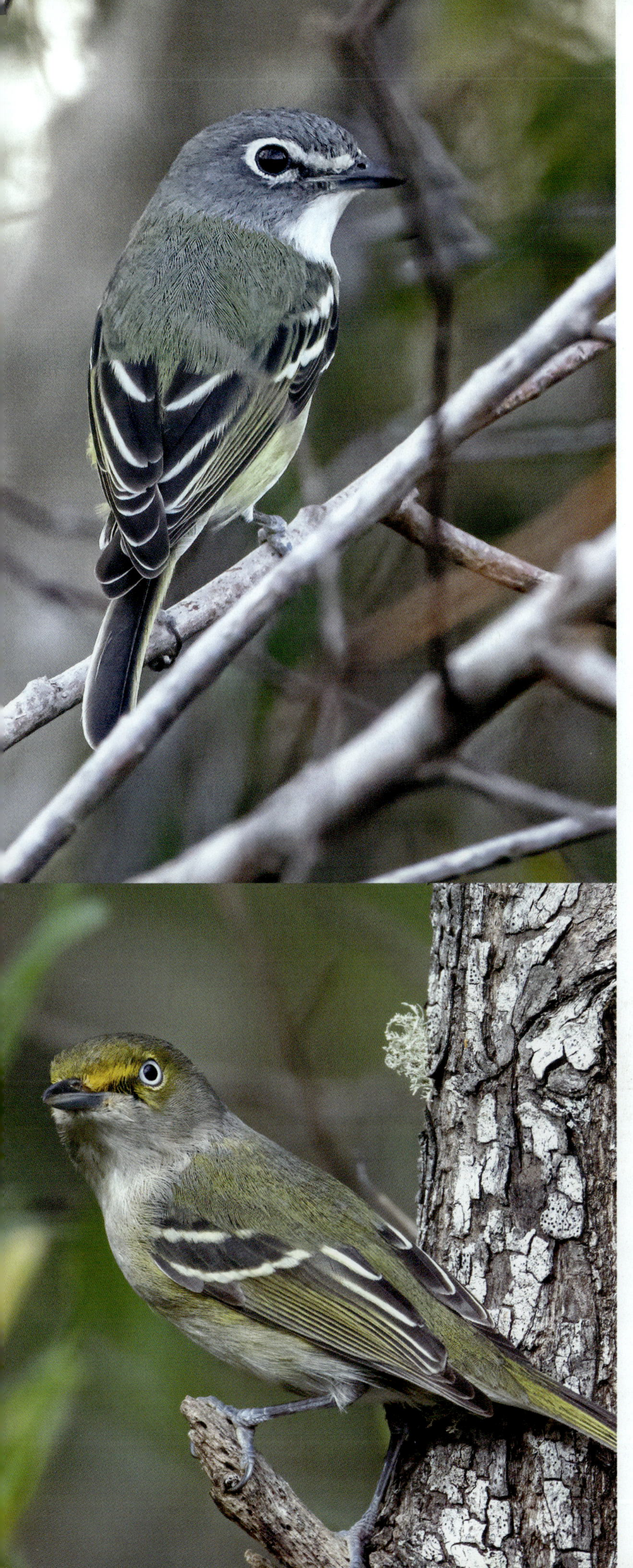

Blue-headed Vireo

Vireos live in tangles of scrub brush, weeds, and thorns, where they subsist on a diet of flies, spiders, caterpillars, beetles, and moths. The most common species in Florida are the White-eyed Vireo and the more migratory Blue-headed Vireo. This is a small five- to six-inch-long bird with a blue-gray head and white eye-rings that look like spectacles. They are only in Florida for a few months before heading as far north as Canada's subarctic forests.

This is one of the few photos I have of the species where the bird is out in the open, not hidden away deep in the brush.

White-eyed Vireo

The White-eyed Vireo is one of only two perching birds in the United States with a white eye. They are yellow-green above and pale yellow below with yellow spectacles. These vireos are common year-round residents in Florida but they are very secretive and rarely seen by a casual observer. They nest low in shrubs along the edges of fields and gardens, making them susceptible to predation by outdoor cats. Usually hidden in thickets and rarely venturing out in the open long enough for a photo, this vireo gives away its location with a distinctive song.

A White-eyed Vireo sighting in Maine triggers a rare bird alert, but one or two are found that far north each year.

Brown-headed Nuthatch

While Maine birdwatchers are accustomed to seeing the common White-breasted and Red-breasted Nuthatches, in Florida we trek to the longleaf pine flatwoods of Saint Sebastian River Preserve State Park to find the Brown-headed Nuthatch.

These small round birds creep up and down tree trunks using their bill as a probe to chisel out insects from under the bark. They are frequently seen with Red-cockaded Woodpeckers.

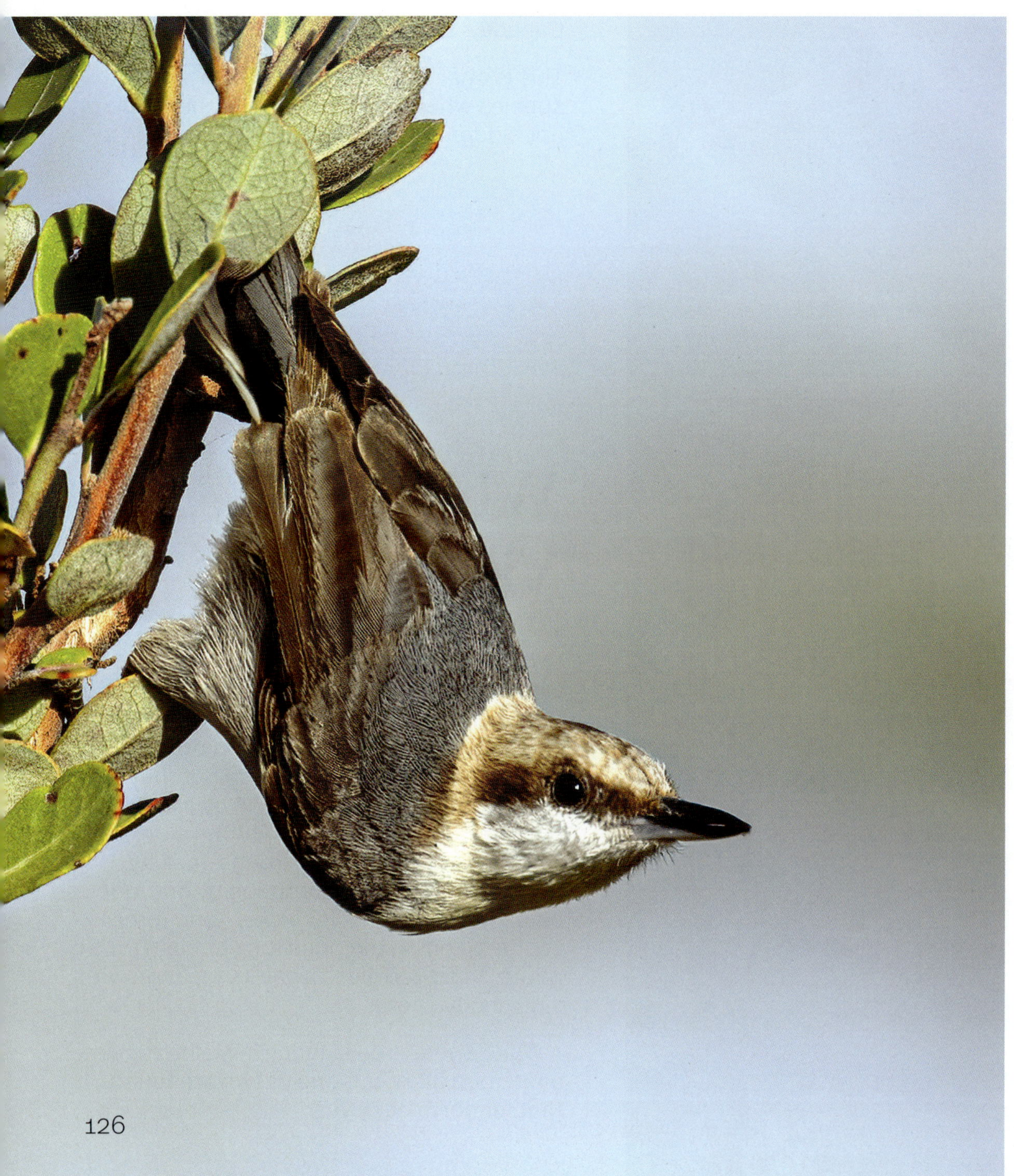

Loggerhead Shrike

Loggerhead Shrikes are widespread across North America and Mexico. Northern populations are migratory, while they are permanent residents in Florida. The Loggerhead Shrike acts more like a raptor than a songbird and is often called the "butcher-bird" because of its habit of impaling prey on a thorn or barbed wire. The gray-and-white bird is distinguished by its large head, black mask, and hooked bill. While the majority of their diet consists of large insects like grasshoppers and dragonflies, shrikes are fierce predators that use their specialized bill to kill birds and small mammals as large as the shrike itself.

Shrike populations have been declining, possibly due to loss of open agricultural land in southern states and heavy use of insecticides having a negative impact on migratory northern birds.

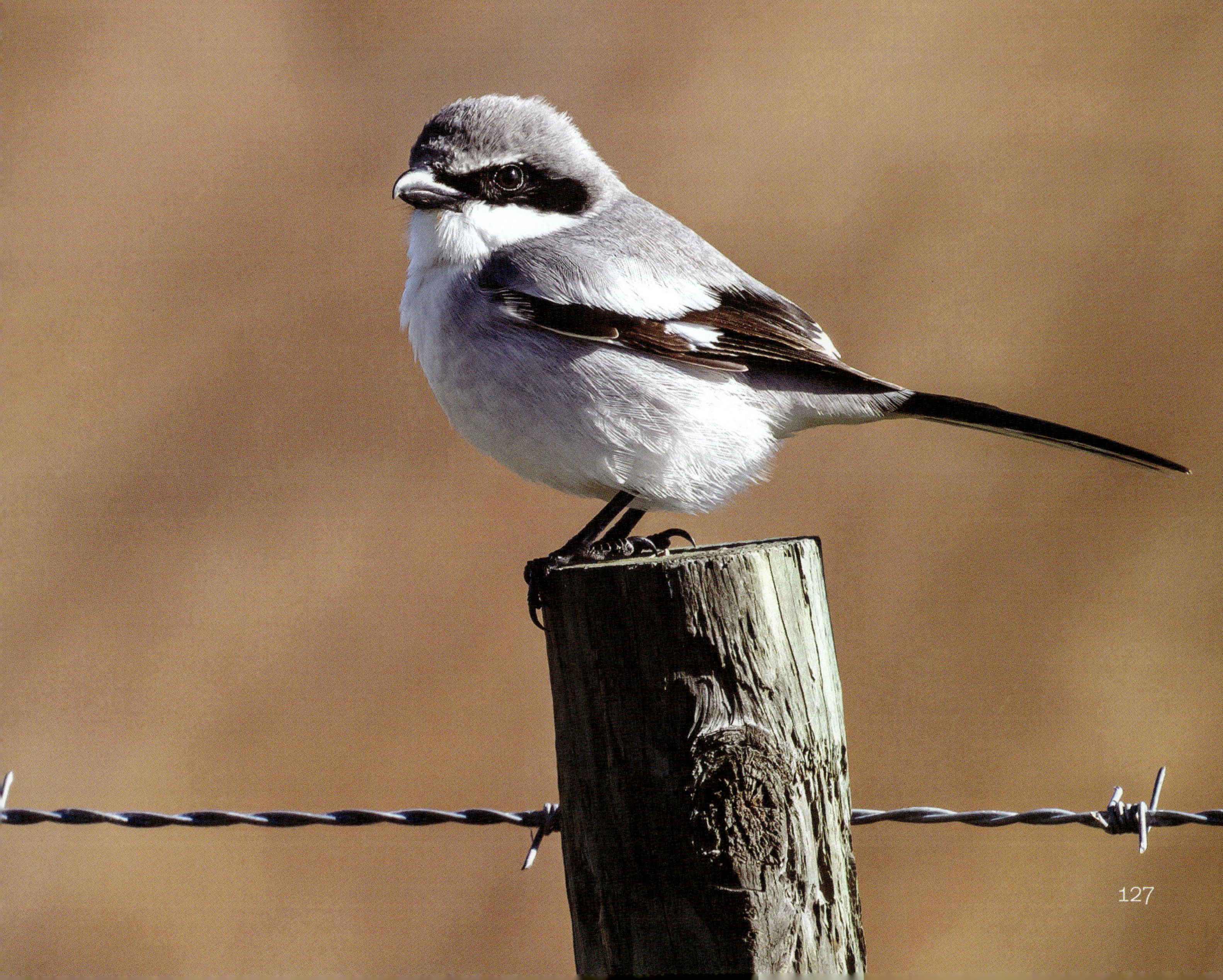

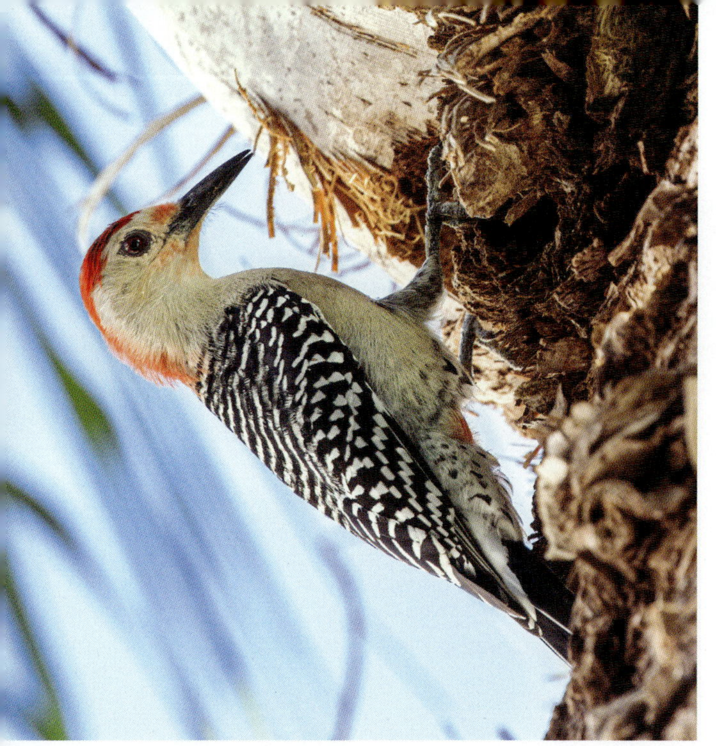

Red-bellied Woodpecker

Red-bellied Woodpeckers are known for their raucous calls rather than their red bellies, which are very faint and difficult to spot in the field. They can be found in backyards, parks, and any wooded area. While they typically eat insects and seeds, they enjoy the fruit of the strangler fig tree.

These southern woodpeckers have gradually spread northward and are now common in New England. Don't confuse them with Red-headed Woodpeckers, which are completely different birds.

Because both species use old nest holes left by other woodpeckers, they are vulnerable to competition for nesting sites from invasive European Starlings.

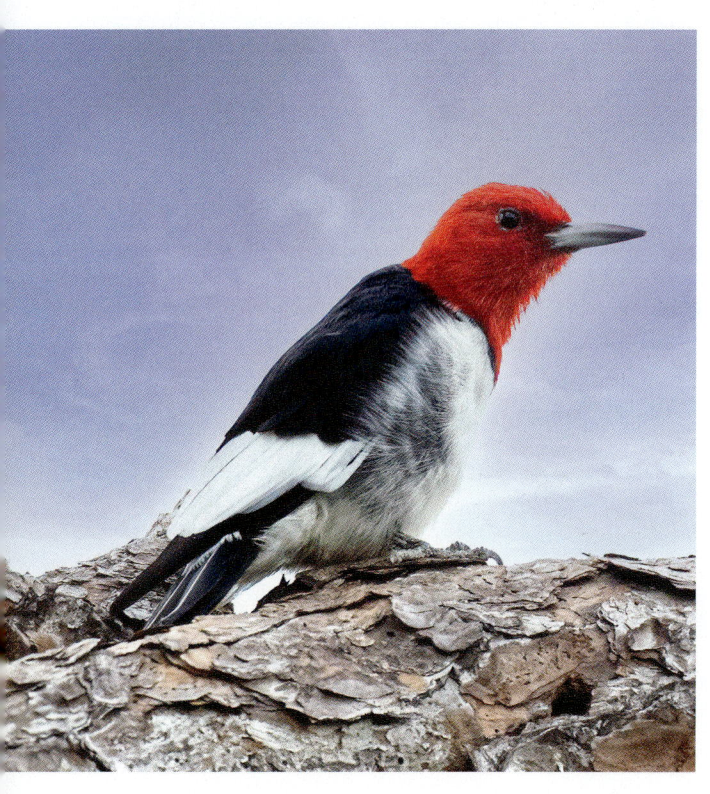

Red-headed Woodpecker

Red-headed Woodpeckers are less common but noisy, eye-catching birds with black-and-white wings and fiery-red heads. They are nomadic and create nest cavities in dead and dying trees, up to eighty feet aboveground. Males do the majority of the excavation work chipping out a cavity that can be a foot deep. Red-heads are unusual in that they are one of the few birds that cache their food. They wedge acorns and seeds into hidden spots to be eaten at a later date and, somehow, they remember where they are hidden. They prefer to live near agricultural fields and open forests. They may be present in an area one year and disappear the next.

Red-headed woodpeckers are less common in South Florida than other species of woodpecker. There is a year-round population, but many birds from more northern areas migrate to Florida for the warmer climate. The best time to find them is during the winter months.

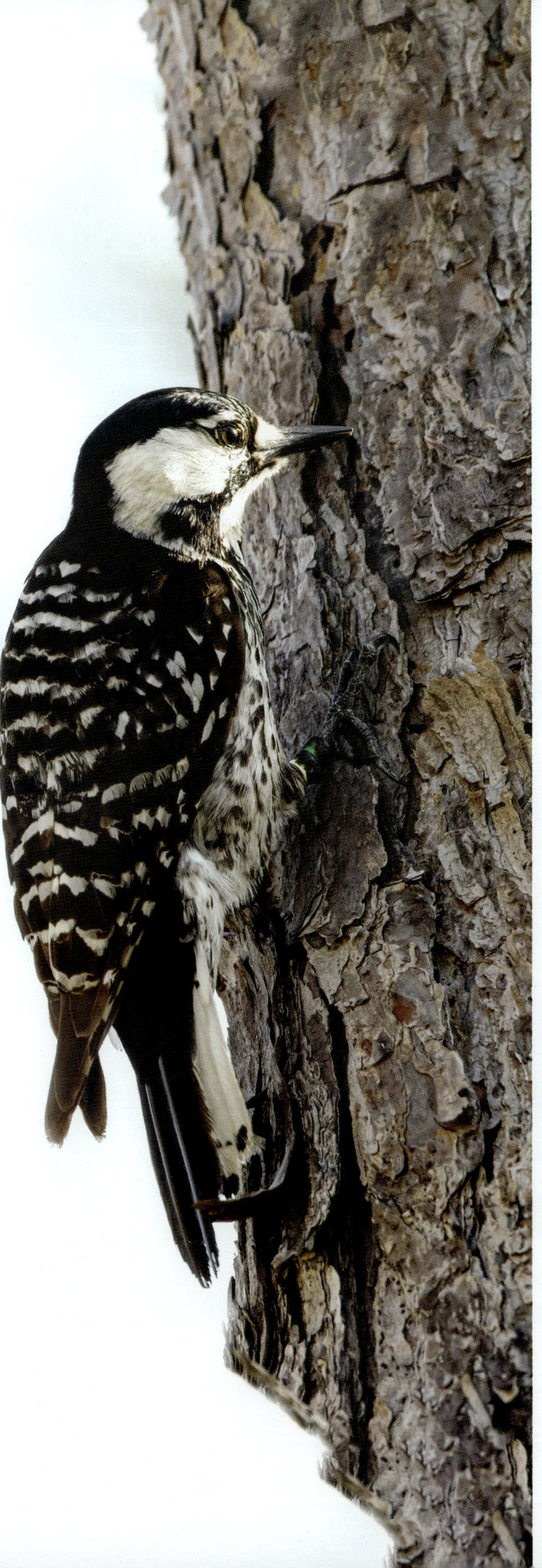

Red-cockaded Woodpecker

Red-cockaded Woodpeckers live in groups, nesting in old-growth pine forests where they excavate holes in living trees infected with red heart disease. This is a fungal infection of the inner heartwood of the tree that usually does not appear until the tree is at least seventy years old. There is one breeding pair in each family, and only one clutch of three to four eggs is laid per season. These are cooperative breeders, as they have "helpers" that will incubate the eggs as well as feed nestlings. They are considered endangered because there are only about 12,000 individuals left in their range, with complete extirpation in several states. The State of Florida and the U.S. Fish and Wildlife Service have extensive programs to preserve appropriate breeding habitat.

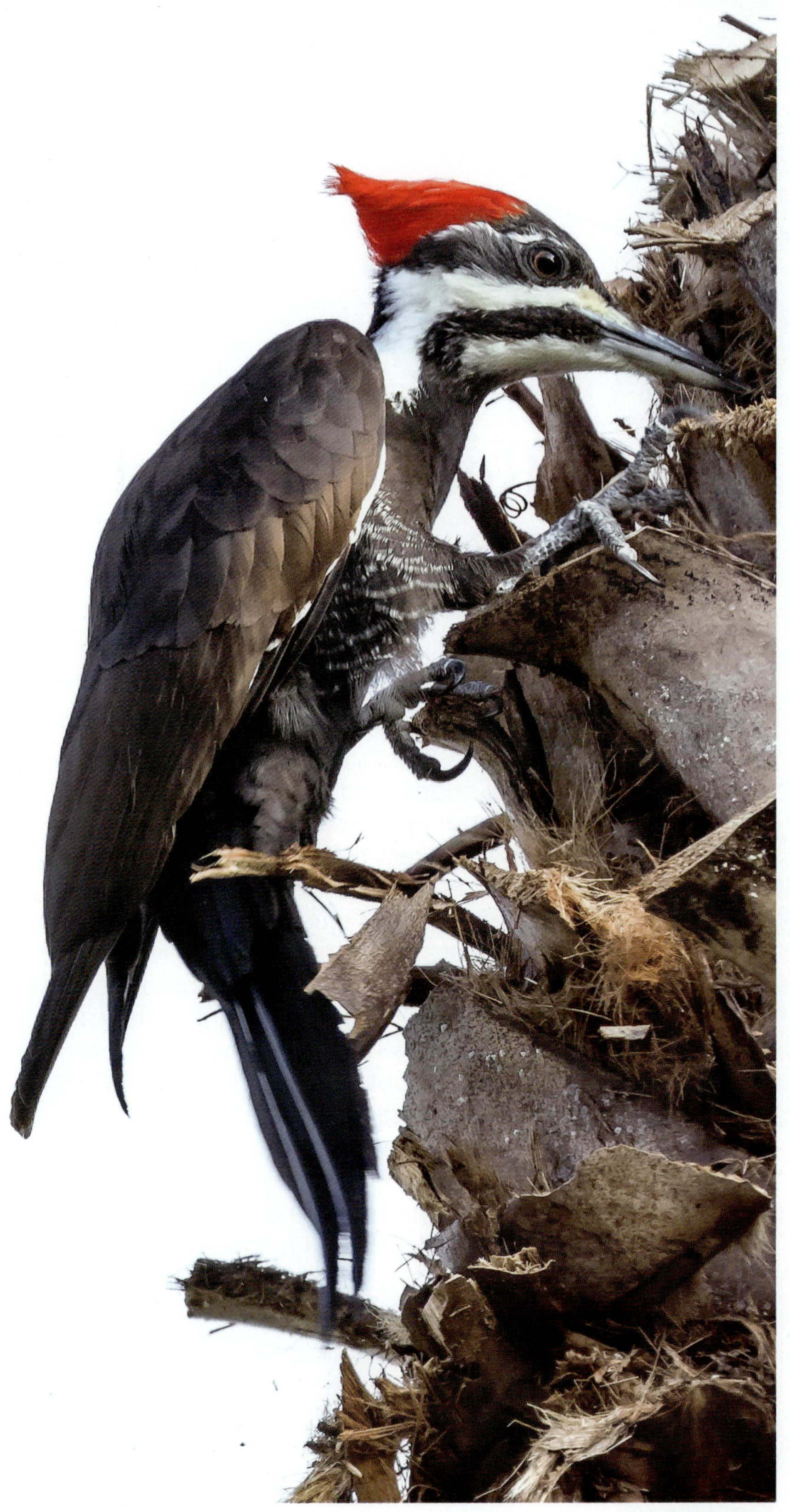

Pileated Woodpecker

Pileated Woodpeckers are the largest of the North American woodpeckers and noted for their large, rectangular nesting cavities. It's quite a sight to watch a Pileated excavate a nest hole, with large wood chips flying everywhere as they bang away. These are unmistakable birds because of their two-and-a-half-foot wingspan and conspicuous red crest. Their populations decreased as eastern forests were cleared but they are increasing again as they adapt to second-growth forests, and they can be found all over eastern North America. Pileated Woodpeckers tend to stay in their winter ranges and do not migrate south like many other birds so any Pileated you find in Florida is a year-round, permanent resident.

I had to pull over to the side of the road to get this photo of a bird exploring a palm tree. The male would sport a bright red mustache, so we know this is a female.

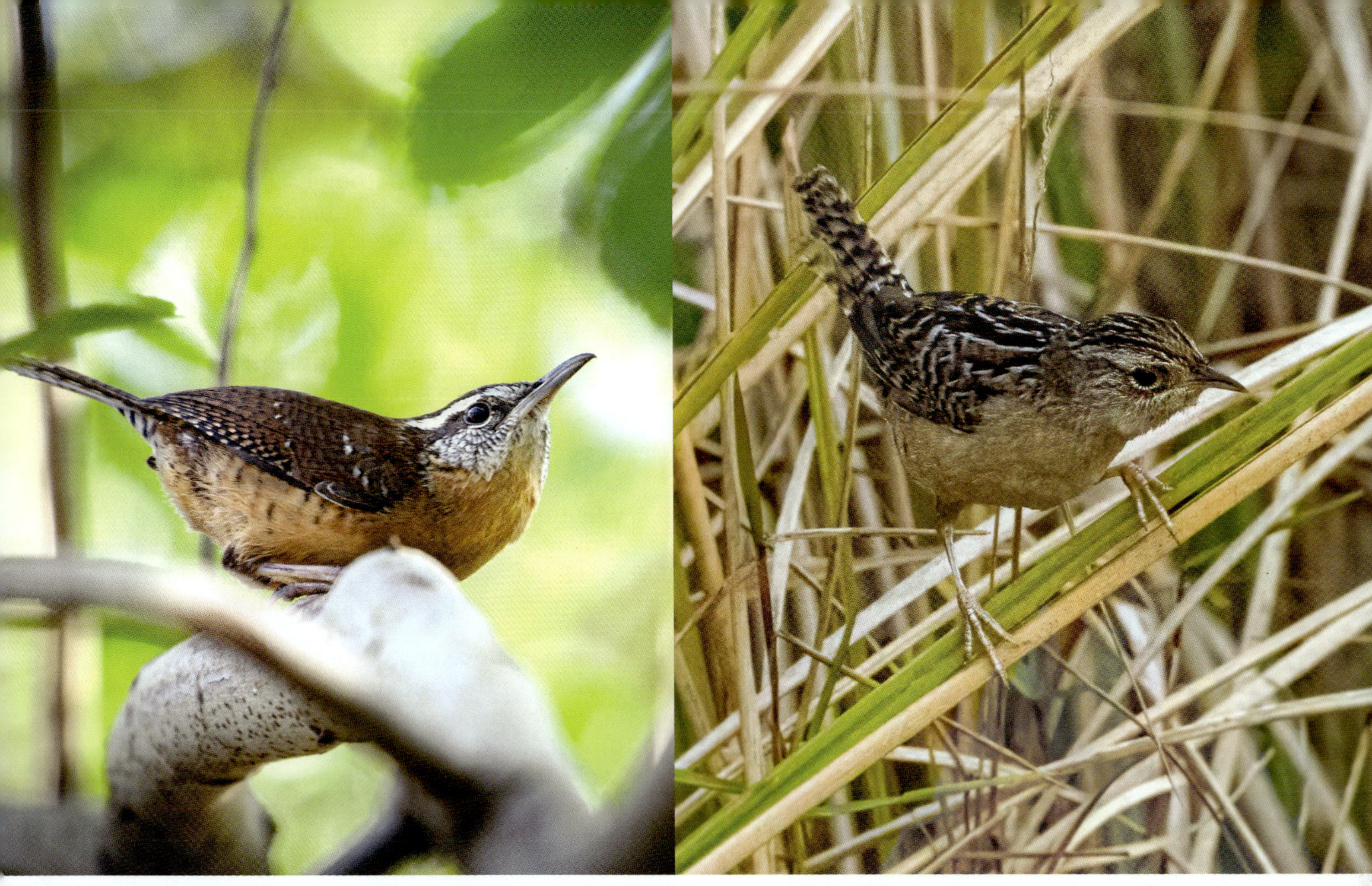

Carolina Wren

The Carolina Wren is a loud musical songster of the southern woods. These are small, reddish-brown birds with a perky upright tail and a distinct white line over the eye. They will nest in suburban backyards and their "teakettle teakettle" song is welcome in any garden. There can be many variations of this song and no two birds seem to sound alike. They spend the mating season in pairs and often sing duets as they forage through tangles of brush and vines. Usually hidden in deep undergrowth, this one came out for a brief moment.

Carolina Wrens in central Florida are nonmigratory, but birds from other southern states have expanded their range north in the past fifty years. After a few mild winters, we have noticed them in our yard in Maine.

Sedge Wren

Even more shy, the Sedge Wren is rarely seen as it runs through thick pasture grasses. They are tiny, dull brown birds that spend the majority of their of their time out of sight in dense marshlands and grasses looking for food on or near the ground. These birds are nomads. They can be present in a certain location one year and then gone the next. My friend Joe and I were able to coax this little guy out to pose for a quick photo before it vanished.

Northern Mockingbird

Mockingbirds are one of the most common and most noticeable backyard birds. In 1927, the mockingbird was declared the state bird of Florida, a distinction it holds with Arkansas, Mississippi, Tennessee, and Texas. They are dark gray above and pale gray below, with large white wing patches that flash as they chase away an intruder. These birds are known as mimics because they will imitate other bird songs or ambient noises in order to defend their home territory. They can sing all night long in the spring. Mockingbirds have steadily expanded their range north over the last fifty years and now can be found across North America and southern Canada.

Northern Cardinal

Male Cardinals, with their brilliant red plumage, are familiar at backyard bird feeders, but in Florida, they can also be found in the deep woods, nesting in shrubs and tangles of vines. This male was quietly hiding in the shadows at the Fort Drum Marsh Conservation Area. Females have the same red crest, large black bill, and a smaller black mask with an olive-brown breast and flanks. Cardinals are very vocal, and their mating song in the spring is a well-known high and clear series of whistles. It has recently been discovered that female cardinals sing as much as the males, and a pair will chip back and forth to keep in touch as they forage through the yard.

Cardinals have always been common in the South, but they did not appeare in Maine until the late 1940s. They were described as rare visitors in Ralph Palmers's 1949 book *Maine Birds,* but within twenty years they were regularly nesting in Maine and now are quite common on any birdwatcher's yard list. Feeders stocked with sunflower seeds may have had a lot to do with their range extension.

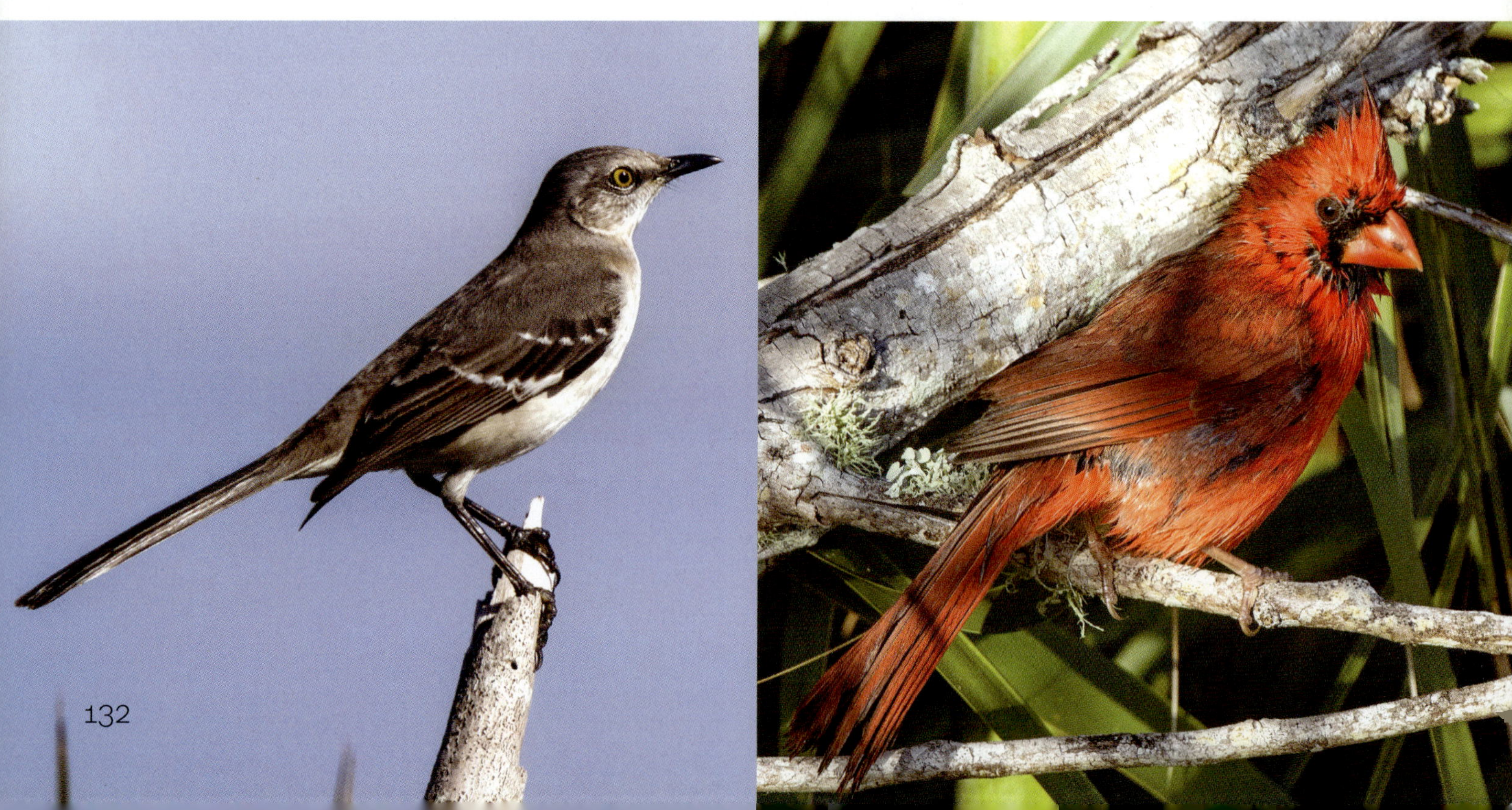

Yellow-headed Blackbird

These birds form huge breeding colonies in the wetlands of central North America, then spend winters in the south, including Texas and Mexico. They are rare in Florida. Other than bright yellow heads, the males also show white wing patches in flight. This bird was discovered at Wakodahatchee Wetlands in December, 2014.

I was fortunate to add this Florida male to my life list in 2014, but I never got to see the lost bird, known as a vagrant by birders, that appeared in Maine's Penobscot region in 2021, so I am still missing one for my Maine list.

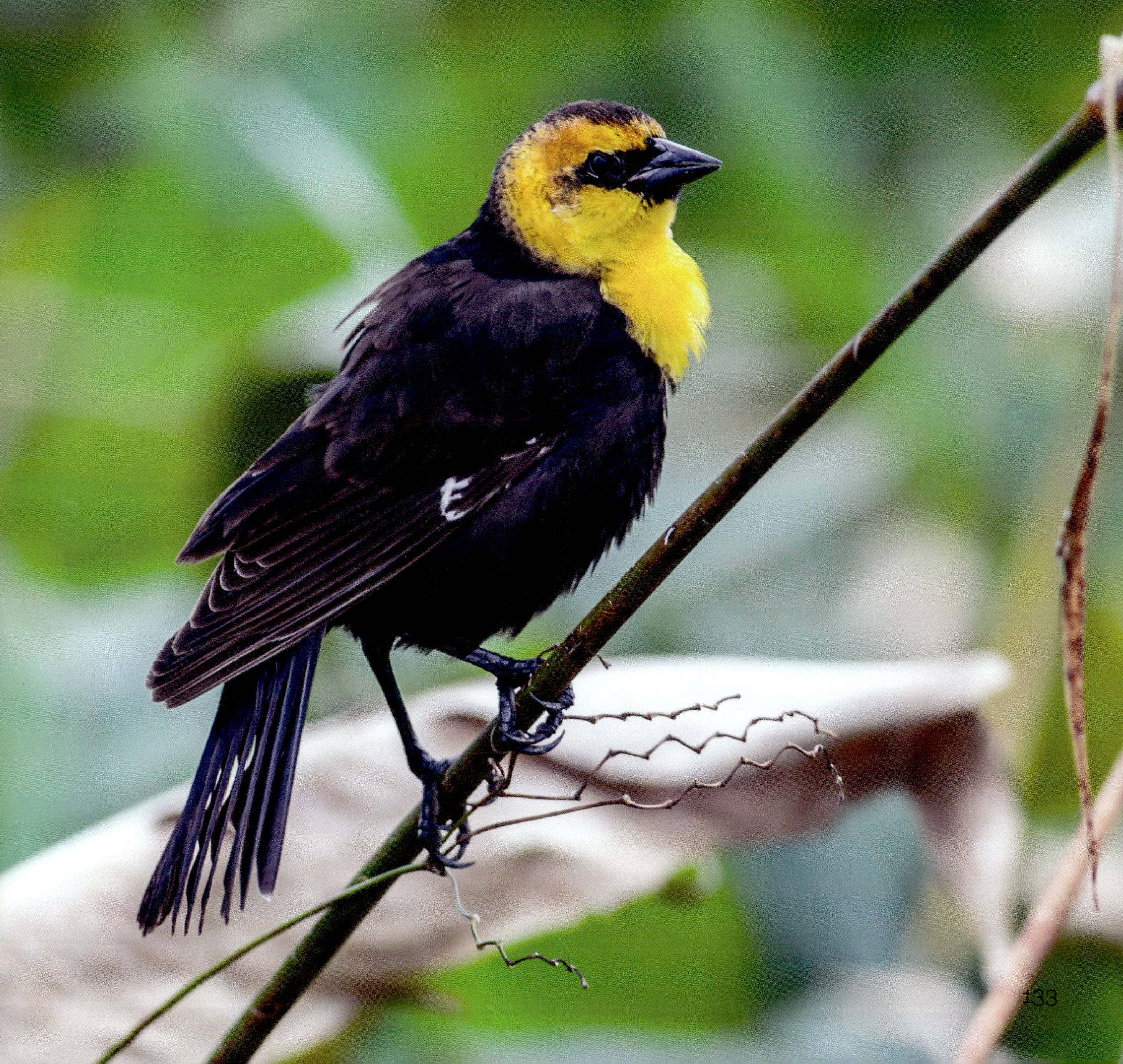

Eastern Meadowlark

With a bright yellow chest and a sharp black V on its chest, Eastern Meadowlarks are easy to identify. When they are on the ground, hunting grasshoppers and locusts, it is a different story, as they can be difficult to find when the brown-and-white striped plumage on their backs blends into the grass. Meadowlarks are year-round residents in Florida and can be found in any grassland, pasture, or open pinewoods throughout the state. These birds are a bird photographer's delight as they perch on fence posts and power lines to sing in the morning sun.

When forests were cleared to create pastures, populations of meadowlarks increased dramatically, though they have been in rapid decline in more recent years. Conversion of grassland to crops, development, and abandoned pastures contributed to habitat loss. Now they are known as a common bird in steep decline with at least a fifty per cent loss in the past fifty years. Meadowlarks nest on the ground from March through August, so they are very susceptible to trampling by livestock. Early mowing is one of their biggest threats, leading to destruction of nests and death of young birds. Also, heavy pesticide use in agricultural fields results in depletion of insects, their primary food source.

Conservation groups are encouraging farmers to make changes in grassland management, such as delaying mowing until after fledging is completed. This not only helps the meadowlarks but other grassland nesting species as well.

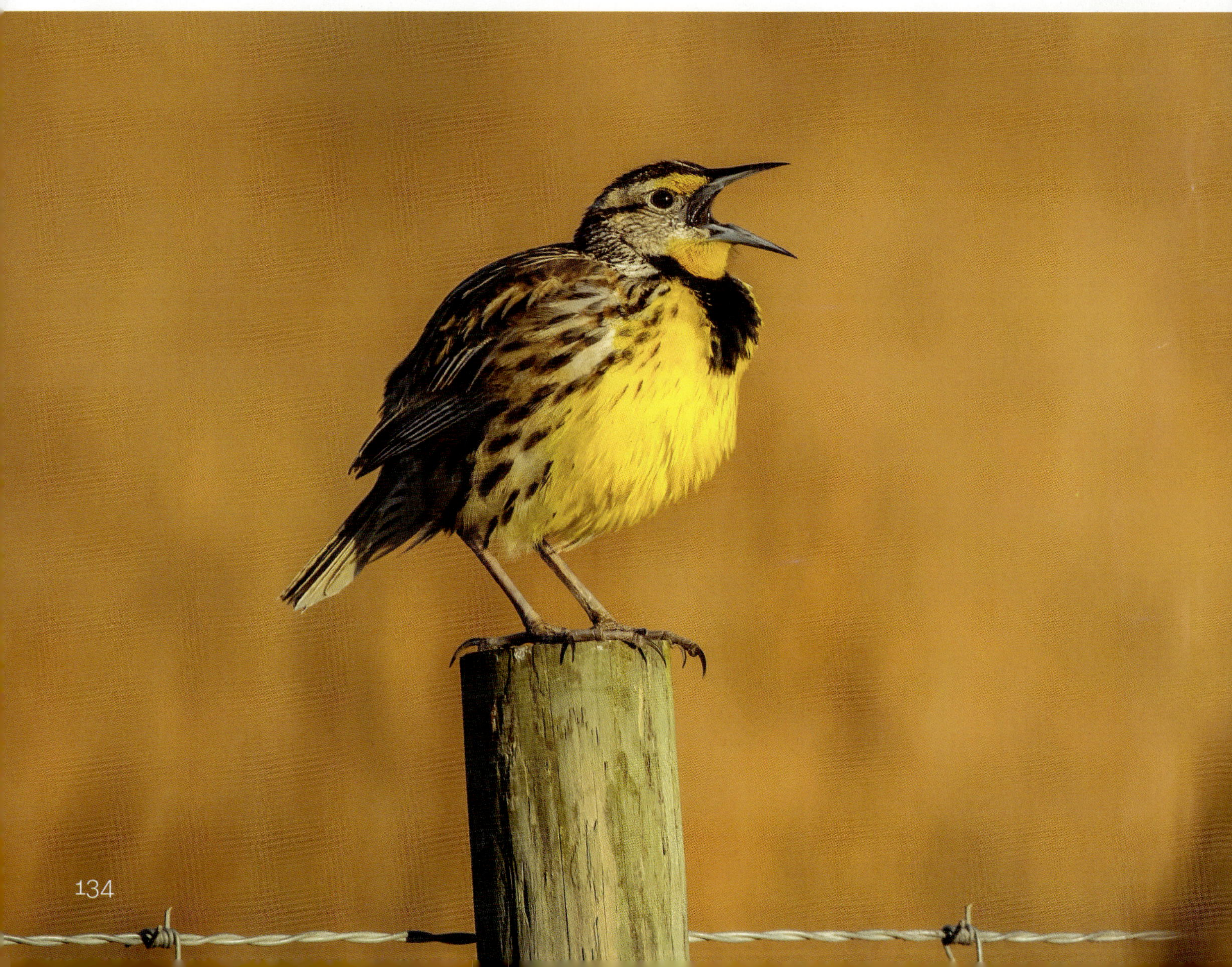

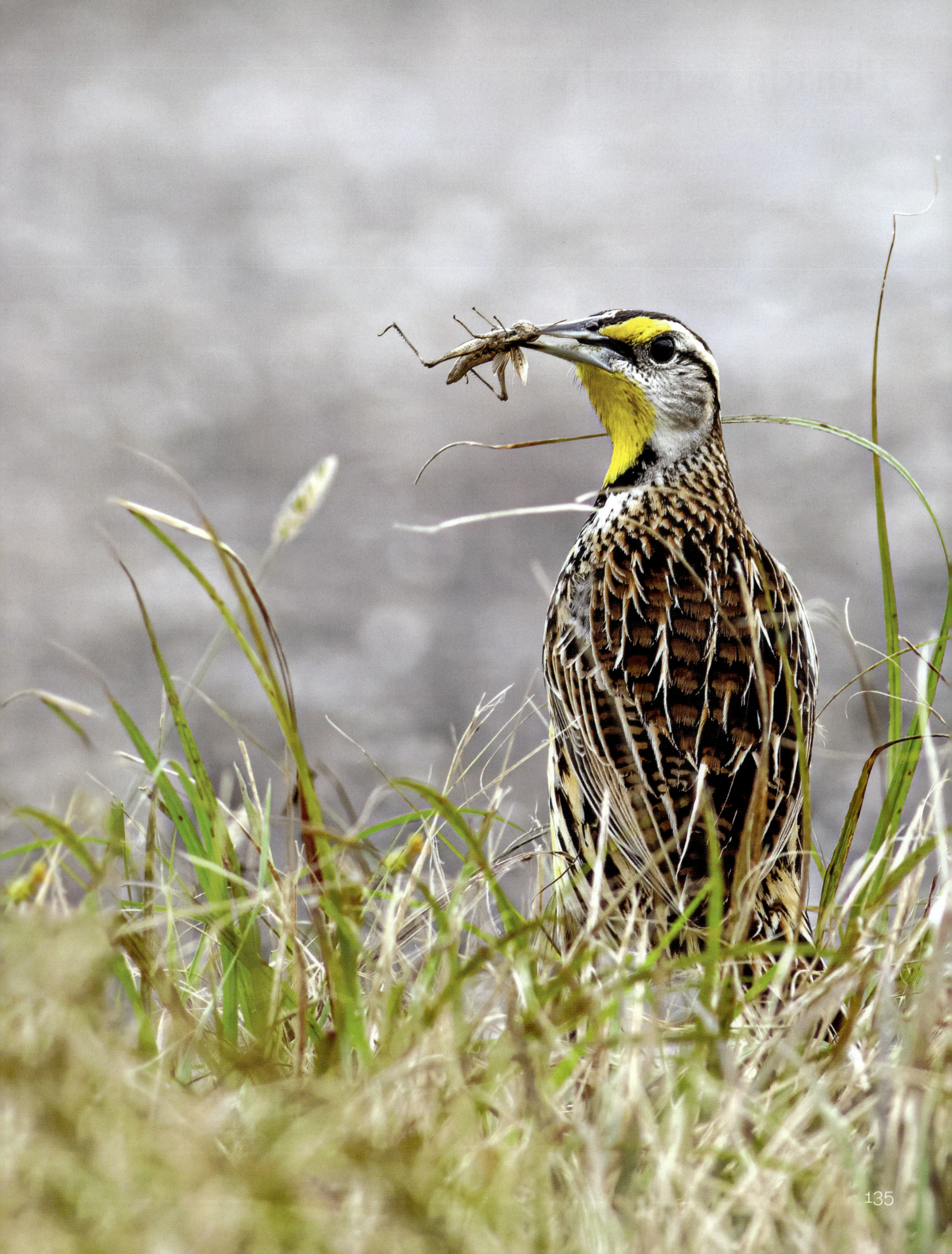

Florida Scrub-Jay

No Florida bird book would be complete without a discussion of the endangered Florida Scrub-Jay. This is the only bird that lives exclusively in Florida. They prefer to stay in one territory and survive in low-growing scrub oak on sandy soils found in areas that have been subjected to frequent fires. Scrub-Jays are now considered threatened because they do not move across non–scrub oak habitat, making them sensitive to habitat fragmentation caused by human development. Their primary food source is acorns buried in the sand for later retrieval, but they also eat seeds, insects, and fruit.

These birds form family groups, with the young staying with their parents to help raise next year's brood. They live in a social and cooperative society with special vocalizations used to alert the group about a nest-robbing snake or predatory hawk. This cooperative breeding behavior is thought to be an adaptation to the harsh and unpredictable scrub habitat in which Scrub-Jays live.

Scrub-Jays are also known for their strong territorial behavior and will defend their territory from intruders. In addition to vocalizing to deter intruders, they will use physical aggression, such as chasing and pecking, to protect their nestlings.

At the same time, Scrub-Jays are extremely tame and will come to peanuts or other handouts offered by well-meaning people. While getting them to eat out of your hand can be entertaining, it has been discovered that this activity disrupts their breeding cycle and can result in loss of their chicks. The Fish and Wildlife Commission does not approve of this behavior, so be aware, hefty fines can be imposed.

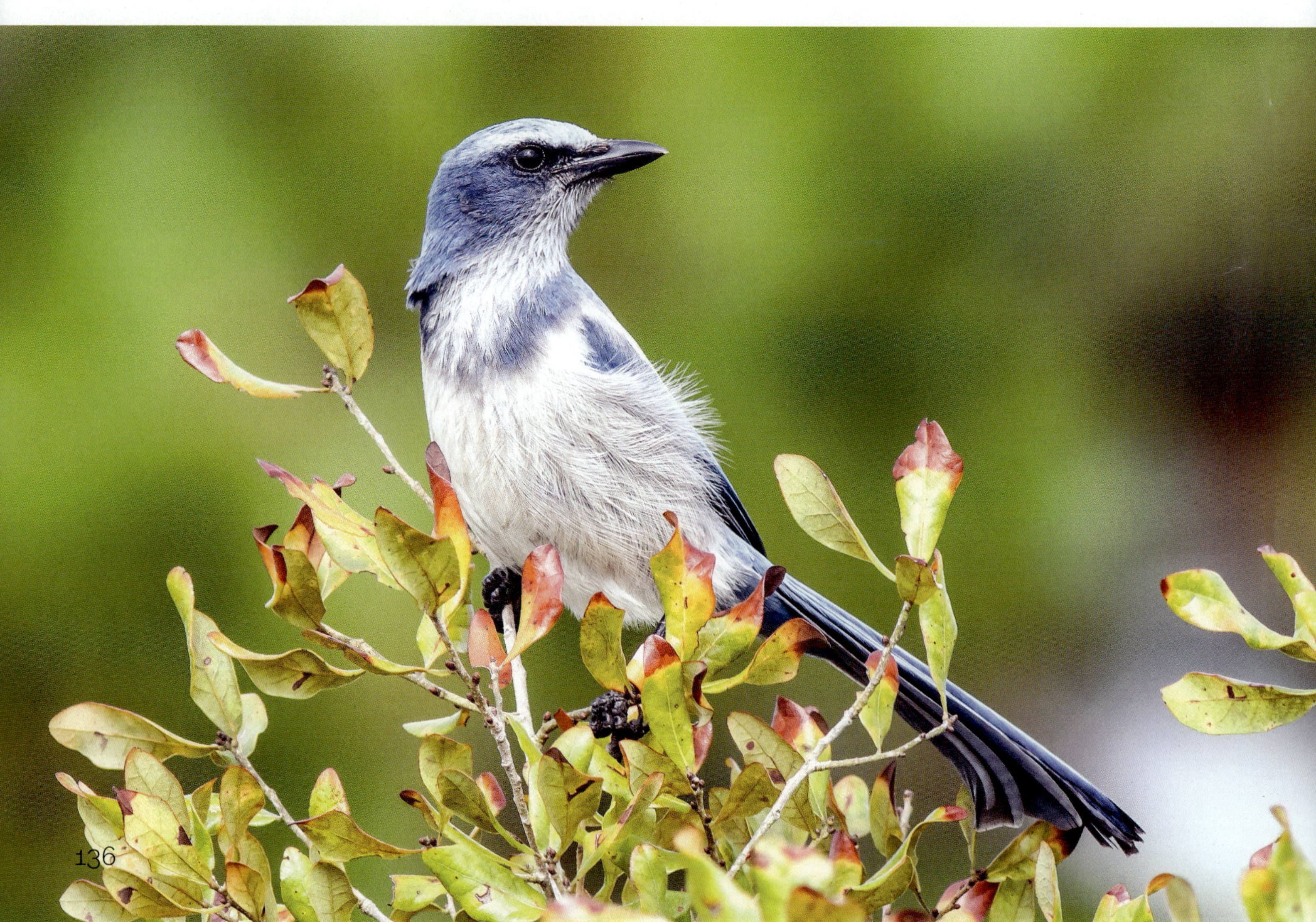

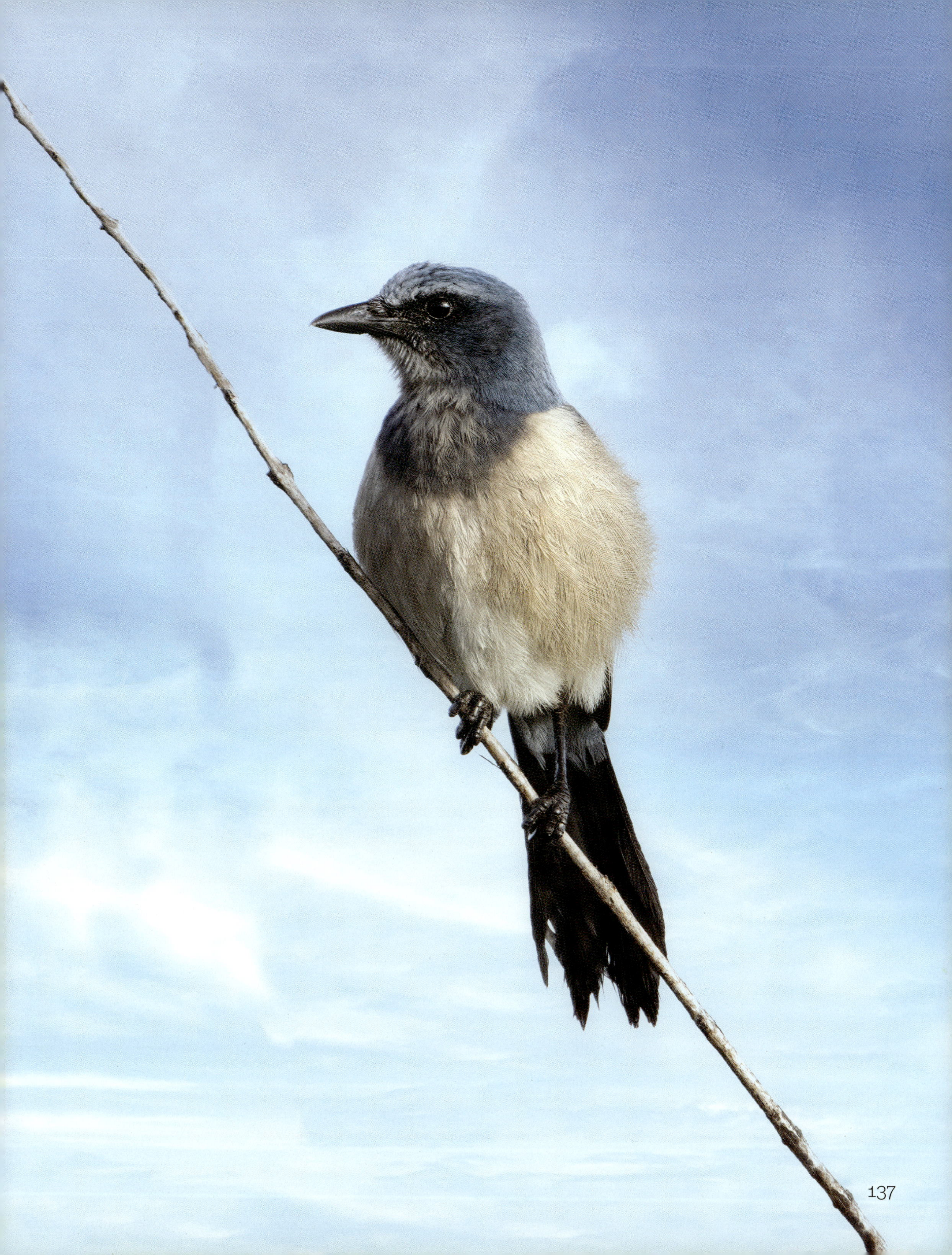

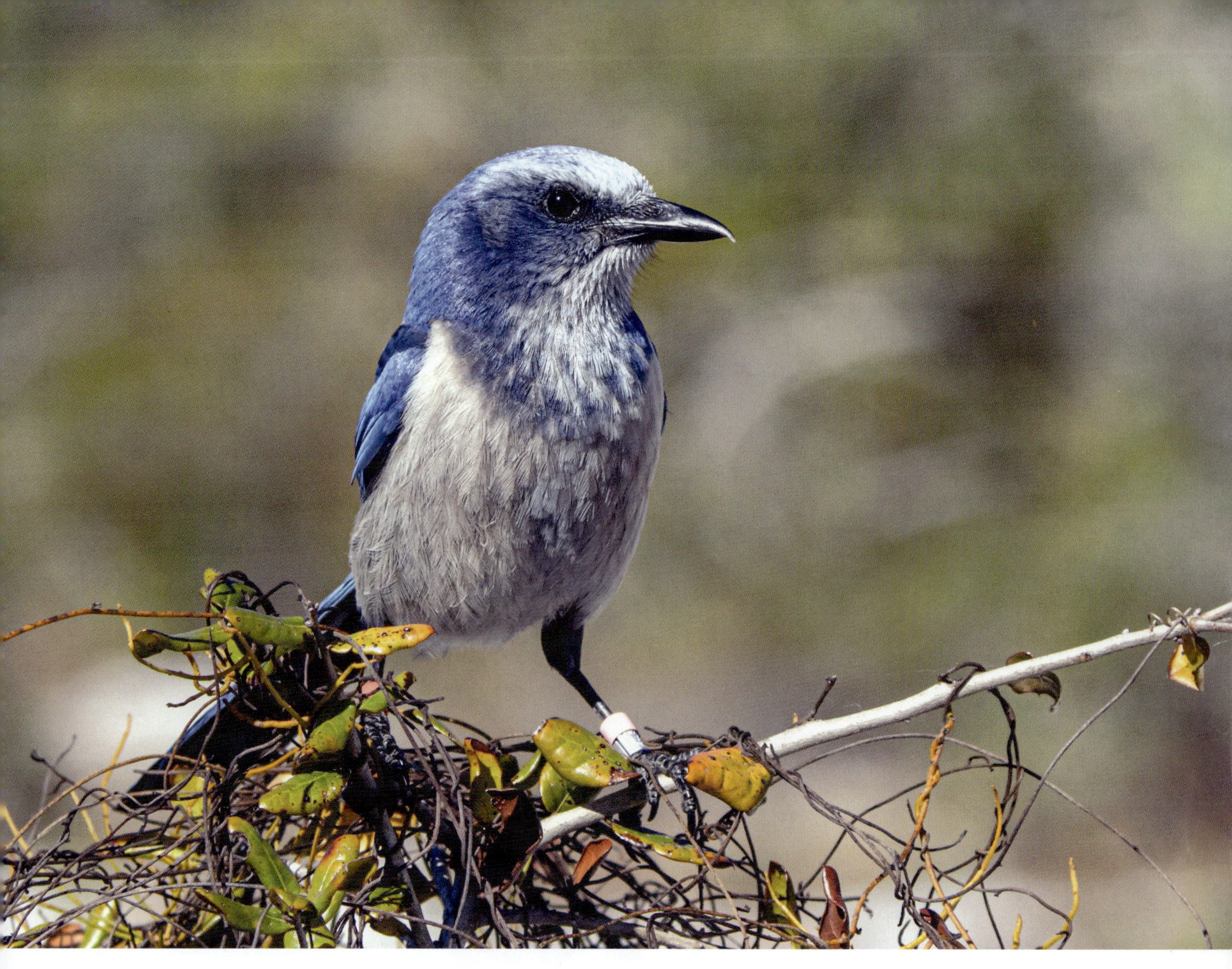

Banded and closely monitored, Florida Scrub-Jays have been studied since 1972 by Dr. John Fitzpatrick, former director of the Cornell Lab of Ornithology.

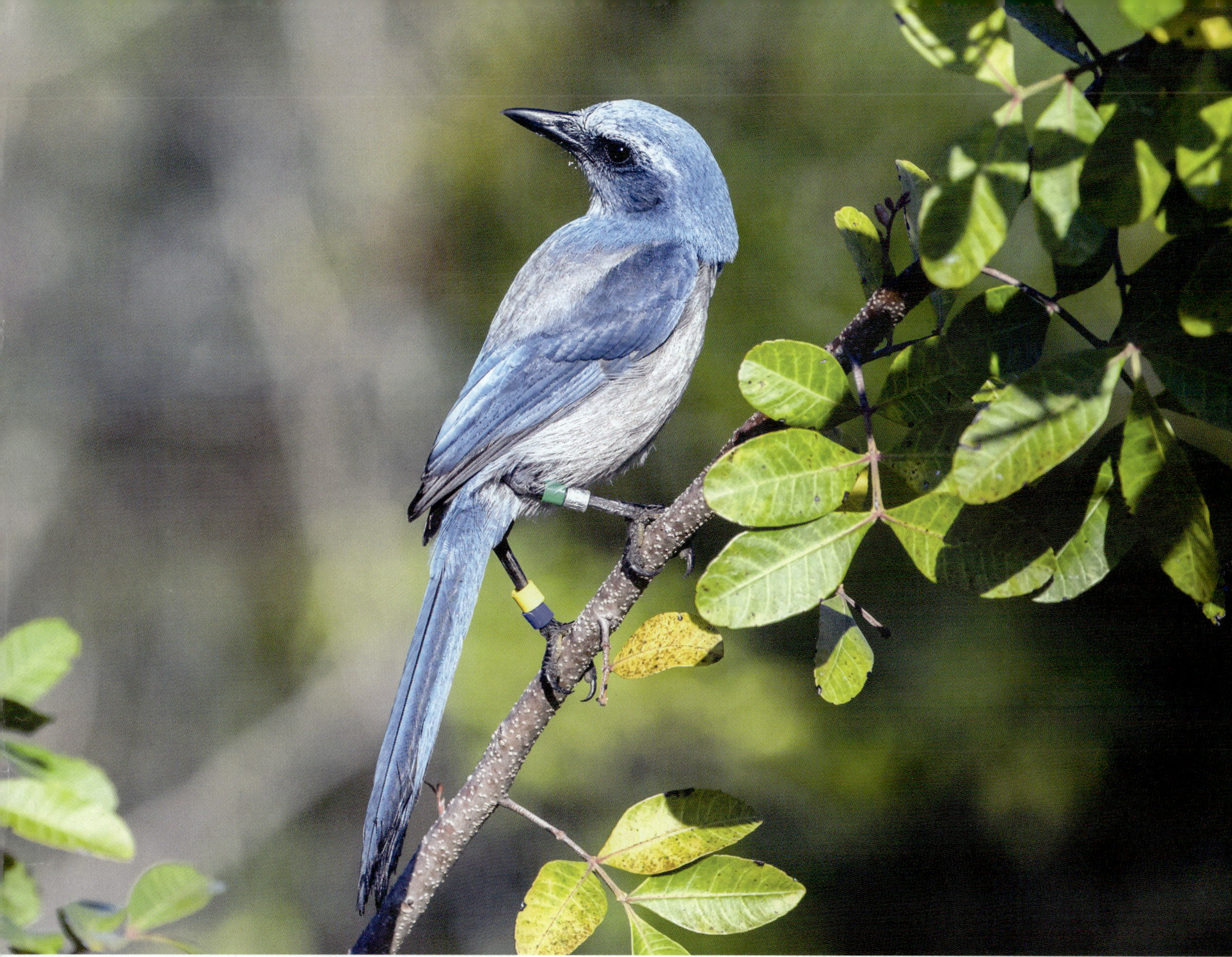

These birds can be quite tame and will readily come to humans offering peanuts or other handouts. Remember, this is a threatened species so feeding the Florida Scrub-Jay is always considered illegal and will result in a fine.

One of the best places to find Scrub-Jays in Indian River County is the Wabasso Scrub Conservation Area.

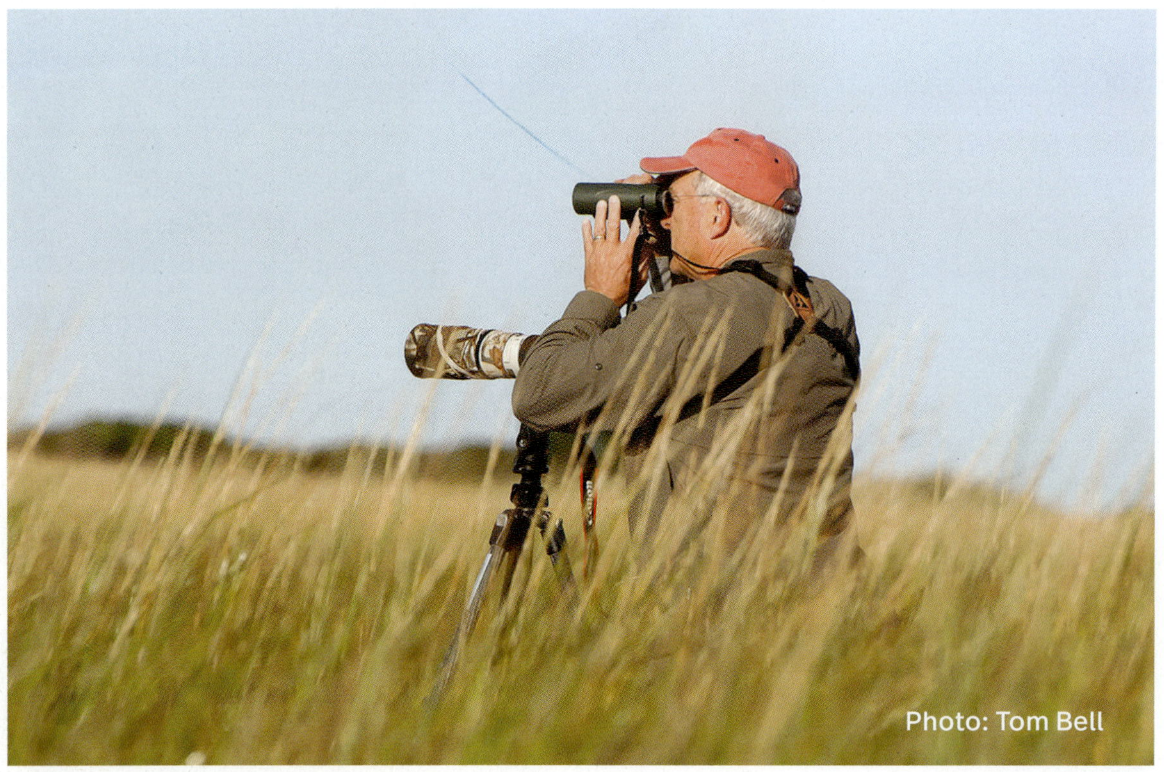
Photo: Tom Bell

At the end of April, another winter season for a displaced Maine birdwatcher comes to an end, and it is time to head north. I always think about staying a little longer because the migrating warblers and vireos from Central and South America will soon be arriving on the Florida peninsula as they make their way back to northern breeding grounds. Maybe one year I will stay, just to get that elusive Black-whiskered Vireo for my life list.

The goal of this book is to highlight some of the more than 500 species of birds that winter in, breed in, or migrate through Florida. A lot of these birds are in trouble with population declines documented in recent decades. However, not all the news is bad. Many species are surviving and making a comeback as a result of enlightened Federal and State conservation laws and successful programs to reestablish native habitats. For example, the Florida Fish and Wildlife Conservation Commission (FWC) is an important partner in bird conservation efforts in the state. The FWC conducts research, monitoring, and habitat restoration projects to help protect and preserve Florida's bird populations. The FWC also works with landowners to develop conservation plans that help protect critical habitats and prevent the loss of important bird species.

Million of people identify as birders, making birdwatching one of the most popular outdoor activities in the United States. Birdwatchers are passionate about birds and their habitats, and they are motivated to advocate for land conservation and support organizations that work to protect birds and their environment. Birdwatchers also play an important role in conservation efforts by providing valuable data and information about bird populations, especially through the eBird website. Perhaps with sensible use of pesticides and preservation of critical territory, we are beginning to see a reversal of the recent negative trends. Hopefully this book will encourage you to focus your binoculars, become a birder, and contribute to the preservation of Florida's bird populations.